W9-CRC-162

BROADCAST MANAGEMENT
Radio-Television
by Ward L. Quaal and Leo A. Martin

CLASSROOM TELEVISION
New Frontiers in ITV
by George N. Gordon

CASE STUDIES IN BROADCAST MANAGEMENT
by Howard W. Coleman

THE MOVIE BUSINESS
American Film Industry Practice
Edited by A. William Bluem and Jason E. Squire

THE CHANGING MAGAZINE
Trends in Readership and Management
by Roland E. Wolseley

FILM LIBRARY TECHNIQUES
Principles of Administration
by Helen P. Harrison

THE FILM INDUSTRIES
Practical Business/Legal Problems
in Production, Distribution and Exhibition
by Michael F. Mayer

THE FILM INDUSTRIES

Practical Business/Legal Problems in Production, Distribution and Exhibition

by Michael F. Mayer

COMMUNICATION ARTS BOOKS

HASTINGS HOUSE, PUBLISHERS
NEW YORK

To my daughter DOE MAYER
and her film-making contemporaries
—young and old.

Library of Congress Cataloging in Publication Data

Mayer, Michael F
    The film industries.

    (Studies in media management) (Communication arts books)
    Includes bibliographical references.
      1. Moving-pictures—Law—United States.
I. Title.
KF4298.M38   343′.73′078   73-8914

Cloth Edition: ISBN: 8038-2299-5
Paper (Text) Edition: ISBN: 8038-2300-2

Published simultaneously in Canada by
Saunders of Toronto, Ltd., Don Mills, Ontario

Printed in the United States of America

CONTENTS

PREFACE

I COME FROM a film-oriented family, so my interest in the area is no accident. My father, Arthur Mayer, operated theatres for several circuits and then for himself, headed advertising for Paramount in the 1930's, and with his partner Joseph Burstyn, brought to this country such great foreign films as *Open City, Paisan,* and *The Bicycle Thief*. He also found time to write his autobiographical *Merely Colossal* as well as *The Movies* with the late Richard Griffith. Now engaged in a new career, he teaches film at Dartmouth, University of Southern California and Stanford, and no doubt will emerge with other new projects in years to come.

My mother represented for years The American Jewish Committee on the ill-fated industry "Green Sheet" which prematurely brought to parental and other attention the nature of current motion picture fare and prospective audiences. This was long before the days of G's, PG's, R's and X's. Her opinions on individual films are still vigorously articulated, particularly when confronted, as is the usual case in our family, with violent opposition.

My brother makes films in Mexico; my eldest daughter has started directing under the aegis of the American Film Institute, and another daughter still to be heard from contemplates, if distantly, a cinematic future. (Alas, two children show only the faintest interest in the medium.)

So my concern with the subject matter came easy and early. I remember calling up to get theatre grosses at age 12, and ushering as well as suggesting advertising copy but a few years later. From these humble origins, a career in film emerged. Lacking the creative qualities I could only envy, I entered the practice of theatrical law. As an attorney, I represented independent film distributors, such as Kingsley International Pictures (who can forget the irrepressible Bardot in our *And God Created Woman?*) and others perhaps more distinguished but hardly so well remembered. And then as executive director of the new-born International Film Importers & Distributors of America, Inc., (IFIDA), suddenly my whole professional, and a good part of my personal life, became film-oriented. The job was the popularization and promotion of foreign films on these barren shores, and a task it proved. I wrote a book on the subject, *Foreign Films on American Screens*. And eventually, I developed a course on industry practices, presently delivered at The New School for Social Research in New York after prior annual sessions at New York University and Columbia University Summer School.

This book emerges from that experience and from the interest and stimulation created in me by students young and old. A whole new generation of film-makers, agents, investors, specialized attorneys and ordinary movie buffs has arisen with a prime passion for the cinematic medium. And that concern, while essentially aimed at the creative function (where I am no help at all), cannot avoid involvement with the practical problems faced everyday in the production, distribution and exhibition of film.

My course, as well as this book, is intended to deal with this concern and this interest. You will judge how well I have or have not done.

Students and film-makers want to know how to get started with their projects. Apart from the rare case, their bank accounts are not overflowing and they need advice, for example, in how to acquire properties and talents by option without laying down a king's ransom in advance. They are interested in the form of their organization best suited for their effort—be it corporation, general partnership, limited partnership or individual proprietorship. They had better learn about taxes or their prospective investors will teach them. The acquisition of adequate financing is probably the single most difficult problem confronted in any motion picture venture and will remain so as long as we are hitched to an economic-political system that subsidizes rich farmers and aircraft producers and undeclared foreign wars, but gives paltry assistance to the arts generally and almost nothing to creative film production. Short of support by a major film distributor, methods and techniques of attracting lenders and investors must be investigated. We seek to look at this problem.

For obvious reasons, there is great interest in production abroad. A major consideration is, of course, the types of subsidies granted film producers in most civilized parts of the world. This subject is discussed.

To help guide the prospective producer, we seek to analyze the significant elements that have created past box-office successes. Obviously, no such chart can predict the future. But perhaps for some, there is a beam of light. Those who do not read history are doomed to relive it—or something like that—as someone once said.

Vital to the practical approach are problems in distribution and exhibition. We look at the normal, old distribution contract—as well as the new versions that are currently replacing it. We analyze the everchanging exhibition license and the chronic problems that have made the exhibitor-distributor relationship the source of unique and bloody economic warfare for decades of film industry history.

The foreign market for American films has been, and remains, a critical source of revenue. Its dimensions and prospects are explored. Perhaps more exciting are the new elements in the cinematic explosion —the non-theatrical areas of homes, schools, clubs, television, pay television, community antenna television (CATV), hotel television, cassettes, and the like—which can bring new life, revenues and popularity to the medium. Here, in my belief (and without demeaning in the slightest the vast theatrical market), is where the great future lies.

Other practical problems cannot be avoided. The impact of censorship, obscenity law and classification is with us and will remain with us. So will problems in title selection, defamation, privacy invasion, idea seizure and copyright infringement.

This book is written for the film creator, his associates, investors, attorneys, exhibitors, distributors and third persons concerned with these problems. Definitive answers are not available—kindly look elsewhere—but doors are opened and questions asked.

I express my gratitude to many who have helped me in developing my course and this project. My partner, Hi Bucher, who writes financing agreements in his sleep; my good friend, Justin Golenbock, a distinguished attorney who now teaches in addition, as he should, Forms of Business Organization at Yale Law School; Steve D'Inzillo of the IATSE; Noel Silverman, a non-musical music expert of the first order; Saul Turell, Jerry Pickman, and Harold Marinstein, geniuses in all matters of distribution; Bud Levy and Meyer Ackerman, exhibitors extraordinaire; Harry Olsson of CBS, king of TV legalities; Howard Gottfried, producer; Jules Stein of American International Pictures who wrote "the book" (if not this book) on foreign distribution; and Barbara Scott who speaks with authority on matters of censorship and controls. My good friend, fellow co-author and film trade-paper publisher, Martin Quigley, is always a source of encouragement. Another editor, author and friend, Joe Taubman, preprinted some of my material in his *Performing Arts Review*. I also salute Jack Valenti for implementing a classification system in the industry which, while not without fault, has in essence (in my view) performed a worthwhile function ignored by his predecessors. While thanking all these worthies, let me make clear that responsibility for contents lies elsewhere. As the late President Harry S. Truman put it, "The buck stops here."

I've had lots of help with the typing of my manuscript. I'll mention only Daisy Lippner, Catherine McGee, Stephanie Murphy, Luba Soby and Leslie Nakon—with gratitude.

My thanks go as well to Russ Neale of Hastings House for his advice and other help, and to my editor, Bill Bluem, for constant interest and enthusiasm.

MICHAEL F. MAYER

July 11, 1973

INTRODUCTION

THIS WORK COMES at a propitious time. By the mid-50's it appeared
to many that commercial television eventually would all but eliminate
motion pictures, radio and magazines as effective national media.
From the movies, TV seemed potentially able to absorb many artistic
and entertainment functions—along with the inherent persuasive
modes which implicitly are involved in popular or "mass" entertainment. From the other media, television seemingly would command
the mass advertising market, becoming what Merrill Panitt once
called "the biggest bang in the mass producer's arsenal of weapons."

It is true that television wrought enormous changes upon national radio and certain great magazines—simply absorbing many of
their traditional communicative functions and forcing changes in the
business practices and procedures they had instituted. What is by
now abundantly clear, however, is that motion pictures have neither
been replaced nor eliminated in their function as a popular art form
or as a major mode of influence and persuasion in our civilization.

The movie industry today has been weakened in some respects,
but it has gained strength in others and has managed not merely to
survive, but to prevail, as a formidable media-system. It is capable of
providing multitudes with art, entertainment, enlightenment, and a
host of messages which can support attitudes, personal values and
actions that are both responsible and responsive to the requirements

of a free society. A few general observations quickly support this truth. The theatrical motion picture is experiencing steady and certain economic revival and growth. Audience figures have risen to 21 million a week—up from a low of 18 million at the end of the last decade. New theaters have been constructed at the rate of over 200 a year since 1964. Television itself has become a prime outlet for creative output. Production starts continue to rise each year among major companies. The general creative outlook is optimistic and further economic growth and expansion are indicated.

We must recall, too, that theatrical motion pictures by no means represent the full range of film activity in America today. Production, distribution, dissemination and exhibition increasingly are affected by a continuing audio-visual revolution in which "non-theatrical" film is a bellwether medium. It is a fact that an aggregate of billions of hours are spent by people witnessing all kinds of non-theatrical films each year under many different conditions and within varying situations. There is a 16mm sound projector for every 200 citizens in the United States. On the American campus the number of 16mm projectors has risen by 300 per cent in the past decade as the number of colleges and universities increased by only 28 per cent. No elementary or secondary school in the nation is without its 16mm projector and a battery of people who can operate it with ease and convenience. More 16mm and 8mm projectors are being sold each year; the educational film rental and free-film markets expand each year, and we are fully aware of the revolution in film study on the American campus.

It is no accident that Michael Mayer would produce this much needed work at this point in media history. All trends and data point to the need for greater emphasis upon study and examination of basic legal and economic practices in the film industries of America. A trained and knowledgeable observer with deep personal commitment to "the movies," Mr. Mayer has long been aware of this need, and he has now prepared a volume which will be of value to serious students of film, whether they are still in the classroom or already engaged in professional activity. His work is a welcome addition to the *Studies in Media Management* series.

A. WILLIAM BLUEM Ph.D.
Professor of Media Studies, Syracuse University
General Editor, *Studies in Media Management*

Part One

PRODUCTION

1

The Option Contract

IN PUTTING TOGETHER a package for film, television or other presentation, a vital tool for the prospective producer is the option agreement. An option is a call—an exclusive right to put into effect for a period of time (or by "dropping," not to put into effect) an agreement for rights or services or any other type of legal acquisition. The option permits a producer, generally without vast expenditure of funds, to tie up these properties and personnel for a prospective project he desires to create.

The producer can then present his proposal in a reasonably definitive form to a distributor or other financial backers. He has a "package" open for acceptance or rejection at a price he can afford without having made final commitments to anyone.

Why would an author, or other party, enter into such an agreement? There are obvious disadvantages in permitting a literary property, for example, to be "off the market" for a period of time. But if the author is anxious for a particular producer to make a film of his work he might well permit it. If he foresees a successful television series he might be similarly inclined. Particularly if his work is aging, and no one else has sought to acquire it he has very little to lose. The option price can be large or minimal depending on his bargaining strength. The author gets something in hand and he may get a great deal more thereafter. He may also have a prospective participation in the project. For a host of motives then, the option grantor will, under certain circumstances, be not only willing but eager to permit his property to be tied up for a limited period of time.

It is vital to note that the option must either contain within itself all the terms of the subsequent contract that will go into effect if it is exercised, or such provisions must be attached in the form of a separate contract. It is impossible to have a valid option agreement without such specification, as an agreement that one will merely acquire rights on unspecified terms to be thereafter determined is unenforceable. An agreement to agree now or hereafter is but a scrap of paper without legal significance unless there is a means or method set forth by which the terms will, in fact, be constructed. A preferred technique is to attach to an option agreement an "Exhibit A contract" which sets forth all the terms and conditions that will spring into effect if the option is exercised. We shall hereafter discuss a typical Exhibit A agreement after examination of the option form.

The option will first set forth as a preamble the nature of the property to be acquired. For illustrative purposes only, we here consider the acquisition of rights in a novel for motion picture production. Nothing stated is intended to limit the potential purposes for which any option may be granted.

After describing the novel, the agreement will set forth the exclusive rights sought. This may be done by incorporating by reference the rights as set out in the Exhibit A agreement attached. In this case, such rights would include the right to make a motion picture version or versions of the work in question for use in the various media.

The option would also restate the same representations made by the author or owner of the novel as to the property as are included in Exhibit A. The thrust of these representations is that the author actually owns and can legally transfer the rights set forth. Clearly if he has already granted such rights to others, he may not do so. In other instances, however, he may have granted selected licenses to the property which do not impair or conflict with his right to enter into this particular agreement. Any other licenses granted should be set forth and attached to Exhibit A.

Further, the author must warrant or promise that he will not, during the option period, transfer or diminish the rights granted under Exhibit A. This is the key to the option—for during its duration, all of the rights required must be available to the purchaser. If they are not, the option is pure fiction.

The Exhibit A agreement should be executed simultaneously with the option but to go into effect only upon its exercise. It should be specified that Exhibit A will be null and void if the option is not exercised in the precise manner set forth. The Exhibit A agreement as executed should therefore be held pending exercise, in escrow or by the parties, as it is not yet an effective document but only a prospective one. If signing were postponed until actual exercise, all kinds of problems might arise which should be studiously avoided. These could include all types of foreseeable disputes arising in the period between the signing of the option agreement and its exercise. In such event, securing the signatures at a later date might prove difficult indeed.

The option will set forth its price, the precise time period of its duration and the exact manner in which it shall be exercised. These are the critical terms of the option. The amount of time granted may well be vital. A producer should keep in mind that he needs ample time to create a screenplay and put together the other elements for filming a novel. He will want an extended period necessary for his purposes. The author, on the other hand, is likely to want to limit the time during which he can make no other agreement to license the novel. He may have in mind other offers that might arise. Such matters must be fought out at the bargaining table.

Time is clearly of the essence in such agreements so if, for example, an option is only exercisable until midnight, April 1 in the prescribed manner, exercise at any time thereafter is not binding on the author. The manner of exercise, as well, must be precisely as set forth. If notice is required, it should be done by personal service, or registered or certified mail (return receipt requested) postmarked or actually received before the expiration of the time period. Frequently an initial payment under the Exhibit A agreement must accompany the notice of exercise. If that be the case, notice without accompanying payment may be a useless gesture. In other words, both the timeliness and the appropriateness of the option terms must be met "to the letter" for the option to be properly exercised. Nothing, of course, prevents an author from accepting late service or faulty exercise, but if he or his agent has had a better offer and is looking for an "out," failure to follow exact procedures may grant him his fondest wish.

If the option is not exercised within the time period, for any reason, all rights granted under it as well as under the Exhibit A agreement are terminated and at an end. Exhibit A should be destroyed as it is now void. Contrariwise, if the option is properly executed, the Exhibit A agreement is immediately and automatically in full force and effect. The purchaser has acquired and the author has granted the rights there stated on the terms set forth.

The Exhibit A Contract

The Exhibit A Contract, after appropriate preambles describing the nature of the property, will set forth the precise rights granted to the purchaser. From the producer's point of view, these should be broad and all-encompassing. The author may look at the matter, however, from quite a different perspective and wish to limit the grant. If there are any reservations of rights to the author for any particular uses, they should be explicitly set forth with any limitations on their use. In any event, the exclusive right to make a motion picture or motion pictures based on the property, including its characters with accompanying music and dialogue (including foreign language versions), should be granted. The matter of whether "sequel" rights or the exclusive use of "characters," etc. are included should be determined one way or the other. So should rights of dramatization on the legitimate "spoken" stage. Other rights that should be specified would include the privilege of copyrighting the film version(s) and foreign language versions of the film(s), the right to make and use trailers and to use or not use the title of the novel in any manner. The availability of any publication rights (in a synopsis or otherwise) for publicity, advertising or other purpose should be disposed of.

The producer must insist on the broadest powers of distribution and exploitation of any films created in all manners throughout the world, including the theatrical, non-theatrical, television, pay television, CATV, hotel television, cassettes and any and all manners of exploitation now or hereafter becoming known. In this connection, use of the phrase "but not by way of limitation" is helpful, as a specific listing of methods may be considered definitive in itself unless so qualified.

A clause of the agreement will set forth the duration of rights. From the producer's view, this should be perpetual but in any event not less than the period of copyright protection of the book. Exclusivity, of course, may end with the termination of copyright protection of the work. Such a clause does not bar termination for breach of the agreement under general legal principles well before such date.

The author must represent that he owns the rights granted "free and clear" and has authority to enter into the contract. He shall set out his copyright number and date of publication, and list any licenses he has previously made of the property of any kind. He must warrant the originality of his work and that use by the purchaser will not infringe copyright or any other right of any third person. He should further warrant that there are no claims or litigation against him or any outstanding commitments or licenses of any type with reference to the rights in question and, if there are, he should specify them. He must promise that in any future grant of rights the author will make reference to the terms of this agreement.

Standing back of the warranties is an indemnity proviso that the author will pay the purchaser for any loss suffered by reason of the breach of any of his warranties. Sometimes this clause is limited in amount to the consideration paid or a part thereof. Sometimes it is broadened to include any costs involved in the defense of the property against any alleged as well as any actual breach as, for example, a suit for copyright infringement. Costs should include, but not by way of limitation, all losses, damages and legal fees incurred in defending the warranted rights. The author's indemnification should not, of course, cover any new matter inserted in the film version by the purchaser as to which the author can bear no responsibility.

Beyond his indemnification, the author should also agree to keep his novel out of the public domain by renewing his copyright and similarly protecting it in foreign countries. To accomplish such purposes as well as others, the author agrees to execute other necessary instruments to effectuate the terms of the contract. In addition to this, the purchaser may secure authority to act as the author's "attorney-in-fact" for such purposes. In this way, a missing or uncooperative author's consent need not be required each time it is needed for a necessary act.

The purchaser must have broad power in creating films to adapt, rearrange, change and modify the novel, its plot and characters. This should be explicitly set forth to bar any claim by the author of misuse of his material for any reason.

The author is entitled to credit as such on any film version of his novel and the size and content of such credit should be contractually determined. The purchaser clearly is entitled to use the author's name for the purpose of exploiting or promoting the film.

A consideration clause will set forth how the author is to be paid.

This is a matter of bargaining strength. The consideration may be cash due in one or several payments (the first of which might accompany exercise of the option) or may involve a guaranteed payment against a percentage of net proceeds. (A participation in gross proceeds would only go to an author with very substantial bargaining power.) On some occasions compensation consists purely in a percentage of proceeds payable to the author. In these events he will require regular statements and remittances and the right to inspect any producer's books. Similarly, the usual clause stating that the purchaser is not "required" to film the novel should be excluded as author's only hope for compensation in this instance would be destroyed if no picture is made. In the alternative, as a protection to the author, the property might revert to him if no film based on it is released by the purchaser within a specified period of time.

The right of assignment is critical to the purchaser who may not be able to produce the film himself and seeks an opportunity to license it to others. Ordinary contracts are generally considered assignable. In this type of situation, however, failure to mention assignability could prove a problem. Purchaser will, of course, remain liable for any payments due unless specifically released by the author.

Other formal clauses are generally included in such a contract. Although litigation is undesirable, it is wise nonetheless to mention the state law applicable in construction of the agreement. Arbitration of disputes as a quick and efficient method of disposition may well be preferred. There are forms for clauses covering this. There should also be a clause as to just how notices to each of the parties are delivered, as well as a provision permitting the curing, within a set time period, of any alleged breach, by written notice.

In the matter of breach, a provision should set forth, in those cases where the author is entitled to payments over a period of time or sharing in the proceeds, that any act of bankruptcy by the producer as defined shall be cause for termination. An author should not, in such event, be tied to a bankrupt producer.

While fraud may not be contractually excluded as a grounds for suit, it is wise for both parties to state that all claims and representations are confined to the instrument and that their agreement represents their entire understanding superseding any prior commitments. This minimizes the risk of a fraud claim.

Oral modification or termination should be prohibited to prevent any claims of verbal changes in written terms. If the parties wish to alter or terminate their agreement, they should do so in written form which avoids such arguments. Similarly, it should be clearly expressed that a waiver by one party of a particular term of a contract is not a continuing waiver and only applies to the instance at hand. An author, at the producer's instance, may for example not insist that one install-ment payment be timely made, but this does not mean that all payments can thereafter be so postponed.

Obviously, we cannot cover each and every term of such an Exhibit A agreement in this limited space. We refer here to the essential provisos. The agreement, of course, should be signed and formally acknowledged by both parties before a notary public.

By use of an option, together with an Exhibit A agreement of the type here set forth, the prospective film-maker may secure a call on rights and services without vast expenditures aimed at the creation of his "package." There can be options on talent, options for the prepara-tion of treatments and screenplays, and step deals which permit the exercise of options at a succession of points in the creative process. By use of this technique, upon assurance of financing and other require-ments, he is then in a position to exercise his options and to proceed toward the production of his film.

2

Contracting
with the Talent

PERFORMERS' AND ARTISTS' contracts range from the modest (pursuant to Screen Actors Guild minimums) to the magnificent in content. As it is easier to scale down from the top, it is best for our purposes to analyze the essential terms of an agreement with a significant actor for a significant film. With that in view, it is simpler thereafter to visualize terms for others of less significant status.

The initial clause may well be a mere statement that the Producer agrees to employ the "Artist," who similarly agrees to perform subject to the terms thereafter set forth. Employment may either be at a set locale or such other place or location as Producer may designate on reasonable notice.

The actor should warrant his availability and indemnify against any loss suffered in the event of his failure to appear. In this connection, the term and dates of employment may prove vital. A prominent performer may well have obligations, by option agreement or otherwise, with a different producer. His contract should warrant his availability and specify any such potential conflicts by stating precisely when and where he is obliged to perform other services, so as to avoid conflict with the terms of this agreement. A minimum term of employment at a guaranteed salary per week is usually established ($1,500 a week for 10 weeks is an illustration), effective on a set date or one to be thereafter designated. A similar rate may then be applied to additional weeks of work required both before or after the minimum period for other necessary activities. When the salary is high, it should be prorated for additional periods of working time less than a week.

In view of various pressures and vicissitudes of film production, a standard work week may not be possible. Actors may be required to work more than five days and on Sundays or holidays. This can be covered by provisions authorizing additional days off at a later time during the guaranteed period, or an increase in payments for any necessary additional days.

Many other contingencies of employment must be covered. A film may be held up from starting or continuing for a multitude of causes. In addition to *force majeure* such as fire, flood or civil disorder, there may be other specified or general reasons for a postponement. A contract may allow, within limited time periods, for such periods of "suspension" during which a performer may be, at producer's option, off salary. Of course, if the suspension runs too long, the performer himself may terminate the agreement.

Suspension may be due, among other reasons, to an actor's incapacity. There may be illness, accident or other disability(s) preventing his performance. In such event, the producer should be able to suspend, and if the condition continues for a significant period of time, terminate his obligations subject to payment for services already performed.

Sometimes there is dispute over "Acts of God" as the cause of an actor's disability. Contracts may require a doctor's certificate, or even a determination among several doctors as to whether an actor may proceed. This may prove helpful in those cases where a dissatisfied performer feigns illness in order to avoid obligations or in order to utilize another employment opportunity.

If an actor willfully fails to perform, he is in breach of contract and, of course, there is no producer's obligation to pay him. This is not a happy circumstance, particularly if it occurs in the midst of production and, in order to avoid it, many agreements specifically prohibit "any" rendering of services to others by the actor during the term. While injunctions against work for others are hard to come by, the law does permit the enforceability of such clauses where the services involved are unique, extraordinary and of special value, and money damages will not suffice to protect the injured party. Frequently, the agreement will specify that the actor concurs in this description of his services and that an injunction against performing for others will be in order in the event of his breach. When litigation follows, however, a court is not necessarily bound by this rigid language.

Compensation payments for prominent personalities may be for straight cash or for a percentage share in the film or for a combination of both. Frequently, a performer is granted a participation in profits over and above his salary. He might receive 5%, for example, of such profits to be determined on the basis of an elaborate schedule attached to the employment agreement. The schedule will set forth a formula for computing profits. Typically, if made by a producer-distributor, it will involve deduction of all costs of production, distribution and financing from gross receipts as received by the distributor (not the exhibitor), before net profits are available. Only then will the performer share.

Other actors with stronger bargaining power may receive a percentage of distributors' gross take in excess of a specified figure frequently estimated to cover various expenses of production, distribution and financing. Obviously, from a producer's view, giving away a percentage of his receipts is a far more dangerous thing than paying part of his profits when and if earned. He may be compounding losses by such an act where the film, for example, exceeded budget and he has not recouped his expenditures, but is nevertheless laying out to the actor 5 or 10 cents on every dollar received from distribution. The dangers are apparent, but sometimes a performer may prove worth it. (See William Holden's multi-million gross participation in *Bridge on the River Kwai,* or Sean Connery's fantastic share in the *Bond* pictures.)

Conversely, the performer who is usually represented by astute agents will want his share from gross proceeds, not profits. Essentially, this is because profitability is rare in film production, and the participation may well be valueless. Furthermore, customary arguments over the deductibility of various costs are avoided. The actor knows that when a certain point of gross proceeds is reached, he will receive additional compensation. The nature of such participation remains a question of bargaining power between the parties—who needs whom most and what each is willing to do for the other. Under current conditions in films, such participations in either category, although not uncommon, are less frequent than in earlier prosperous times. Producers' risks are generally too great.

Profit participations are to be distinguished, of course, from deferments, which are simply payments of compensation postponed

to a later time and frequently conditioned on the receipt of certain
moneys. Deferments are common in low-budget productions, where
both producers and actors want to see a film completed, and the job
cannot be done with the funds at hand. An actor's salary may be
deferred until the picture is in distribution, and it may well be a first
charge against producer's receipts. If several artists are involved in
deferments, they may be granted *parri passu* with each dollar divided
on a proportionate basis per the amount of each obligation as and
when received. (If Actor "A" is entitled to $9,000 deferred payment,
and Actor "B" to $1,000, Actor "A" would get 90¢ from the first
dollar available, and Actor "B" 10¢.) All kinds of formulas are
possible, and no standardized technique is determinable.

Payments of gross, profit or deferred compensation, should be
accompanied by relevant statements on a regular basis. They generally
are made to the actor's agent, who represents him in the negotiations.
The performer or his representative should have the right to inspect
books and records in this connection to verify and extract information.
All this is covered by the agreement where applicable.

The actor's duties involve not only appearing for work on camera,
but following all the necessary and reasonable directions of his
employer in all respects. Times may be set by the agreement for
appearances on the set, rehersals, make-up, wardrobe, retakes, voice
recordings and the multiplicity of other details that go into film-
making. Additional compensation for such services may or may not
be payable. Employment is, of course, exclusive during any "minimum
period" of employment, unless otherwise expressly agreed.

Control over the artist's work is in the hands of the producer,
which includes not only production, but artistic efforts as well as
cutting and editing. (This, of course, is subject to modification in the
case of employment of directors who may exercise substantially such
controls themselves.) The performer frequently waives his alleged
right of *droit morale,* or artistic recognition of his work, enforced in
some foreign jurisdictions if not under American law. This could be
particularly pertinent where he winds up as the face on the cutting-
room floor.

The performer may also be required to cooperate with the
producer in the matter of publicity for the film. He may, for example,
be obliged during the contractual term to help in exploitation and
publicity for the film. Such services should not be considered "extra,"
but a part of the basic consideration for the employment agreement.

Transportation to the place of work outside a normal radius from the actor's home is a producer's expense. Similarly, where living expenses are necessary "on location" or in a foreign country, they are, of course, for producer's account. Return transportation reimbursement after completion of work may be conditioned on the performer's actually returning or not performing services elsewhere outside his domicile. Double payments of transportation by two producers are inappropriate.

Producers, of course, are granted the right to use the actor's name, photograph, likeness or voice (simulated or otherwise) in all ways, in connection with his film. This may include commercial tie-ins, although it is frequently stipulated that the performer cannot be shown as endorsing any other product without his consent. There is no "right of privacy" in the artist's performance as that goes to the essence of his employment.

Beyond this, unless otherwise stipulated, all rights in the film of every type and nature created belong to producer, as his property. This includes the right to distribute and exploit in all media now known or hereafter becoming known. Various efforts by performers to limit such producers' rights (i.e. the film is not his for use with "sound" or for television distribution) have rightfully foundered where no specific exception is provided.[1]

The subject of performer's "credits" has been amply disputed and should be clearly defined in the agreement. They might, for example, specify first position in the cast above the title of the film in no less than equal-size type to such title in all paid advertising controlled by the producer-distributor (except teaser campaigns or other specialized publicity and advertising). These placements should be spelled out in detail. With lesser performers, such obligations are reduced. Care should be taken to exempt certain uses. Actors have been known to have their representatives measure the size of their names on billboards to enforce such provisions, so they require considerable care in draftsmanship.

A producer may well desire to insure his performer's life to cover losses in the event of death or disability. An actor must cooperate in securing such insurance. This must be authorized by the contract as colossal losses are quite possible when a principal actor dies or is

[1] See *Autry v. Republic Productions* 213 F2d 667 (1954); *L. C. Page v. Fox Film Company* 83 F2d 196 (1936); *Bartsch v. MGM* 391 F2d 150 (1968).

injured during shooting. (Such an incident occurred when the late
Tyrone Power had nearly finished a film in Spain and the picture
reportedly had to be entirely reshot.)

Union productions involve membership of performers in the
Screen Actors Guild (SAG). It is normal for the actor to agree that
he will during the contractual term be a member of this, or other
pertinent organization, in good standing. While SAG dues are the
actor's obligation, if production is abroad, for example, and membership is necessary in a foreign labor organization, the producer should
pick up that check.

Some star performers require specialized provisions in their agreements. These might include a commitment to retain a "stand-in" who
can substitute for the star during preparatory camera work, elaborate
star dressing rooms at a studio or on location, the gift of a 16mm print
of the finished work for home, but not commercial, use. "Morals
clauses" still abound in performer agreements despite the changing
standards of our age. A performer must not, at the risk of discharge,
commit offences involving "moral turpitude" or "offend against
decency or morality" or be held up to "ridicule and contempt." It
all reads rather obsolete in the 1970's.

Another holdover from the day of giant studios is the option
provision that allows a producer to pick up a performer for an additional term(s) or film(s) following completion of this contract. Such
provisions, while not uncommon, are less utilized today than hereto-
fore as independent producers are rarely sure of their plans so far in
advance. Nonetheless, it is sometimes practical to insert an option
clause to secure further rights to an important performer.

As in other agreements, certain general commitments are frequently included. The contract should confirm what state or national
law is applicable to disputes: jurisdiction of controversies may be
delegated to some definite tribunal or to arbitrators where permissible.
Places where notices are to be sent as well as the manner of notification
should be established. Assignability of the agreement by the producer
should be included if acceptable to performer. It should be clarified
that, while the intention of the agreement is to produce and release a
film or films, there is no obligation to do so, and no action can be taken
if producer fails to do so. Remedies such as injunctions should be
"cumulative" rather than singular, which simply means that their use
does not imply that no other action can be taken to enforce the contract. Exercise of one right is not to be considered as exclusive. Simi-

larly, waiver by a party of one breach by the other should not be regarded as a continuing waiver of all such breaches. The agreement is entire and supersedes all other writings, and covers the full understanding of the parties, there being no representations or undertakings not specifically included within its terms. The agreement should not be subject to waiver or modification except in writing signed by the parties.

In essence, these provisos should be a part of any contractural undertaking of performers. However, it must be noted that, as in the case of other contracts, without good faith the agreement is of limited value. Particularly in such a delicate operation as making a motion picture, mere language on a piece of paper will not suffice. While the contract is essential to specify terms of employment, it is only a limited tool in the creative process.

3

Problems in Financing Feature Films

THE FINANCING OF independently created motion pictures of feature length has become, and remains, a most difficult problem facing many producers. Short of a long "track record" of successful films or an outstanding "package" of literary material, star and directorial names, there is unlikely to be a long line of prospective financiers waiting to be of assistance to his effort. How is the project to be expedited or lifted off the ground?

For those with the requisite reputation or skill, the modern tendency of major distributors to finance 100% selected projects while leaving essential artistic control to the producer has been an infinite blessing. In this regard, the modern management of United Artists Corporation, which led the way in this development, deserves full credit. Others have since followed in similar paths.

Where a powerful distributor desires to see such a property produced, the production problem is vastly simplified. The distributor can and does see to it that financing, to the extent of an approved budget, is made available to the project. This can be done either with its own funds or upon its guaranty to a bank that the funds advanced will be returned with interest. More often than not the loan is for the entire budget.

The arrangement is relatively simple when and if the package is approved. A production-financing agreement is drawn granting full distribution rights in the property to the distributor. Generally a modest amount is allowed for pre-production activities to cover essential priority expenses, such as acquisition of literary rights, screenplays, etc. Budget, script, directorial and major performance credits must, of course, be agreed upon in advance.

The loan will be payable in stages based on production advices indicating each requirement as it occurs. There is no quick "hand-out" of the budgeted sums. Payments usually come from a separate bank account, with counter signatory by a bank-distribution representative and the producer. Windfalls and free rides are rare in today's atmosphere.

Depending on his bargaining strength a producer's fee will be set. This is payable over a period of time, and occasionally reserved pending completion of the picture within its budget. One apparent way to encourage such effective completion is to hold up producer's payments in full or in part pending such eventuality.

Completion of the film at or near budget is, of course, essential, particularly from the financier's point of view. Thousands or millions invested in a project are wasted and gone if there is no completed film. To assure completion, the financier-distributor may require other more drastic provisos. If a producer has other films in distribution, he may be required to pledge the use of their proceeds to complete delivery of the new film. If he owns stocks or bonds or other securities, these may have to be made available for purposes of completion of the film if it is not properly accomplished pursuant to contract. In some cases a completion guaranty, or an agreement by a well-heeled third party committing himself and his assets to assure completion in any event, has been required. Such guaranties are currently difficult to acquire, as the potential outlays when a film exceeds its budget are literally fantastic.

In effect, the completion guarantor, for a consideration usually in the budget, plus a profit participation, agrees that the financier-distributor will receive the film he bargained for regardless of cost in excess of budget. To achieve this purpose the guarantor must have the right, if necessary, to assume control over the entire project when called upon and to utilize specialized personnel to finish the job, as well as first recoupment for monies expended.

It is not a business for the faint-hearted, and disastrous losses have been suffered both in the U. S. and abroad in completing films. The creation of a feature involves major hazards, not all of which can be insured against, and budgets are frequently exceeded. If the overage is modest, frequently the distributor will pick up the check or rely on such matters as deferred payments to producers, directors and actors. But if the excess funds required are substantial, the guarantor's position is highly vulnerable. It is little wonder that there are few persons or corporations in the completion-guaranty business here or abroad. Even in the more favorable climate of Great Britain where a quasi-official agency entered the business, its losses have proved substantial.

In most distributor-sponsored efforts, however, completion at or near budget is usually less of a problem than in the purely independently-sponsored effort. Skilled representatives of the distributor are on hand to aid, or prod, the producer to see that the work gets done and, with their guidance together with the natural desire of most producers to meet their financial responsibilities, the modern trend is toward realistic budgets and completion figures.

Where the distributor finances or causes financing, he generally uses his traditional distribution agreement for the film (see chapter on distribution agreements) under which the producer is allotted a fee for his services and thereafter shares in such profits as the film may achieve after all costs, including distributors' fees and charges and the loan with interest, are recouped. Frequently this share is 50%, but this is not an inflexible rule. As the great majority of films never achieve profit status, the producer's fee is generally his sole means of compensation under the contract, and is therefore essential to him—unless he is otherwise wealthy or is creating the film for non-monetary motivations.

The distributor will seek and deserve other security devices necessary to his purpose. His contract will retain security interests in the film pending repayment of his loan, any laboratory will hold materials for his benefit, a promissory demand note payable on default may be required (sometimes individually endorsed), other creditors will be subordinated in their interest to the distributor's loan, and a chattel mortgage against the film filed as security. The contract is thick and substantive but the essential terms are as set forth.

Family-Friend Financing

Unfortunately few producers are able to attract this form of 100% distributor financing. They are required to look elsewhere for the support of their projects. This is most frequently true for unusual, imaginative or different type films from new producers who have little status and less funds. Fortunately, however, their budgets are generally far smaller than those of major-sponsored theatrical features.

Here the hoped-for financing may be acquired from friends or relatives, hopefully without any "public offering" as might be required under the Securities and Exchange Laws—these would require substantial difficulty and expense and are to be avoided if possible.

For a modest film, family-friend financing may not prove too difficult a task. The form of organization may well be dependent on the interest and involvement of the investor. From the point of view of flexibility and freedom from individual responsibility, the corporate form has much to recommend. Investors may be offered shares or profit participations by either the producing corporation or its shareholders in the total amount of the needed investment. There are advantages in making a reasonable proportion of such investment loans, as opposed to stock participations, as the investor will pay no tax on any loan recoupment, as opposed to dividends on his stock which will be taxable. On the other hand, the producers generally prefer as few definitive obligations as possible, and a loan is repayable at some point while a shareholder as an equitable investor need only be paid dividends when earned and declared.

More likely the investor, foreseeing the possibilities of prospective loss, so frequent in film investment, will prefer a limited partnership form of organization. Under this structure, after the limited partner has made his investment he has no further financial responsibility (unless otherwise agreed) and, most significantly under present tax laws, he can write off any loss incurred against his ordinary income. In other words, were he in a 60% income bracket and he lost $100,000 in the venture, his loss would be sharply limited by his write-off against his ordinary income. This he cannot do with a loss suffered by virtue of a stock investment or loan in a corporation which, as a rule, is a limited deduction applicable only against capital gains or a modest amount of income.

While there are various forms of corporations taxable in a manner akin to partnerships (Subchapter S, et seq. of the code) they appear to exclude film rental income which would make them of dubious applicability to such ventures.

Consequently, the limited partnership form is probably desirable to wealthy relatives and friends making a film investment. The disadvantage is for the general partner, who bears full responsibility for all obligations incurred beyond the invested funds. Sometimes, however, even this can be avoided by use of a corporation as general partner, which is now permissible under New York State law.

It should be noted that, under the limited partnership form, only the general partner may participate in the production. Were a limited partner to involve himself in the business, under the law he is liable to creditors precisely as a general partner. This, too, is a plus for the producer who wants artistic control of his film. In any event Uncle Joe and Aunt Harriet are not likely to be too inclined toward this responsibility!

"Friendly" investors are less likely than "arm's-length" investors to insist on all the protection of form contracts. They do not usually insist on completion guarantors or pledgeholder agreements or the like, so dealing with "friends" has collateral advantages. They are not usually available, however, to finance million-dollar budgets or to take participations in excess of moderate sums.

Derived from the legitimate stage, a frequent but by no means general, profit formula for these operations is 50% to investors, 50% to the productive talents. This, of course, assumes the initial repayment of all production expenses to investors. In a limited partnership, the limited partners would receive their allocable share each of 50% of profits while the producer (general partner) would receive the other 50% after all costs are recouped. Once again, producers must generally look to production fees or limited office-overhead charges for any financial participation beyond their dubious share of profits.

Interim Financing and Security Devices

In recent years a number of varied financial sources have assumed an interest in motion picture financing of a specialized variety. Religious groups, wealthy Indian tribes, manufacturers and others for a multitude of motives have made film investments. Securing such support is difficult for the average producer without high status or intimate connections. Such financing may run from 100% of budget to a much smaller provision, and is usually subject to the kind of rigid contractual terms as apply to major production financing. The investor's interest will be carefully protected by security devices, he is more likely to be a lender than an equitable participant, but the investor will probably insist on a share of profit participation. As the new industry investor will usually have a secondary motive (apart from profit participation), it is less likely to give full artistic control to producer and may seek to retain some influence in film content itself.

If a producer seeking outside financing can convince a reputable distributor to guarantee the return of his production "costs" (or a large portion of them) over a period of time (18 months or two years from film release), he may be able to secure the necessary interim financing from a bank or other lending institution. (A similar situation exists where a distributor agrees to "pick up" a finished picture for a set amount upon delivery.) This guaranty of payment is, of course, unconditional, and the sum is to be paid whether or not earned as producer's share of revenues under a distribution agreement.

In such circumstances, a bank or lending institution may be willing to make the actual production advances, relying on the subsequent payment by distributor. This type of financing is not uncommon in film but it is difficult to secure. First, the guaranty must be achieved and while, from the distributor's point of view it is not immediate cash out-of-pocket, it is nonetheless a substantive eventual risk in today's difficult market. In two years or on delivery he *must* pay, for example, $1-million. No distributor can afford too many unrecouped guaranties or pick-ups and stay permanently in this business. The proposed venture must therefore be most attractive and prospectively profitable.

Secondly, the interim lender must be quite satisfied with the distributor's credit. This will be carefully investigated before any advance is made. The interim loan may become the final loan if the distributor should fail, and such failure is not unheard of in today's conditions.

Financiers in this category are not generally sentimentalists or film-esthetes. They are hard-boiled lenders and not equity participants, although they are rarely averse to a prospective profit participation over and above the return of their principal plus a high rate of interest. But they cannot, in any sense, be regarded as mere profit participants. What they basically want and need is security that their loan will be repaid. Lending, and not investing, is their business.

In part they receive this security from an agreed "pick-up" (i.e., payment by a distributor upon the turning over of a completed film) or guaranty (payment within 18-24 months after delivery). In each case, the payment is to them and not the producer. But what if the film is never delivered? What if producer runs out of funds before completion or for any other reason cannot finish his work?

Here a reputable and financially responsible completion guarantor seems essential. If the producer has funds or other assets, perhaps these will suffice to satisfy the investor. More likely a third-party guaranty of completion will be required to secure the loan.

Other security devices as well must secure the lender. Until his loan is paid, he will require subordination of the rights of all other creditors, any copyrights should be assigned to him, a chattel mortgage on the film for his benefit and a laboratory pledgeholder-agreement to hold for his account. A promissory note personally endorsed for use in event of breach, and a security agreement specifying the lender's special interest in any proceeds are essentials. Where the distributor is guarantor, contractual relationships must be spelled out in an agreement securing the lender's interest from that source.

A multiplicity of problems arises when several groups provide differing shares of interim financing. The interests of each must be geared together—some may require preference in security over others, some may be profit participants, while others share from gross proceeds—the problems are too many and varied for discussion here. Suffice it to say that one lender or investor, if practical, is far superior to a host of participants under such arrangements.

Financing Through Foreign Production

A practical approach to financing frequently involves production abroad. Here, the advantages are manifold. The producer may be able to take advantage of foreign subsidies, frequently in effect, to pay for a substantial portion of his film. Sometimes banks or other groups have available large funds for investment that cannot be removed from the foreign jurisdiction. Finally, by virtue of a co-production arrangement, he may secure a large portion of his financing by sharing territorial and revenue rights with foreign groups, frequently either producers or exhibitors or studio owners. Many such groups exist, willing to participate in projects to a substantial extent if assured rights of exploitation in their own areas of the world. The producer's financial risks are sharply limited.

A studio in Copenhagen may, for example, pay all the "below the line" or studio costs of production as an advance against Scandinavian or European rights of exploitation. A German distributor or exhibitor group may advance funds against a prospective film with similar rights reserved. There are no rules to the applicable formulas. The parties may cross-share their rights—following the recoupment of any party's investment from his share of the world territory, the next proceeds from that territory will serve to recoup any unpaid investor.

The dangers here are also apparent. Production will be abroad and some foreign technicians are not adequate for first-class production. Language and formalities are frequently a barrier. Sometimes, a major distribution deal is out of the question because many companies will insist on world rights and not just the Western Hemisphere or other limited area. Nevertheless, co-production abroad has proved a most useful tool and a simplified means of securing financing for an individual or selected group of film projects.

"Public" Financing

Going to the public for substantive film financing has proven a difficult but not insurmountable problem. Here, the producer must face the problem of security registration. A full and complicated registration statement is required if the issue is substantial—the more modest "Regulation A" prospectus if it is limited. An underwriter must be found to market the issue. The prospectus must be full and complete and, if the issuer lacks experience and a record of success, it is likely to fail. Considerable legal fees are involved and all relevant information set forth. The prospective investor must be informed of all the risks of his venture and, in the film business today, these are obviously substantial. It is a difficult route, but a handful of determined and intrepid enterpreneurs have accomplished it.

It must be kept in mind that any "public offering" must meet these requirements. The term is one of art but generally involves offering an investment (be it stock, debenture, note or profit participation) to more than 25 interstate investors. To fail to register not only violates the Securities Act but creates the risk that an unsuccessful investor may sue to recoup his loss on the grounds that there was a public offering without a registration.

The ways of film financing are many and arduous, but short of a truly subsidized industry which does not appear foreseeable, must all be explored. The recent export subsidy advance is a step, but only a modest one, in the right direction. But it is no panacea. It offers small sums on a limited basis against foreign revenues.[2]

    This brief chapter touches but a few techniques that have been utilized to finance theatrical and televised film. Other methods must be, and are constantly being found. There is hope in the new industrial interest in promoting film ventures. Banks and other lending institutions may loosen their purse strings with new incentives. Co-production abroad remains a favored instrument. Public or industry subsidy may eventually develop. The ways and means must be found to utilize the great creative capabilities of our rising generation of young and talented film-makers.

[2] The Export-Import Bank of the United States announced on October 12, 1971, that subject to risk participation by other institutions, it will finance or cause financing of selected film projects for up to 50% of the cost of production for films to be exhibited or distributed abroad. The program is subject to rigid rules available through the bank and covers the value of export rights as well as production costs for approved features.

4

Production Subsidies

OUTSIDE THE UNITED STATES, most serious film-producing countries have searched for and found means of helping their local industries in one manner or another. The theory is that locally made films support important national interests and that employment and economic conditions as well are improved by sponsoring a film industry. A technical work force is secured employment, industry is activated and local production as opposed to American films and other worldwide productions is encouraged.

It must be added that, because very few films return their negative costs, a viable industry is a difficult thing to create. The experience in most countries has been that, unless there is sponsorship, support or subsidy, no significant motion picture industry can be locally envisaged. The possibility of recouping negative investment from merely the local market is difficult if not impossible. Costs have risen sharply, markets are insufficient in size or population and film, therefore, must be regarded as international rather than national in its economic implications.

The worldwide techniques for film sponsorship are many and varied. In some situations, actual cash is laid out toward production by a governmental or quasi-governmental body interested in such development. Elsewhere, low interest loans are made by or guaranteed by governmental bodies to producers. These loans bear modest interest or sometimes no interest whatsoever.

Governmental or quasi-governmental guaranties to prospective investors or lending institutions are another method of making sure that a producer gets the necessary financing to create his film. As an alternative, partial production costs may be advanced by means other than direct cash payments through subsidies to studios and technicians. In this way, the producer gets his film without having to put up all of the necessary expenses.

Still another technique, which occurs after the fact of production, is the payment of cash or other prizes for films found eligible by selective governmental or quasi-governmental groups. These funds may be conditioned to apply toward financing a future project of the winning producer.

Admissions tax rebates follow a similar path. They are in effect subsidy after the fact, generally to a film that has proved its value at the box office. They perform the subsidy function insofar as they encourage and may be directed toward the payment of new and additional films.

The most well known subsidy is the EADY Plan formulated in Great Britain to encourage production following World War II. The plan is named after Sir Wilfred Eady who had sponsored an earlier voluntary plan for the British treasury.

In essence, the scheme levies an exhibition tax on all of the exhibitors of Great Britain. Over and above a specified base amount, a percentage of gross admission price is set aside to be paid into the subsidy fund. This is a tax in effect on the British movie going public, local exhibitors and to the extent that they share in such proceeds all distributors. It is the yield of this levy that goes to subsidize the eligible film makers.

The requisites for eligibility for participation in the fund evolve essentially around the British nature of the film. A British quota film is eligible to participate and others are excluded.

What makes a non-quota film? There are restrictions on labor costs and if the labor costs are minimal the film is non-quota and may not participate no matter how British it may be. Similarly if 10 per cent or more of the film's playing time is derived from previously registered films that film cannot qualify. If the film is older than a specified period (recently four years) it too is excluded.

The included films for the general subsidy are those made by a British subject or corporation with a majority of directors British or Irish, in 35mm., at a British studio where no less than 75% of the costs of the film have been paid to persons who are ordinarily residents in the British Commonwealth. The films must also be "long films"—recently defined as over 33 minutes in length. Government films, TV films, 8mm. and 16mm. films are not included within this aspect of the plan although there are certain limited benefits of different characteristics for films other than "long films" in 35mm.

For the benefit of certain foreign interests that have utilized the plan, exceptions are made in the labor costs provisions so that a foreign actor or actress or director may be paid a substantial salary which is deducted before the requisite amount of labor costs must be paid locally. In other words, a production will not be discouraged simply because a British company desires to use an American director or performer which, by the ordinary rule-of-thumb, would exclude it for lack of the requisite payment percentages to British residents. This is done by excluding particular salaries of one or two participants from the total salaries paid before applying the eligibility rule.

It is essential that the "maker" of the film be a United Kingdom company. This rule appears to be more form than substance, however, as the United Kingdom company may be financed from elsewhere and may in fact be substantially controlled by foreign interests. It is the formality of the production company's origins that appears to be the critical point rather than the domicile of its principal backers. Although at first blush this seems strange, it is quite understandable, because the plan is trying to encourage the making of pictures in Great Britain and is far less concerned with those who may profit.

Based on the actual box office take of all eligible films, at the end of the year, the subsidy funds are then divided among the participants. The films share in the same percentage of the fund as their gross relates to the other films so qualified.

In other words, if any eligible film grosses £1. out of every £100. gross by all British quota films, then it is entitled to 1% of the net subsidy fund at the end of the year.

The system obviously places a great premium on success. Movies like the James Bond series which had fantastic box office receipts in Britain received vast sums as a bonus based on their remarkable performance. One might argue that this is hardly the essential function of a subsidy, (i.e., to make the rich richer). It may be counter-argued however that such large emoluments encourage others to produce popular films and therefore support the domestic film industry. It should be noted that the British do have some subsidy programs for minor experimental films not based on popularity as well as the general EADY Plan and that in their practical way they have tried to meet all the logical objectives of subsidy.

For many years the plan was considered a substantial success even though its principal benefactors may have been essentially American firms. In more recent times, however, it has fallen on more difficult days. The British box office is sharply down and the fund is thereby diminished. American financiers are currently loath to make substantial investment in production in Britain. This may be temporary as it follows the disastrous years of 1969, and 1970 during which the major American film companies succeeded in losing hundreds of millions of dollars.

Overall the plan must be considered the most successful of the subsidy programs. In essence, it has now been followed in Germany with a similar formula that unfortunately like its counterpart is encouraging the production of the current fad, i.e. sex education films which have proved popular in the markets of West Germany.

Elsewhere in the world, under more rigid rules, the French government has taken steps to subsidize its local industry. To qualify as a French film the motion picture must be in the French language, utilizing local nationals as players and technicians and must be processed and edited in a local laboratory. Subsidy payments are determined by the Minister of Cultural Affairs and come from the proceeds of an admissions tax, a release tax on distributors and prior loan reimbursements.

The subsidy fund payments are in the form of credits against which a producer can draw when he makes a new film. He is not entitled to cash as such, but only to such expenses as may be allocated by the authorities to the picture in production.

Under this plan the maker of the film must be French. The rule is applied much more rigidly than in Great Britain in order to encourage French Film production as such. The subsidy plan does not appear to have succeeded in particularly encouraging a declining French film industry.

In Italy producers may be entitled to subsidy if their film is produced in Italy and made predominantly with local personnel. The prime source of subsidy comes from a high admissions tax charged to national exhibitors. The Italians also have prizes and awards and low interest loans may be made available from a governmental bank or with governmental guaranty.

Many countries have established screen quotas for films made elsewhere. Local exhibitors may suffer consequences if they play more than a specified percentage of foreign films. The idea once again is to encourage play dates for the local variety.

Another fertile source for film funding has arisen in Israel. There the government through the Film Center in the Ministry of Commerce and Industry grants benefits both to "approved" Israeli features and another category known as "other films." The "approved" group involves films whose scripts have been accepted by the Film Center and which have committed themselves to the payment of at least 25% of wages and technical services to be spent for Israeli crews and local services.

Producers in both categories, however, get a significant rebate for each dollar converted into Israeli currency and actually used in production as well as an exemption from customs duty on raw stock and equipment imported into the country.

Approved features get still another benefit in the form of a partial refund of admissions taxes collected when the film is distributed. This takes the form of cash advances on account of the refund to a prescribed maximum during subsequent production. In addition loan guaranties up to 20% of the projected budget and reduced income taxes from film distribution proceeds may be allocated.

In many countries of the world, of course, there are substantial advantages of a similar nature.

There are numerous grounds for an American producer to contemplate foreign production. With American standards and union practices, Hollywood and New York costs sometimes approach the astronomical and while rates abroad have risen a large gap still remains. It has proved quite possible to produce equal quality films on far lower budgets elsewhere in the world.

Authentic backgrounds present another motive for production in the land where the plot is laid or at least one strongly resembling it. Authenticity is certainly a key factor in determining locale.

Still another motive for production abroad is the free availability of private local financing to aid in production. Various types of arrangements can be entered into to divide territories and give participants a chance to recoup investments from chosen areas. The splitting of such financing by territories may make the raising of substantial funds far easier than it would be under ordinary circumstances.

In the same connection, the tremendous significance of the foreign box office to films generally cannot be overestimated. Production of films abroad contributes to these markets and on an over-all basis may be helpful in establishing a healthy climate for a producer's films in the local territory.

In earlier years there were also substantial tax advantages for American stars and other participants resident in foreign countries over prolonged periods. Several of these rules have now been repealed which limits but does not entirely destroy this financial advantage of production abroad.

Perhaps, however, the most significant advantage to filming in foreign climes is the policy of subsidy in so many parts of the world that recognize the true value of the motion picture medium.

5

The Elements
of Popularity

"IF YOU'RE SO SMART why aren't you a millionaire?" A favorite client of mine often used that phrase when we attempted to analyze business problems related to the success or failure of any particular film enterprise. It seems peculiarly appropriate when one approaches the hazardous game of analyzing what elements make for popularity on the screen. The factors are there all right but the trouble is that for every success based on these criteria one can find a failure—for each flashy novelty a dim photostat—and today's hero is tomorrow's anti-hero. Nonetheless, some effort to identify the considerations that create a strong pull at the box office seems essential. How else to struggle, in an unsubsidized American industry that must support itself, toward the goal of public acceptance?

We limit ourselves initially to the American-Canadian area which, while less than half the world market for most domestic films, still represents a crucial segment of the paying public. What types of films have shown the ability to draw huge numbers of patrons? Can we, in brief, explain their popularity?

Variety magazine annually publishes lists of winners—both for the entire history of film and for the particular year just ended. The listings may not be entirely accurate and may contain some omissions. Nonetheless, their significance is apparent. A recent schedule specifies

31

these blockbusters as leading all-time successes: *The Godfather*
(1972); *Gone with the Wind* (1939); *The Sound of Music* (1965);
Love Story (1970); *Airport* (1970); *The Graduate* (1968); *Doctor
Zhivago* (1965); *Ben-Hur* (1959); *Ten Commandments* (1957);
My Fair Lady (1964); *Mary Poppins* (1964); *MASH* (1970); *Butch
Cassidy and the Sundance Kid* (1969); *West Side Story* (1961);
Thunderball (1965).

Gone with the Wind, based on a highly successful novel with an
indigenous American theme, opened with a vast fanfare of publicity
in Atlanta in 1939. Far and away the most expensive film of its time,
it ran an unprecedented four-and-a-half hours on the screen. It featured distinguished stars (Clark Gable, Olivia DeHaviland and Leslie
Howard) and an element of surprise casting—the British Vivien Leigh
as Scarlett O'Hara. The story was romantic and sentimental against
the stirring background of the Civil War. The great sequence of
wounded and dying in the Station Plaza at Atlanta truly met the cliché
"unforgettable." *Gone with the Wind* continues on its rounds of
revivals and re-revivals for every new generation with tremendous
appeal.

The Sound of Music again employed sentimentality. This time,
in a sugar-sweet musical form as far removed from the real problem
of escape from Nazi occupation (the ostensible theme) as the world
of 1973 from that of 1920. Based on a Broadway musical of limited
impact, it did contain a remarkable book and lyrics by the immortal
Rodgers-Hammerstein combination. Its appeal was unique, running
across all barriers of age, race and sex. A quasi-religious theme was
coupled with an all too-adorable Trapp family and a saccharine Julie
Andrews singing her way from nunnery to mistress of the house. The
beautiful background mountains and meadows of the Austrian Alps
added to the scene. Vast millions of dollars have been lost in efforts
to copy the scope and character of this fantastic-grossing film.

Love Story, also based on a highly popular novel, again featured
sentiment and unreality in the real world of strife and difficulty. A
young, if cynical Italian girl (the stunning Ali MacGraw) and an
unbelievable Boston Brahmin (Ryan O'Neal) find and lose, and find
and lose each other again amid happiness and tears that near drenched
the theatres of America.

Airport, based on Arthur Hailey's strong-selling novel, has been
gratuitously referred to as 1970's prospective Academy Award winner

for 1944. A melodramatic, old-fashioned plot; a host of stars (Burt Lancaster, Dean Martin, Helen Hayes) involved with the dangers of modern flight, combined to make a surprising and overwhelming theatrical smash. The old and regular theatrical audiences of another era came out to see *Airport*.

The Graduate was quite a different story. Here the novel had no broad appeal and the stars (Dustin Hoffman and Anne Bancroft), although experienced, had little box office appeal at the time of release. Mike Nichols, who directed, however, had already started a distinguished career. The film broke new ground in its frank and open appeal to the youth market. Here was a picture that defied ancient conventions of American films—ridiculing the traditional dreams of success in business and matrimony as well as all the other middle-class standards of morality. "I have just the place for you—plastics," says a friendly business tycoon to the young and disillusioned Hoffman. Popular theme music, anti-Establishment sentiments and brilliant performances helped create an outstanding critical reaction for the film. Once again, fortunes have since been lost trying to recreate its unique and remarkable appeal.

Dr. Zhivago harked back to an earlier day of spectacle and drama. The broad canvas is wartime, revolutionary Russia. Within this scope we find the heroism of men at war, sin and retribution and the overpowering force of love as human emotion. There are stars (Omar Sharif, Julie Christie, Geraldine Chaplin) but they are dwarfed by the majestic setting. Spectacle and high drama would seem the key.

Our next two films may be combined for analysis in view of their similarity of appeal. *Ben-Hur* and *Ten Commandments* were both spectacles with historical-religious themes. They fit closely within traditional formats for film success. There is once again true love, majesty, sacrifice and redemption. They return the spectator, albeit unrealistically, to earlier and simpler times—they eliminate his daily problems and cares and make the theatre a place of escape with large-scale, high-budgeted entertainment.

My Fair Lady was still another expensive musical, this time based on Shaw's well-read *Pygmalion* and a successful Broadway musical, featuring Rex Harrison and Audrey Hepburn and emphasizing a fine score, delightful humor and overwhelming sentimentality. From guttersnipe to lady, the tale is told against an anachronistic setting of an obsolete British high society. The theme was classic, the adaptation brilliant and the results tremendous.

Mary Poppins, from a well-known fictional character, was a surprise. What might have appealed merely to a children's audience found a far broader scope with Julie Andrews' delightful personality and an imaginative, if saccharine, screenplay. In spite of these factors, it is still difficult to understand its overwhelming results at the box office.

Mash and *Butch Cassidy and the Sundance Kid,* while entirely different in theme, appealed again to a young anti-Establishment audience fed up with war and traditional heroes. *MASH* was clearly an attack on Vietnam (although situate in Korea), phrased in terms of black comedy, while *Cassidy* reversed the roles of traditional Western heroes. Both films had "names" (Elliott Gould and Donald Sutherland in *MASH,* and Paul Newman and Robert Redford in *Cassidy*). Although both were well made and entertaining, the extreme popularity of either would have been difficult to predict.

West Side Story was a musical version of the Romeo-Juliet saga set against the background of modern Manhattan with its gangs and racial hatreds. The Bernstein music, brilliant dancing and direction, and the sentimental theme coupled together to create a magnetic audience-pull for a very worthwhile film.

Thunderball, and the other James Bond films, took advantage of the modern acceptability of casual violence and easy sex. Using the perfectly cast talents of Sean Connery (without whom Bond films seem to fail) and a host of gorgeous and willing sex symbols, the pictures had no story-line worthy of mention but simply jumped from thrill to thrill, be it violent, sadistic or prurient. The entertainment is pure escapism and one should not ask for what end or purpose.

The most recent and greatest winner was, of course, the remarkable *The Godfather* based on a highly successful novel by Mario Puzo. It too had violence but coupled it with moving performances, particularly by Marlon Brando, and a strong sentiment of love within the criminal "family." Fine critical comments and an outstanding campaign added to the film's fantastic box office impact.

The Popularity Factors

Looking, then, at these various theme elements that have gone into financially successful films (we do not deal here with artistic success), we find a host of factors which, if properly presented, may achieve the golden prize of popularity. These would seem to include:

Spectacle. Of the all-time winners cited above, no less than five have elements of high spectacle. Their backgrounds may run from Biblical times to civil wars of more recent vintage, but they are vast in scope and overpowering in scene. They use the film medium to its broadest extent in showing that which cannot be successfully displayed on stage or on a small screen. Historical partisans parade in great numbers, battle sequences show huge armies in desperate clash, the personal story is frequently diluted—the background is the theme. Great historical events, military or revolutionary incidents and religious movements all hold a firm place in films of this nature. Why one spectacular may fail when another proves a bonanza remains mysterious, but that spectaculars have been a major factor in success is simply undeniable.

Sentimentality. Here the appeal is primarily to audience "feel" rather than any intellectual experience. Emotion takes priority and rationality is far in arrears. Generally the context is romantic—the love of sweethearts, or husband and wife, or family or country. Music is frequently an effective additive for films of this genre—*The Sound of Music* and *West Side Story* are illustrative. On a separate level, *Love Story* is a perfect example of pure sentimental appeal. That inexplicable item called love remains, perhaps, the most potent factor among human emotions and the sentimental film aims straight at the heart.

Family films. While this type of picture may include the two categories above, we are speaking here of materials primarily created for a very young audience. Not infrequently, these pictures break out of that pattern as in the case of *Mary Poppins* and a succession of Walt Disney hits. It is not only the children who find values but their parents as well. Simplicity (some might call it oversimplification), domesticity, nonviolence, antisexuality, trick animation and the frequent use of pets or other animals—all are characteristic of these efforts. Today, as rarely before with television's competitive appeal and a vast market to be tapped, there is room for this type of film. Few, however, can find the proper formula. For if the film is purely a children's picture its box office grasp is limited. It must go beyond that, in all its simplicity, for a broader scale appeal.

Musicals. While music may be a key factor in successful films of

sentimental appeal, the old-fashioned musical *qua* musical appears to
be losing favor. Here we are concerned with the film in which music
is the prime quality—for example, the old-fashioned backstage story
(*42nd Street*). This type of effort appears passé. We are not referring,
of course, to the successful rock concert documentaries such as
Woodstock, Gimme Shelter and *The Concert for Bangladesh*. These
pictures seem generally more representative of anti-Establishment
sentiments although they do combine musical interest as well.

Adventure. This is a recurrent theme among top-grossing features. Here the producer has found an audience in the lure of action,
frequently coupled with unusual, different and spectacular atmo-
spheres. The Bond series is indicative but numerous other successes
have capitalized on the escapist desire to visualize (for a few hours at
least) an active life in a brand-new setting. The traditional "western,"
long an industry staple, emphasized this quality.

Violence. Here is another element traditional in nature (i.e., the
ever-present Western), but which has developed new and broadened
boundaries in recent years. Violence has moved from the routine (if
any killing can be considered routine) to the shocking as a box-office
element. Mere mayhem is insufficient. Now there is torture, rape,
brutality and sadism in such successes as *Dirty Harry, The French
Connection, The Valachi Papers* and that terrible nightmare of 1984,
A Clockwork Orange. See also the "Kung Fu" hits of 1973 such as
Five Fingers of Death.

Sexuality. Pure sexuality as opposed to romantic love has shown
vastly increased potential draw in recent years. As indicated in our
chapter on foreign films, while the initial breakthrough came in that
area, American producers have learned quickly, broadening the scope
and increasing the candor of activity in their films. The remarkable
success of a pure sexploiter, *The Stewardesses,* in 1971, and *Deep
Throat* in 1972 is indicative of the large audience available for explicit
films of this character. There is indeed, as well, a substantial audience
for male homosexuality, lesbianism, explicit intercourse, *fellatio* and
other aberrational acts on the screen. While much has been shown,
there remain many things that have not been—and if success in this
area is to be enjoyed in the future, one can predict with certainty that
it will involve new techniques and new shocks not presently available.

Whether this will be permitted by local and state authorities is another story discussed elsewhere. (See *Obscenity Laws*, page 126).

Humor. The funny picture is a species unto itself. Many films in diverse categories have amusing situations but they are not premised merely on the comical. There are, however, cases where films aimed purely at laughs have proven substantial winners. Stanley Kramer's *Mad, Mad, Mad World* and the Woody Allen Comedies are illustrative. *Bob & Carol & Ted & Alice* hit with a comedy sex theme. *Odd Couple* and *Plaza Suite* also show that situation comedy has power in theatres as well as on television. The ability to make people laugh is clearly also the ability to draw them to theatres, although few of these pictures are listed among the top winners.

Another aspect of humor is "campiness" or an amused view of some habits of the past. Successful revivals of several old films have shown this special, if limited, appeal. Although there was little funny about it, the surprising popularity of *Bonnie & Clyde* was essentially "campy" as it seemingly related to style and time rather than to its content. *Thoroughly Modern Millie* was more traditional in its direct take-off of a way of life of a bygone era.

The Bizarre and Unusual. American films in these categories do not generally make the top listings above but nonetheless show considerable potential in the modern market. Science fiction can occasionally hit the mark (*The Andromeda Strain*). In 1971, an extraordinary shocker entitled *Willard*, dealing primarily with a young boy's relationship with his rats, garnered huge receipts. No doubt, nauseating as it may seem, similar efforts will be forthcoming.

The Horror Film. Akin to the bizarre is this category which has long been a staple of the American market (*Frankenstein* and *Dracula*) and will undoubtedly so remain. New filming techniques have made them more realistic and chilling, with such delightful sequences as severed limbs, cleft heads, flowing blood and miscellaneous gore. *Tales from the Crypt*, a 1972 success, is a good example of this ancient species modernized.

Racial Themes. While not unprecedented (*Birth of a Nation, Gentleman's Agreement*), films with racial and religious backgrounds have taken on an added impact with the rise of ethnicity in American life. In particular, black-white difficulties and a new view of the American red man have taken precedence. This has been reflected in some important pictures. *Shaft* and *Sweet Sweetback's Baadasssss Song* were two tremendous successes of the 1971 season. They were followed by a black flood in 1972 (*Superfly, Shafts Big Score, Legend of Nigger Charlie,* etc.) Each film has pro-black and anti-authority thrust and each is coupled with strong action melodrama. Numerous other pictures with varying success have indicated a renewed interest and sympathy with the American Indian (*A Man Called Horse*). These racially oriented films have, in some instances, shown appeal to white as well as black audiences. There is no doubt we will be seeing many more of the same including, in all probability, *The Grandson of Shaft*. Other special interest groups are also producing films and will continue to bring them to the screen, including homosexuals (*Out of the Closet*), women's rights and other minority efforts. It has been a traditional, if somewhat inaccurate, slogan in the film business that "if you want to send a message, go to Western Union," but some of these films seem to belie that doctrine and to combine message with popularity. The growth of minority audiences and increased maturity and selectivity of audiences would seem likely to make this a continuing trend if the nature of the themes can be expanded.

Neo-realistic Films. The type of realism which hit the jackpot for Italian producers in the late 1940's (*Open City* and *Paisan*) and the British angry young men of the 1950's (*Room at the Top, Saturday Night and Sunday Morning*) has rarely had equivalent success for local producers. It runs counter to the tendency to escapism which is a more usual theatrical motive. Nonetheless, under existing circumstances, it is hopefully possible that we will have a return to this type of film which has shown the power to deeply stir human emotions (*Sounder*). Similarly, straight documentaries which have generally fared poorly at the box office short of some special shock value have a role which they will undoubtedly continue to play.

Anti-Establishment Pictures. We have mentioned several leading productions in this category (*The Graduate, MASH, Butch Cassidy*). There should be added the extraordinary case of *Easy Rider,* produced cheaply but rolling up fantastic grosses with a young audience. These are films which have caught the strong sentiment of self-criticism developing in this country since the early 1960's. The causes include such things as the Vietnam conflict, the debate about drugs, the racial issue, Watergate, and a general tendency toward disillusionment with materialistic American dreams. This is a stream of thought of many young, and some not-so-young, of our citizens and they will pay their dollars to see these thoughts illustrated on the screen. It must be added, however, that there are a great many examples of where this quest for a "youth-oriented" market has failed. In particular, we have in mind nearly all of the films about the campus revolts of the late 1960's (*Strawberry Statement*).

What Makes a Successful Film?

We have cited many elements that have been involved in large-scale successes. But obviously, merely to load these into a property and hope for the best is clearly the producer's road to economic ruin. It takes the right thing at the right moment to catch the public fancy. This is hardly a predictable, particularly when we keep in mind that major films must be planned long before their public exhibition. It is not what the public wants now (difficult as that is to gauge) but what it will want two, three or even five years from now that most producers must project in selecting their projects. The difficulties of such determinations are apparent—and all too real.

A few things are clear. With but a handful of exceptions copies of a prior formula have proved unsuccessful. The woods are strewn with the disasters that followed attempts to imitate *The Sound of Music, The Graduate* and *Easy Rider,* and the unbelievably horrible financial statements of major production companies in the period 1969-71 are ever-living proof. One of the rare exceptions to this principle would seem the James Bond films, so long as they utilize the services of Sean Connery as 007. Without him, even these famous adventure yarns appear to lack viability.

Is the story the thing? To a very great extent this seems to be the case. Success after success appears to accompany popular novels capably translated to the screen medium. Illustrations would include *Gone with the Wind, Love Story, Airport, Dr. Zhivago* and *The Godfather.* The pre-sold market for such works appears immense. Even a successful novel, however, is no certainty and there are numerous examples where best-sellers have failed in a different medium.

Star appeal is notoriously fickle and, while bankers like the security of a "name" for their loans, there is little to indicate, at least for now, that the presence of a particular personality spells success. The true indicia of movie stardom is the ability to draw a large public regardless of the accompanying property. With the possible exceptions of John Wayne and Clint Eastwood, it is hard to think of a single player who presently performs this role. Burton and Taylor certainly do not. Brando has more downs than ups and while George Scott hit beautifully as Patton and the beleaguered doctor in *The Hospital*, he was unable to save *The Last Run* or *They Might be Giants*. Bill Holden had his *Bridge on the River Kwai* but more recently fared poorly in *Wild Rovers*. Dustin Hoffman scored in *The Graduate* and *Little Big Man* but not so well in *Who is Harry Kellerman* . . . Casting, while vital to the right property, is insufficient unto itself for broad appeal.

With but few exceptions the box office records of most directors are equally erratic. There are some who may be counted on regularly for films of artistic importance but few with a continued box office appeal. Stanley Kubrick with *2,001* and *A Clockwork Orange* appears to have high prospects, but it is early in the game. David Lean has had a remarkable record of appeal (*Bridge on the River Kwai, Lawrence of Arabia, Dr. Zhivago, Ryan's Daughter*). Mike Nichols, with *Who's Afraid of Virginia Woolf, The Graduate* and *Carnal Knowledge*, also, however, had his *Catch-22*. The mere hiring of an outstanding or competent director is obviously no assurance of popularity, particularly in these days when directors services come high.

Certainly a large budget is no guarantee of anything. Today's public wouldn't care less what a film costs to make—the repeated failures of multi-million-dollar pictures is clear proof (*Star, Dr. Doolittle, Hello, Dolly, On a Clear Day You Can See Forever, The Mollie Maguires*, etc.). Today's sharply reduced budgets are a consequence of such disasters.

If one must generalize, and perhaps one should not, the key factor in addition to the themes we have set forth would emphasize the juxtaposition of time and content. To come out at the right time with a theme significant to the moment is a vital factor. Perhaps a few themes are significant at all times, as the record indicates with reference to religious spectacle. Others, however, have proved far more mercurial.

We close with the usual clichés. The film must be well cast, capably directed, broadly advertised and publicized with a strong word-of-mouth reaction. The ingredients must all be there. " 'Tis a puzzlement," as the King said to Anna of Siam—but a fascinating puzzlement that will grip us as long as the public seeks entertainment.

Part Two

PROBLEMS IN DISTRIBUTION-EXHIBITION

6

The Distribution Agreement

DISTRIBUTION AGREEMENTS for motion pictures, like other agreements, vary sharply with the respective bargaining power of the parties. There are very few simple forms which can be blindly adapted to any situation. The financial terms, in particular, are subject to drastic differences. If the distributor is financing the project in whole or in part an entirely different set of terms may apply as opposed to the produced or independently financed film (foreign or domestic) that is being subjected to license. The financing distributor will, of course, with great justification, insist on certain privileges where it has already invested substantial funds in a project. On the other hand, where it is merely acquiring a limited license in a film completed with other people's money some of those terms need not be applicable.

Nor is acquiring a film invariably done by a distribution license. Where producer-distributor creates the product itself, it is the owner by definition and while it may grant certain rights in the proceeds to artistic creators or others for one reason or another, there is no transfer of rights. The negative belongs to the distributor.

Other film rights may be acquired in toto and without license. A negative may simply be purchased outright by sale or transfer with all attendant rights and no spelling out of other terms is necessary.

However, the most common transaction for distribution purposes, where a previously created film is transferred or where an independent producer contracts to develop a cinematic property, is a license. We deal here with some of the terms inherent in such arrangements. Forms are available elsewhere.[1]

The License

Generally the initial provision is the granting clause under which the rights licensed to the distributor are spelled out frequently in great depth. The distributor will nearly invariably insist that the rights be *exclusive* for the agreed term. It is the rarest of licensees who will accept less than exclusivity for his grant, as competition is, of course, violently destructive of potential exploitation values.

The question of term should also be specified in the granting clause. To properly exploit a film requires a substantial amount of time. In your author's experience, terms of less than seven years are exceedingly rare and frequently rights are granted for periods far in excess of this running from ten years to perpetuity. (The latter phrase is closely akin to an outright sale.)

The grant is generally not only to the distributor but his licensees and assigns, as he may wish to sell or license to others some or all of his rights, or may reorganize in a new corporate or other form. A limited right to dispose of such rights is to be expected (i.e., a distributor frequently may not itself deal with such items as nontheatrical rights). In that connection, it should be added that the matter of who pays for the charges of subdistributors or other limited assignees of rights must be covered and clarified. A full assignment clause may pose problems as the grantor may feel he is relying on a particular company or individual and may not wish to see the contract transferred, at least without further compensation to himself. The ordinary rule of law, short of unusual circumstances, is that a contract without any assignment provision is fully assignable but there are enough exceptions that the matter should be covered. A full assignment clause is normal (although without a release provision the assignor remains liable to the grantor under a contract) but it is not extraordinary for assignment to be conditioned in one of several ways. The distributor may be limited to assignment to a corporation he or it controls, may be obliged to make further payment on an assignment or may be forbidden to assign without grantor's consent in writing.

[1] See Lindey: *Motion Picture Agreements,* Matthew Bender 1947; Lindey: *Entertainment, Publishing and the Arts,* Clark Boardman & Co., Ltd. 1963, with annual supplements.

The granting clause spells out the rights licensed. For a theatrical feature they will undoubtedly include all rights of theatrical distribution within the territory covered. Generally a distributor, under presently difficult business conditions, will also insist on television as he may not be able to recover his advance or expenses without it. Still, some contracts omit it or leave TV with the licensor. A distributor may then validly ask for a protection provision against premature TV or other exploitation for a period of time to protect his essential grant. Periods of two years for such non use are not extraordinary. Television is a broad term and the distributor will most likely break it down to include free television, pay television, community antenna television or other means of televised distribution. As cassettes are a means for televised projection as well as home and other exhibition, they too may be included.

The grant will ordinarily include other nontheatrical rights as well. There may be great values involved in showings to schools, clubs and universities in all gauges of film and the distributor will either want to exploit these or have the right to permit others to do so.

Because of the constantly changing technology, the prudent distributor may well insert a clause authorizing his right to distribute by any and all means known or hereafter becoming known within the territory. There have been many arguments over such clauses in the past. Did a general grant of rights in the pre-sound era include distribution of a "talkie?" Did a grant of all rights of distribution or use without more specifics include or exclude television? No one is looking for litigation and these are litigious points, particularly where a film acquires great value during the term of the agreement.

Territorial and Other Rights

Rights should include distribution in foreign language versions where pertinent. Even in local arrangements for the U.S. and Canada, for example, problems can arise over distribution of pictures in or about "French Canada" with particular reference to television from Montreal and Quebec City stations. Including the French version in the grant should remedy the problem.

Territory is, of course, a vital term and should be spelled out explicitly. If the world is the area that simplifies matters, but for many films (foreign in particular), grantor's rights may be limited. General geographical terms should be avoided to exclude "ambiguity"—what, for instance, is included in the Western Hemisphere? What is a United States "territory" or "possession?" What is Puerto Rico? What Dominions of Canada, if not all, are relevant?

A territorial problem may arise where televised broadcasts cover a non-included area of distribution. If one holds, for example, television rights in the U.S.A. but not Canada, what is the effect of a broadcast in Detroit or Buffalo? The contract should clarify, from a distributor's point of view, in view of improving technology, that territory means the place of broadcast and that this is not limited by the territorial grant. A grantor might look at it differently.

Other important rights would include distribution to ships, aircraft, trains, hotels, motels and the like. With particular reference to communications, a distributor should if possible get the right to license to ships and aircraft departing ports within the territory. Limitation to national carriers of a particular country is difficult as many ships, for example, sail under foreign registry and important sources of revenue may be lost by a misplaced word. Domestic distribution should also include U.S. military and Red Cross or related bases or installations throughout the world.

Beyond the initial grant of rights, including territory and term, other adjacent rights may prove important. If the producer-owner will grant it, the distributor may desire the right to cut, edit, change, dub, subtitle or otherwise alter or add to the film. Disputes have arisen as to the right to do this, particularly for television where time slotting becomes vital. Of course, the producer or director of an important picture (and to what producer is his picture not important?) may be concerned with any cutting or changes. In such cases, the right may be limited for censorship or classification or television purposes or not to be exercised without licensor's written consent.

Copyright ownership should belong to the licensor as it is an important indicia of ownership but is frequently demanded (not without reason) by the distributor (with an agreement to reassign at the end of the term). The rule at law, at least until recently, has been that a copyright owner must be party to any copyright litigation and, in case of infringement, the distributor may not wish to have to go looking for an itinerant owner-producer whose availability may be questionable.

As a distributor wishes to publicize his trademark, he usually insists on a clause allowing him to add his logo and mark to a film. He should be instructed by the licensor as to other necessary credits both on the film and for all advertisement and publicity purposes. When a distributor is authorized, as is the occasional practice in foreign films, to add scenes to the film, additional credits may be allowed.

Musical rights to synchronize and perform can prove most significant. Producer-licensor must grant such rights. In many foreign countries, performance rights societies control performance in theatres (not in the U.S.A.) and their clearance may also be necessary. Whether the grantor owns the right to publish and record such music may prove a problem in the matter of granting recording rights. A distributor, of course, desires to participate in the proceeds of any album of soundtrack music or other separate recordings when available.

Frequently a clause grants advertising rights in all media, including use of trailers on television and otherwise. This may be necessary, even where TV rights are withheld by the owner, as promotion by the medium may be essential. Publication rights for a synopsis (7500 words) or limited edition of the literary work may also be desired by the distributor for publicity and exploitation purposes or even ordinary royalties. What the owner can give here is frequently limited by the rights he himself has acquired in the basic literary property itself.

The right to change a film title is frequently granted, and seems reasonable as titles may prove problems in exploitation. Sometimes the right is limited to require grantor's consent (not to be unreasonably withheld).

An owner should also turn over copies of artwork, stills, outtakes and other materials he has on hand to help in exploiting the film.

Commercial tie-ins for merchandising may prove valuable in connection with the film and the distributor will endeavor to secure broad rights in this area. They might include such items as toy manufacturing based on principal characters, premiums for sponsors, comic books and strips, and costumes. Such grants are, of course, subject to whatever limitations the grantor may have by virtue of his own acquisition.

Warranties

It is usual and normal for a distributor to insist on certain warranties in connection with the licensing of a film. These would include that the grantors have full title and the free and clear privilege of entering into an agreement and granting the rights set forth; the fact that no other contract interferes with or limits the grant of such rights; that distribution/exhibition of the film will not infringe on copyright or privacy rights or other rights of third parties; and that there are no claims or liens against the product of any type or nature (except as explicitly set forth).

The grantor should also warrant that there are no litigations or claims pending against him involving the film (except as specified), and that distribution/exhibition of the film will not require any further payments to third parties.

If it be the fact, the owner should warrant that the film has not been previously publicly shown in the territory. He must further warrant (particularly with reference to foreign films) that good and commercially usable prints can be made from the negative or other materials that are being delivered.

To avoid dispute and the frequent legal defense that a distributor "should have known or might have reasonably investigated some condition of fact," it is usually agreed, with reference to the warranties, that the distributor may completely rely on the contractual language and need not look or search elsewhere for information. If there are limitations on the warranties they should be fully set forth in the document. This again avoids future argument over allegedly "known facts."

Backing up the warranties is an indemnity proviso that requires the licensor to indemnify the distributor in whole or in part in the event of any breach of warranty to the extent of his loss. This clause generally includes not only the direct loss suffered but counsel fees as well. Sometimes the same protection is asserted as to losses suffered in defending against any "alleged breach" even if not proven, so as to put the burden of upholding the warranties on the licensor and not on the distributor. Various techniques have been established as to how the defense of warranties will be conducted, whose counsel will be utilized, notices and the like. Some distributors insist on the right to withhold monies that may fall due to the owner during any period of litigation or thereafter if breach is shown, in order to protect the right of indemnification.

Financial Terms

As previously indicated, the financial terms of such agreements vary with the bargaining power of the protagonists. Sometimes the price of the license is a definite and flat sum of money to be paid on delivery or over a period of time. Sometimes there is a non-returnable guaranty against a percentage of monies received by the distributor, payable to the owner. Frequently there are simple percentage terms payable from the first net dollar received by the distributor (not the exhibitors' revenues which is an entirely distinct item). Under some modern agreements, percentages may be due licensor from the first dollar received as opposed to the older practice of payment only after initial deduction of distributors' fees and allowable costs. All this is a matter of negotiation between the parties.

Keeping in mind that there are many variations on the theme, a not unusual formula would call for the licensee to retain as his theatrical distribution fee 30% of all revenues from the United States, 35% of such revenues from England and the Dominion of Canada and 40% from other territories. This is compensation for services rendered as distributor.

Distribution fees for other forms of exploitation vary. If outright sales of prints are permitted for non-theatrical use, 25-35% might be allowed for this. For licensing in smaller gauges (8mm. or 16mm.) the range might be 10-25%. Television charges vary from outright network deals (10-25%) to syndication or license station by station (30-35%) drastically. All of these figures are illustrative rather than definitive for the areas concerned and subject to change without notice.

The balance of proceeds are frequently initially allocated to so-called deductible costs—an item which has proven a fertile source of argument in many past instances.

The prime costs include items of laboratory costs for negatives, duplicating materials and particularly prints, and the dollars expended by the distributor for advertising, publicizing and exploiting the film in the territory. These can involve extremely high sums of money and, in the case of most financially unsuccessful films (which means most films), are likely to be of such a nature that, together with the distributor's fee, they eat up all the available revenues. To protect against such eventualities, grantors frequently limit the number of prints to be made or advertising expenses allowable as deductions despite their interest in the broadest possible exploitation of their film. The so-called gross deal where grantor shares, usually on a sliding scale depending on gross, a percentage of distributors intake from the first dollar, is a consequence of this condition.

Many other costs, usually of a less important nature but still significant, are also frequently deductible. These might include dubbing, retitling, editing, checking (the process of investigating exhibitors' gross receipts to see that distributor receives a fair share including legal charges), screenings, censorship and classification, copyrighting, insurance, trailer preparation, tariff and other duties, print examination, trade association dues, junking prints, advertisement accessories and certain types of taxes. This listing is intended to be illustrative rather than all inclusive and distributors may well endeavor to add further specifics and a catch-all phrase covering other costs not specifically enumerated.

After the deduction of these costs and the distributor's fee as well, under the older arrangement, all revenues go to the licensor. This, of course, is subject to distributor's right to recover any advance he may have made as consideration for the contract. This sum is then the "licensor's share." Under a so-called "gross deal," the licensor's share starts from the first dollar and rises with gross revenues as distribution costs are paid.

Where a distributor has financed or borrowed the financing for an independently produced film, a similar arrangement is followed except that "licensor's share," i.e., the sum left over after deduction of the distributor's fee and costs plus the negative expenditure on the film with interest, may be thereafter divided (frequently 50-50) between producer and distributor.

The licensor or producer is entitled to regular statements accompanied by his share (if due) on a clear and definitive form. They shall indicate collections as well as all allowable deductions. Statements are frequently on a monthly basis for the first 18 months of prime distribution and thereafter quarterly. They are, generally, premised on the distributor's actual collections and not his billings as, in the film industry, the two may not have the remotest relation to each other. Frequently statements are deemed "conclusive" unless objected to within a period of time. Whether such a provision would protect against a fraud charge, however, is dubious.

The owner should have the right through his representatives to inspect distributor's books and records and take extracts with reference to his film, during normal business hours. This is a normal checking procedure to which no reasonable objection may be made. Frequently, however, limits are placed on the number of such inspections that may be made over a period of time. A "statute of limitations" or time restriction is also not unusual. Distributors claim that such examinations are time-consuming and wasteful for their staffs. Producers may view the matter quite differently.

Where films are licensed for various parts of the world, problems arise as to blocked currencies, moratoriums on payment and the like. Reasonable disposition of such special problems can usually be made under the contract.

Delivery and Other Terms

A crucial clause in many distribution agreements is delivery. The problem has particularly plagued distributors of foreign films. A prudent distributor will not advance important monies before actual delivery of the film, which is accordingly carefully defined by contract. A list of items including primarily (but by no means limited to) negatives or other duplicating materials, prints, music and effects tracks, trailers, and a host of other items in appropriate condition must be delivered to distributor or a selected laboratory within a specific period of time. Delivery is not generally complete until the laboratory certifies that first-class prints can be manufactured from the materials submitted. In addition, most distributors will insist on typed copies of the dialogue, music cue sheets, stills (positive and negative), advertising materials, copies of underlying contracts and related items.

Failure to deliver on time all required items may be cause for optional termination of the agreement of distribution or other sanction and goes to the essence of the contractual relationship. Delivery is also frequently accompanied by a so-called "lab letter" addressed to the laboratory by owner instructing him to honor all distributor's orders for prints and not to withhold same regardless of any other indebtedness by licensor to the lab. Usually materials are left in the owner's name but with irrevocable, if limited, rights to the distributor to utilize the film for the purposes permitted.

If a third party shall infringe or otherwise interfere with distribution of a film, the contract establishes techniques for dealing with the problem. Usually distributor is authorized to act in licensor's name to prevent such activities. Any recovery collected may be divided or go to the party asserting the claim.

There is invariably a notice provision requiring that notices of default or otherwise be promptly served by a particular means on parties at an address previously set forth. There should be a provision permitting each to cure any default before any right of termination comes into play. Essential breach could include such matters as failure to render proper statements, pay remittances, release the film within a time setting or any act of insolvency by the distributor.

Sometimes the parties prefer to arbitrate their differences rather than have them settled in a courtroom, and a valid clause may so state. Arbitration is quicker, less legalistic and frequently cheaper than other methods of determining disputes. Where a contract involves parties from different states or countries, the law applicable to interpretation of the contract should be set forth. This may avoid a conflict of rules in case of any dispute.

The contract should state it is entire and represents the full agreement of the parties. All representations should be within the document and it is wise to expressly negate any claims of any collateral obligations. In this way, hopefully, allegations of fraud and the like may be avoided when the returns are in and hopes fail to become realities.

Any modification of the contract must be in writing signed by the parties so as to exclude any claim of an oral change. Similarly, any waiver of enforcement of a particular term should expressly not be regarded as a continuing waiver of a repeated offense. This should avoid the oft-repeated claim that one accepted inappropriate treatment earlier and should not complain of it now.

There are, of course, multitudes of additional terms that are omitted here that may well apply to particular contracts. We are seeking a broad overview in a complicated area and the parties should rely on experienced counsel for guidance. Set "forms" and "boilerplate" are to be avoided and, where possible, the occasional distributor's approach of "this is standard" or "the way we have always done it" negated.

This is a time of new approaches and new thinking, and the film distribution agreement must be no exception. In a difficult business where participants in production and distribution are simply going to have to learn to get along better, the search must go on for more equitable agreements and arrangements to solidify their relationships.

7

The Exhibition License

THE EXHIBITION LICENSE is the agreement between distributor and exhibitor that sets the terms under which exhibition of the film will occur. In the motion picture industry, in the matter of theatres, many of the terms of the agreement have become "standard" over a period of years, but even here change has begun to emerge in the form of annual revisions of agreements. In most other areas of exhibition there has been less time for formalization and consequently change is constantly occurring. In this chapter, for purposes of simplicity, we deal primarily with normal theatrical licenses although many of the terms required have equal application to other areas of exhibition.

Although the trade term is "sold," actually, of course, except in the rarest of cases a film is only licensed to play a theatre. There is no sale or transfer of title to a print but merely an authorized grant of a particular playing period (playdate). Ownership or title to the film remains in the distributor or party for whom the distributor acts.

In the normal manner, the exhibitor files an application which is, in fact, the contract for the distributors' approval, This is customarily done on distributors' forms (although nothing bars an exhibitor from using or presenting his own form). A salesman may solicit and exhibitor execute the application, which is generally subject to approval by an officer or representative of distributor. Upon execution by him the agreement is theoretically in effect.

We say theoretically because, by custom and habit the terms we are about to discuss, and in particular the financial arrangements, have been diluted and diminished by years of trade practice to the point where your author has, on a previous occasion, referred to the agreement as a mere "scrap of paper." [1] The major thrust of this development is that, in most cases, exhibitors now unilaterally set film rentals at what they regard as a fair rate, regardless of contractual terms, and that as a rule their determination is accepted as the price of the license. Little has happened in recent years to modify this fact of life.

While the exhibition contract may then, in some respects, be merely a citation of prospective terms, it is still important in areas other than pricing, and may even be ultimately binding in that regard regardless of custom and practice. As an important tool of the trade its terms require analysis.

Generally the critical terms of the license are typed into blank spaces set forth on the form agreement. These include the name of the exhibitor, the proposed pricing arrangements, advertising allowances, the "run" and "clearance," and the dates of the engagement.

Specifically, the pricing arrangements are the contemplated rental terms of the film. Generally, for important engagements, this is a percentage figure based on the gross of the picture at the theatre. The distributor is, for example, to receive somewhere from 25% to 80% of the exhibitor's gross receipts (elsewhere defined). Under another common arrangement for first runs, distributor receives 90% of gross receipts, after an allowance to the theatre for so-called house operating expense or "nut." For this purpose a figure is set—assume $5,000 as house expense—and the gross to that point belongs to the exhibitor. Beyond it there is a 90%-10% split to the distributor. Such an agreement, in effect, guarantees the theatre its expenses and allows it to share modestly in any "overage." It is closely akin in nature to a flat rental of the theatre or "4-wall deal."

There are many other financial arrangements that are utilized. At a minor theatre, or as a second feature with a percentage film, a picture may be booked "flat"—i.e., on a straight cash basis for so many dollars. At other houses the scale may be sliding—with the distributor's percentage increasing as the gross goes up. For some important films there may be a guaranteed amount paid in advance, to be deducted by

[1] See *The Movie Business:* edited by Bluem and Squire, Hastings House 1972— "The Exhibition Contract—A Scrap of Paper" by Michael F. Mayer.

exhibitor before the payment of final film rental. Any financial arrangement is possible—the problem has proved one of enforcement of terms.

Several distributor form contracts have written provisions aimed at preventing unilateral determination of film rentals by exhibitors, which we have just discussed. They may provide that there be "no review" of film rental terms except as expressly provided or, in any event, until the prescribed rental is first paid and then to be modified only in distributor's discretion. Such terms remain, however, generally honored in their breach and exhibitors, on a plea of unsatisfactory business, will ordinarily prescribe the rental. In the case of a handful of major films the contract expressly states that the film rental set is final and not adjustable. If the picture is strong enough this may prove enforceable, but it is the rare film that meets this qualification. Similarly the price is firm where exhibition is the result of competitive bidding between theatres for the film.

The "run" proviso deals with the sequence of exhibition in the area. The theatre may be "first run" in its locality, in which case that status is set forth. If it is a later (second or subsequent) run, that too should be described. Modern distribution techniques for many films involve multiple runs at the same time in groups of theatres. If a theatre is part of such a "showcase" or "carpet" its position is contractually recognized.

The concept of run involves a time of reasonable "clearance" over subsequent engagements, the period of which should be set forth. Unless the first run is so protected—and if, for example, the film opens elsewhere in the neighborhood at a lower price immediately after the initial showing—patronage can be adversely affected. Only reasonable clearance as defined by the courts is permitted, however, to protect the prior "run."

Another practice forbidden by the courts is the conditioning of licensing of one feature on another. (See our chapter on antitrust.) This does not mean, however, that there must be separate contracts for each film. Several films at different theatres owned by the exhibitor may be included on the same document even though separately licensed.

How advertising expenses are to be allocated is an important proviso of the contract. Where there is "cooperative" or shared advertising, the terms will establish the relative burdens of expense. Frequently, on important runs, all advertising expense is paid by the distributor through deduction from film rentals. The contract should so establish. Elsewhere, the advertisement expense may be shared—frequently in the same proportion as film rental is to gross.

Turning to the form clauses of the license, the grant is generally made under copyright (assuming the film is copyrighted) so that, in the event of breach, the distributor has available the remedies allowed by copyright law. These are discussed elsewhere in this work and may prove of value.

The license clause specifies that it is only for the time period set forth at the theatre specified, and for no other time or place. This is to avoid such ancient and abusive practices as additional (unreported) showings or "bicycling" of prints to other nonlicensed theatres. The clause has modern application as well, to the twin- or triple-type adjacent theatres where an unscrupulous exhibitor might find it to his advantage to play the licensed film in a different auditorium within the complex than that to which it is licensed.

Nor may the exhibitor use any print of the film other than that submitted by the distributor. Obviously, it is contrary to the license to permit the exhibitor to manufacture new prints (which can be done by creation of a duplicating negative) as inventory control of all prints is essential to the distributor.

Another clause carefully defines the gross receipts upon which distributor's share is to be determined. It should include all monies received for admittance, less only any "admissions tax payable" or other agreed deduction. The exhibitor (despite some controversy) retains all rights to concession income. But this clause bars the practice of selling parking space, or a pizza discount or some other commodity or service, as part of the purchase price of the ticket—and deducting this from gross proceeds as reported to the distributor in percentage engagements. Such practices, in addition to the "under reporting" of proceeds, have been a habit of some unscrupulous theatre owners.

In order to allow a check of proceeds, exhibitor is instructed to use only consecutively numbered tickets including price and tax in each price range utilized. Tickets are generally to be torn with half a stub to the patron so it cannot be resold and reused. Of course this is impractical where turnstiles are used.

A reporting form will call for verified daily box office statements, and payment to distributor with a weekly recapitulation of all sums due. The form should include all the information previously set forth.

This, of course, as previously indicated, is rarely honored and it is not unusual for the distributor to have to wait weeks or even months after an engagement before receiving this information and his money.

The distributor is specifically authorized to check any engagement by having its authorized representative present at all times during the engagement, with free access to the theatre for all such purposes. In addition, noncontractually, some distributors check "blind" by having their representatives buy tickets at various times, and count audiences in theatres or cars at "drive-ins."

The exhibitor further agrees to keep available relevant books and records for a period of years and to make them available to audit by distributor's representatives. In some cases, following checking discrepancies discovered, vast amounts have been recovered as a result of such audits. The right to audit and inspect appears indispensable.

The contract appears more theoretical than real in its provision that, on flat rentals as well as percentage engagements, distributor's agreed license fee shall belong to him and shall be "held in trust" or segregated by the exhibitor from other monies. This simply is not the practice, and your author knows of no case where it has been enforced.

In theory, as well, the contract is terminable on breach of these financial provisos but it is the rare case where such a privilege is exercised. In effect the exhibitor plays the film, reports and pays later, and segregates no monies from his own.

A separate clause deals with the subject of open or unscheduled playdates, which are frequently altered in the fast moving film business. The agreement may well provide for a technique of establishing first playdates where, for one reason or another, the film is not available or the theatre occupied.

Prints are to be returned in appropriate condition promptly after the engagement by the exhibitor, who pays transportation charges. The print may be necessary elsewhere and the exhibitor is subject to a charge if he fails to ship promptly on conclusion of an engagement. Damage to the print, beyond fair wear and tear, is the responsibility of the exhibitor.

Other provisions forbid presentation before the agreed clearance period is over, or even advertising in advance of an agreed date. These terms are aimed at protection of prior runs in the locality.

The exhibitor, of course, may not cut or alter the film (although the practice is not unknown) and is forbidden to copy, duplicate or sub-rent the print.

There are various default provisions in the agreement. If distributor fails in his duties, his liability is limited to exhibitor's prospective profits on exhibition. Your author knows of no case where this vague and questionable provision has been determined.

In the event an exhibitor fails to play a film for the number of days specified in the license, a method is established of reconstructing the gross for the period in question, applying the figures for the time in which the film actually did play. Saturdays, Sundays and holidays are given extra weight under the formula. Similar methods are applicable by applying the grosses of other films where an exhibitor repudiates or breaches the agreement in its entirety by refusal to play a film once licensed. There may, of course, be other sanctions for breach as well. Once again, litigation under these provisions is most infrequent.

8

Foreign Films—
Yesterday and Today

IN DISCUSSING FOREIGN FILMS in America, one is obliged to make certain distinctions, some of which are quite arbitrary in nature. Although British and Canadian (or at least English-speaking Canadian) films are foreign in origin, they are not what we customarily talk about as foreign films. Nor are a large number of American-sponsored or dominated co-productions produced in foreign climes, but not actually indigenous to the area of production. These are essentially American films that have been filmed abroad for purposes of atmosphere or subsidy or tax advantages or currency arrangements. Accordingly, for the purposes of this chapter we are omitting any discussion of English-language films from abroad albeit that they are foreign-made, many of them using foreign personalities in their creation.

Still another category of foreign films has been popular here but is not the subject of this discussion. We refer to foreign films distributed in the United States in their native tongue without either dubbing or sub-titling. Such films have proved in some instances highly popular among Spanish-speaking Americans, Italians, Greeks and those of Oriental extraction. Very little effort is made to distribute these films broadly in theatres, and their engagements are usually confined to specialized houses for foreign-language films. In some parts of the country, such as Texas and New Mexico, Spanish-language pictures will play in their native tongue in barns or almost any other type of auditorium that the distributor can find. It is reliably reported that such films have in some instances grossed very substantial amounts of money. In particular, the Cantinflas comedies, made in Mexico, have a huge native Spanish-language audience. In New York City and other cosmopolitan centers such films, as well as Greek and Chinese, appear to have found a good response.

The type of film we are talking about here is the indigenous product of a foreign land, distributed either in its native tongue with sub-titles in English or dubbed by the use of English voices over and above the foreign sound track. The history of such films in the United States over the past 25 years has been one of extreme volatility and unpredictability. Successes have followed failures; surprise hits have emerged and anticipated bonanzas have turned into financial disasters.

It should also be added that, in this area, the television market has not had the lucrative side effects that it has had with reference to American or what we will call American foreign-made films. Frequently these latter types of pictures could be bailed out of their financial difficulties by virtue of a successful sale to television. In view of our language limitations and the difficulties of reading sub-titles on television screens, to date foreign films have not had this good fortune. Nor have they had great success in the much-touted market of aviation transport, where American audiences again appear to strongly desire the domestic variety of entertainment.

All of this does not necessarily hold true in other non-theatrical markets to be discussed in another chapter. There has, in fact, been great interest on the college campuses, in schools, in churches and in other similar areas in foreign films. Some such films that have failed in the theatrical media have had positive success in these markets. I have particular reference to the Comedie Française and certain other French and Italian films, which lacked appeal at the theatre box office but found a responsive audience in the schools and universities.

It is too early to say whether that appeal will be translated into additional new markets with the developing new media for film distribution. I have in mind play dates on community antenna television (CATV), pay television, cassettes for televised and other distribution, and other new devices. It should be said that there is a good possibility that specialized foreign films will have a substantive appeal in these selective markets. But in this business, perhaps more than in any other, prediction is a most dubious activity.

Factors Favoring Development

Foreign films, while long prevalent on the American scene, developed strongly following World War II. A host of factors could be considered as accounting for this. These would include:

1. A trend away from isolationism involving American interest in many foreign things. This is best exemplified by the explosion in the travel business. Where once a handful of Americans visited Europe annually now the numbers run in the millions.

2. The presence in the United States of the United Nations, which has included the televising of sessions in foreign languages (with translations), has also created a broader interest in foreign customs and practices.

3. For good or ill American involvement worldwide in economic, political and military activities have brought millions of our citizens into contact with foreign countries and cultures and made the unusual ways of different peoples more visual.

4. Part of the worldwide trend since the Second World War, of which the United States has not been immune, has been an increase in sophistication of tastes. One need not look far to find this. There is an interest in the unusual and the symbolic which would hardly fit with one's earlier assumptions of an insulated America. Even more significant is the fantastic, if somewhat alarming, change in sexual mores. This need hardly be spelled out. Filmed presentation of such matters as pre-marital intercourse, casual infidelity, homosexuality, lesbianism and perversion in assorted forms certainly was not symptomatic of the America of this author's youth. Today it is discussed openly in vast social circles and, while rural America may still be shocked, I do not think the same can be said of most urban communities. Foreign films reflected much quicker than American films this worldwide change in standards and their early appeal was magnified by this recognition.

5. Certain economic factors also played an increase in interest in films of an unusual sort. Under the various motion picture decrees brought on by governmental anti-trust action American production and distribution of films was divorced from exhibition (see our chapter on Antitrust). This meant that there was no longer an assured market for the films of many domestic producers who previously could rely on their own theatres to play even their worse pictures. Production

was cut back. This helped to open up the doors of many theatres to foreign films where they would not previously have been welcome.

6. Another factor sharply diminishing American production for theatres was the television revolution. The habitual theatre patron no longer had to go out to buy his entertainment but could see it home on the "free" television screen. Despite annoying commercial interruptions, films on television have remained an important staple and audience draw. This factor caused a reduction in the number of films produced in Hollywood for theatres (in particular, secondary films) and again opened the door for the engagement of many foreign films.

7. Originally and in their period of novelty after World War II, an extraordinary critical reception for foreign films played a part in their increased popularity. In particular, Bosley Crowther of *The New York Times* proved a devotee of many of the new films and his influence was substantive.

8. The new theatres, frequently built in shopping centers as well as in the more elite sections of the cities, proved prime vantage points for their exhibition. An aura of "elitism," coupled with fine-flavored Brazilian coffee, added something to the theatre-going experience.

9. New stars and directors were vital to the popularizing of foreign films. Large numbers of Americans appreciated their new styles and distinguished talents.

The Negative Factors

Unfortunately, in more recent years these positive factors have been very much negated by a series of contravening difficulties which have obscured the promising popularity of foreign films in the late 1950's and early 1960's. The up-to-date record has, with but a few exceptions, not been a healthy one. A variety of negative factors accounts for this.

In the key area of sexuality where American films had lagged in frank expression, they now excel their foreign competitors in numerous instances. Films like *And God Created Woman, The Lovers, La Dolce Vita* and *I am Curious—Yellow* which earned substantial grosses, at least in part based on their shocking candor, are now surpassed, if not artistically at least in graphic description by domestic efforts. All types of sexual activity are now openly portrayed in many American films. A recent example would be *The Stewardesses*, which racked up tremendous grosses based on no particular merit other than

frank and open portrayal of any and all kinds of sexual activity. Similarly *Deep Throat* has proved a sensation. Other "sexploiting" films
have come out of the old pattern of downtown "grind" theatres of the
42nd Street variety and into the neighborhoods and chain theatres with
remarkable box-office results. The collapse of the old motion picture
code has also had impact.

There is, as usual, much talk of a decline in the appeal of sex-
oriented films and it is true that a good many of them, both foreign and
domestic, fare poorly at the box office. But it remains undeniable that
the filmmaker who can exploit this subject with new and shocking
material can find a ready market. It is naive to assume, despite legal
and other difficulties, that the end of this road is in sight. One might
wish hopefully for the day when public interest turned equally avid
toward other subjects but human nature being what it is sex, of course,
remains a highly potent factor. And it would be a serious overstate-
ment to say, as many seem to, that "everything has been shown."
Everything has not been shown and there are a multitude of sexual
acts, normal, abnormal, perverse, masochistic, sadistic and otherwise
that remain available for the imaginative producer. Note the 1973
success of *Last Tango in Paris*. A recent foreign film showed exposed
male genitalia in erect state, which was a novelty at least for this observer. Provided that a new wave of censorship and repression is not
touched off by the new Supreme Court decisions of 1973 (see page
126), one can assume that this was not the end of a trend but more
likely the beginning of one.

Other limiting factors for foreign films have included a general
dissatisfaction with dubbing and sub-titling. While a limited and select
audience will accept these methods, and they have improved, vast
numbers of people prefer a pure English sound track and will not
accept language substitutes except in the rarest films.

On another level, the modern "international film" has utilized the
services of foreign stars and performers who previously popularized
foreign films. Such stars as Sophia Loren, Marcello Mastroianni,
Jean-Paul Belmondo and many others act in films under American
auspices which can no longer be defined as foreign. One does not need
to see a foreign film to enjoy their performances.

Similarly with the great directors who were so vitally important
in promoting foreign films in the 1950's, their services as well are being
utilized in American-sponsored international productions. Ingmar
Bergman has made such films; so have Jan Kadar, Vittorio De Sica,
Francois Truffaut and Luchino Visconti. Again, one no longer has to

go to foreign films to see the works of some of the world's great directors.

The "new theatres," formerly known as specialized art theatres, have now been seized in great bulk by either the major American companies, for their own films on long-term arrangements (not considered violative of the anti-trust laws), or booked for the modern sexploiting trade discussed above. These theatres are no longer so often available for the distinguished type of foreign film which utilized their capacities in earlier years.

It is also the author's judgment, and obviously a purely subjective one, that there has been an American reaction in recent years against foreign entanglements of many sorts. This may have originated with the disastrous Vietnam experience but it would appear that large numbers of our citizenry, movie-going and otherwise, are less anxious today to hear about foreign problems and foreign difficulties. This applies particularly to the neo-realistic film which was popular immediately after the Second World War. With but few exceptions, this type of picture has proved far less successful in the more recent era. One thinks back to such great efforts as *Open City, Shoeshine, Bicycle Thief* and *Paisan* which ignited the American screen in the late 1940's and early 1950's. Experiences of a similar nature in recent times are few. An exception would be the remarkable *"Z"* which captivated a youthful anti establishment audience in the late 1960's.

The major companies have also succeeded, to a very great extent, in driving independent distribution away from the foreign film business. By bidding up prices on imports, by their international productions utilizing stars and directors at increased compensations, and by their tendency under conglomerate influence to grow and expand, they have assumed a large part of the distribution of all such films. This has driven from the field many of the innovators and inventive minds that helped popularize the business in the first instance, and have made it more of a rationalized industry as opposed to an area of individual effort. In the case of many films, it was the individual touch of the distributor that helped popularize the foreign effort and, when that becomes merely a matter of one more picture in a large group, that individual touch is frequently lost. The point may be overstressed, but there is something to the theory of individual handling of a specialized film, and the great foreign films of the 1940's, '50's and early '60's were frequently so distributed.

Another factor in the decline of foreign film distribution grows out of the abuses of the practice of sub-distribution. Many importers and distributors of earlier years had but one office and licensed their films, apart from a few major territories, through local agents. They did this because they could not afford the overhead of branch offices around the country and wanted to simplify their procedures. Unfortunately, the sub-distribution system has not worked effectively. Without condemning the trade as a whole, numerous local agents failed to pay their proper shares of film rentals to distributors, held onto monies long after they should have released them and engaged in a series of other abuses of many varieties. These might include double-billing a producer's film with a film owned by the local sub-distributor on terms unfavorable to the national distributor. Sometimes local sub-distributors owned theatres and distributed films in their own theatres on favored terms. Inside deals were made with other local exhibitors to the detriment of the national distributor. Under the circumstances, the independent distributor with one office, either East or West, has been seriously and adversely affected. This, in turn, has reduced the flow of specialized foreign films.

Despite all the negative factors, their occasional relative success shows that there still is a demand for outstanding indigenous foreign films.

As examples, one might cite *Z, The Garden of The Finzi-Continis, The Conformist, Fellini's Roma, The Sorrow and the Pity, Investigation of a Citizen, Claire's Knee, The Discreet Charm of the Bourgeoisie*.

The qualities for success can no longer be so easily categorized. We have discussed the sexual aspect which certainly did improve the box office for many foreign films in the earlier period. It still does with an occasional *Fanny Hill or Pornography in Denmark*.

The appeal of foreign comedies appears to have declined following such earlier successes as *Divorce, Italian Style* and the Jacques Tati films from France (*Mr. Hulot's Holiday*). As indicated previously, the foreign quasi-realistic picture, with but few exceptions (*Z, The Shop on Main Street* and *The Battle of Algiers*), has declined in appeal.

Shockers which were something of a staple in the foreign market have now been outdistanced as well by the domestic variety. There appear to be fewer *Rififi's* or *Diabolique's*.

Bizarre pictures are now equally bizarre, domestic as well as foreign. Hence the failure to repeat the success of *Mondo Cane* despite numerous imitations.

Still available for the imaginative exhibitor are the extraordinary and unusual symbolic films, but these too are produced by domestic as well as foreign film makers. The efforts of Antonioni in *L'Avventura* were followed by *Blow Up* and his domestic fiasco *Zabriskie Point*. Nonetheless, there is room for the unusual and no doubt it is in this area that the new indigenous foreign films will find a market.

One other aspect should be mentioned. The foreign film award of the Academy of Motion Pictures Arts and Sciences has always proved an important incentive to box office receipts. It will no doubt so continue. The growth of film festivals around the country should also create a more hospitable atmosphere, although experience to date does not seem to prove the point. The International Film Importers and Distributors of America, Inc. (IFIDA) have attempted, through their awards, to broaden the popularity of the medium but the results have proved disappointing. Perhaps new techniques and new ways may be found to develop and improve the distribution of the efforts of foreign film-makers. For the present, the industry remains challenging but limited in its impact.

9

Distribution Abroad

THE WORLD OUTSIDE of the United States and Canada now accounts for more than 50% of distributors' revenues for American films. The figure has gradually appreciated since World War II and is now probably closer to 55% than one-half. The importance, therefore, of the global market for American-made pictures is hardly to be underestimated.

Obviously, these general figures do not apply to each individual picture. There are, of course, films of a domestic nature grossing heavily in the home market, but poorly abroad. Conversely, however, some pictures have far broader appeal in foreign markets than in the U. S. and Canada. On balance, the primary appeal now lies narrowly on the foreign area side.

This amazing world-wide strength has been a major factor in the survival of the American film industry in the face of recent intensely difficult periods of retreat and recession. Despite the powerful competition of foreign made pictures as well as numerous other obstacles, the world market has remained an essential and vital consideration of business health.

It is difficult to account for this phenomenon. Of course some "American" films are international in flavor, produced abroad sometimes with local directors, stars and backgrounds. Their appeal is aimed for international attention and is no accident. But other efforts

66

are highly domestic in story, cast and production values. They, too, may on occasion thrive overseas. "Action" films have traditionally shown strength in many markets. Similarly classic and so-called "women's" pictures have found a place. The world markets are nearly as unreliable as the domestic in predetermining success or failure. They, too, are subject to increasing audience selectivity. There does, however, appear to be a general interest in things American, be it material values or some assumed "way of life" that encourages the popularity of U. S. films. Stories, stars, production "values" and new directors seem important. It can hardly be said that pure esthetic qualities account for their success.

The most significant foreign revenues come from Europe (including England). A fair estimate would place 50% of non-U. S.-Canada distributors' receipts as emanating from this source. The leading units are Great Britain (despite the decline in attendance and number of theatres, this is probably still the #1 market), Italy, France, West Germany and Spain. Elsewhere prime strength is in Japan, followed by Latin and South America. Of course, individual films vary sharply in appeal from territory to territory by virtue of their local characteristics. Competition from television, as in the U. S., has proved a limiting factor to foreign theatrical markets. As TV rises in popularity, receipts decline but there appears to be, in most countries, a point where this levels off.

The major American companies have individual or joint exchanges in most foreign territories from which they service accounts in a manner somewhat similar to their domestic operations. From these points, films are licensed and shipped to theatres in the exchange area. As initial runs are of vital importance in most jurisdictions, the selling of first dates on appropriate terms is a special consideration. Film rental terms, as contractually expressed, appear slightly lower than in the United States—rarely exceeding 60% of theatre gross— but all kinds of arrangements are possible here as at home. (See Chapter on Exhibition). Renegotiation of terms, however, is rare (unlike the U. S.).

Subsequent runs are also licensed by the exchange, on a percentage or "flat" fixed-fee basis, as conditions dictate. Ordinarily, television licensing (subject to a period of delay after theatrical exhibition) and non-theatrical showings are handled by a separate branch of the distributing organization.

In recent years in a series of economy moves, the majors have combined and merged some of their foreign distribution facilities. Paramount and Universal have joined forces as Cinema International Corporation; MGM and 20th Century are sometimes partners, as are Columbia and Warner Bros. In this manner, economies are achieved, although the high costs involved in terminating personnel in some territories may reduce the savings.

Exchanges may also be jointly operated by majors with domestic distributors in each territory. This frequently gives the organization some additional locally-made films to add to their line of product which may be essential on several scores. Film playing-time quotas in the country concerned may require that theatres utilize a certain percentage of their screen hours for homemade efforts and, of course, an occasional box office winner may come up in the process. Other governmental regulations may also have a softer impact where local personalities have an interest in the operation.

Non-major American distributors frequently distribute their films through locally-owned film exchanges in the various countries or territories. They make a distribution deal generally on a percentage basis akin to sub-distribution as described previously with respect to the United States. In a hypothetical arrangement, a distributor licenses his film or films for a term with costs (prints, advertising, etc.) advanced by the local office, but recouped from gross revenues with a sharing of gross thereafter (50-50 or 60-40). Experience and human nature teach that where the local distributor has a financial stake, he will exert himself more studiously to recoup his costs and earn revenues, than where he does not. Of course, his percentage share is also increased under such an arrangement. If, on the other hand, the American distributor is advancing costs, the local participation declines to a more modest percentage—30-35% of the distributor's take.

The advantages and disadvantages of these different approaches of the American distributor include the abolition of overhead where films are sub-licensed, a lack of necessity for a continuous flow of films to support a local office and the flexibility of the various licensing arrangements available. Conversely, the American-owned distribution operation omits the licensing fee, controls costs more effectively, assures prime attention to the distributor's own films and limits the type of abuses frequently prevalent when a sub-distributor may have conflicts of interest with his licensor.

The latter danger exists, particularly when, as is often the case, a local distributor owns or controls theatres where the films may play. This opens the door to "inside deals" or advantages when one deals with oneself wearing two different hats. The advantage, however, for a foreign distributor in dealing with a theatre-owning licensee is also substantial as it may well assure important runs that otherwise might not prove available. In any event, controls must be exercised, as in the U. S. market, to assure proper reporting of receipts by both theatres and sub-distributors and to prevent misuse of prints and other materials.

A third, and entirely separate, form of distribution is the outright "sale" by an American producer or distributor of his rights in one or more films to a local distributor. Frequently a producer, or his representative dealing directly, will license his film on a flat cash basis and avoid the difficulties of supervision and overhead that a continuing operation requires. This would be particularly likely in the case of a single film distributed by a small company in the U.S.A., with world-wide rights remaining in the producer.

The problems involved in foreign distribution, apart from its form of organization, are legion, and their successful resolution is a significant accomplishment of the American film Industry. In this regard, the Motion Picture Export Association of America is entitled to great credit. This unified body, acting on behalf of the major companies, functions as a "trouble shooter" to locate and determine difficult situations in the world markets; and it is obvious from the results that its mission has been performed with great aptitude. Without such an organization, it is highly questionable whether the substantial revenues from abroad which have done so much to alleviate the vast difficulties of the domestic industry could actually have been achieved.

Impediments and Restrictions

A leading impediment to foreign distribution is a collection of financial and legal measures imposed in foreign jurisdictions—frequently aimed at preventing or limiting remittances of net proceeds of U. S. films to the United States. Such techniques include the direct blocking of the outgo of funds by currency controls. Vast sums, for instance in India and Pakistan, remain earned but not remitted. Elsewhere, less odious restrictions than a complete embargo control or limit the export of funds. In difficult world economic conditions, more such situations can clearly be anticipated. The funds involved, however, may be reinvested in the subject countries in films or otherwise, or may be transferred to other industries holding dollar balances in the U.S.A. While hardly a satisfactory remedy, the situation is thereby made "livable."

In many parts of the world, including France, Italy and Japan, there are screen quotas requiring that theatres play a minimum number of weeks of domestically-made films during each year. This freezes out foreign (including American) films during that period, as do import restrictions on the number of films admitted. The distributor faces a discriminatory market. The popularity of American films reaching the screen mitigates this problem, but it cannot be overcome unless playing time is freely available everywhere. This is an unlikely development as many countries desperately need favorable trade balances and seek to develop their own local film industries by such effective, if artificial, measures.

In some countries, there are higher theatre admissions taxes on U. S. films than on their competitors, reducing the box office take. These can be levied directly or by a system of rebates to distributors of domestic films. In either event, they are discriminatory in impact. A greater burden is placed on the American film than on its competitor.

In nations which subsidize local film-makers with the proceeds of an admissions tax, obviously the American film is charged for this purpose without sharing in the revenue. While this is disadvantageous in principle, American companies in England, for example, have successfully produced eligible films through British affiliates or subsidiaries, thereby sharing in the tax subsidy and limiting or eliminating their revenue loss.

Elsewhere, by a system of governmental pressures or controls, film rental terms to theatres are limited and minimized to protect or cushion local exhibitors. The market is not free and open to all but weighted to protect national theatre interests. The imposition of such controls prevents the distributor from securing full and fair rentals for his films.

Similarly, price controls on theatres in certain territories sharply limit exhibitors' revenues with the indirect effect of reducing percentage film rentals. Obviously, where exhibitors' take is reduced, distributors' share must also diminish as the pie is smaller for each to slice.

Income and other taxes, against American companies generally, may sometimes be imposed on a higher basis than against local industries. While not specifically aimed at American film companies, this type of discriminatory treatment will also limit net revenues and favor local competitors. Again, in a world of economic disparity of "have" and "have not" nations, the continuation of such conditions must be anticipated.

Dubbing and subtitling is inherent in distribution in those parts of the world where the English language is not primary. Films are dubbed to the native tongue in several important markets (France, Italy, West Germany, Spain), and subtitled elsewhere (Latin America, South America) to meet local conditions. Here again, in various territories, restrictions have been imposed by some countries to favor such work and printing by local nationals and studios, rather than permitting it to be accomplished elsewhere on the best and most economic terms available. Once again, free competition is limited. In addition, there may be special dubbing or release taxes or fees to be paid to the national treasury as a punitive measure against foreign films.

There are similar restrictions in distribution of American films to television, particularly in the area of available time. Large amounts of TV playing time are reserved for locally created product and are simply not available to American efforts.

This listing of governmental controls and restrictions is not intended as a "chamber of horrors" or an indictment of all foreign states that regulate film practices. Certainly they are entitled to attempt to bolster their own economic and social status and promote their local film industries. As a matter of sovereignty, their legal powers over foreign instrumentalities are clearly broad (short of expropriation without compensation). So, both morally and legally, they appear to have acted within their rights. We are merely indicating the nature of the problems that have been met and frequently overcome by persevering distributors.

Piracy, Censorship and Other Problems

On a different level, there are other difficulties not unlike those faced by American distributors at home. We have already mentioned exhibitor under-reporting of grosses and other techniques for reducing percentage film-rentals. Such challenges should be met there, as here, with checking and auditing services, but no doubt vast losses are incurred in this drain.

The problem of bootlegged and pirated prints is substantial in several foreign territories. Unauthorized prints resulting from theft or illegal duplication have a bad habit of showing up in private homes in South Africa or in theatres in the Caribbean or Latin America for local viewing at a price. Every such exhibition dilutes the value of the true owner's films and jeopardizes his revenues. The practice of film piracy abroad and at home must be vigorously fought and controlled or it will imperil all motion picture industries everywhere.

Censorship, too, is universal, or at least nearly so throughout the world. The contents of American films are, of course, such as to easily bring down the wrath of national and local control bodies in many countries. The troublesome twins of candid sex and unbridled violence are constant problems in many places. While violence is probably the major culprit when it comes to controls, the new sexuality of American films also creates problems. As if these elements were not enough, a host of other specialized local impediments may ban a particular film in one area or another. Religious dogmas, political theories, racial or personal prejudices all work against the free flow of films to all countries. Films are banned from various countries for a multiplicity of causes. Other pictures must be cut to protect local sensitivities. The censorship mechanism may also be misused as a device simply to keep out films competing for the local market.

Still another problem in many areas of the world is the element of corruption in public officials, or the "outstretched hand." Regardless of legal rights, there may be a critical individual with discretionary authority to ban a film, impose a tax or create other difficulties. Such informal restrictive activity may be as great a problem to film distribution as many of the direct impediments we have noted. And its solution poses excruciating problems for its victims.

When faced with all these difficulties, it is remarkable that American films have fared as well abroad as they have in the post-war era. As previously indicated, the industry's own organization is clearly entitled to vast credit for meeting and ameliorating the manifold concerns. But the preeminent fact is and remains that, in the universal language of film, the peoples of this vast and diversified world like, enjoy and will pay their currencies in large amounts to see American films on their local screens. So long as they want this entertainment badly enough, it is unlikely that all the restraints and barriers will block the consummation of their wishes.

10

Non-Theatrical Markets 1
Schools, Clubs, Universities and Related Areas

THE NON-THEATRICAL MARKET is a huge area for exploitation of film that is still seeking to be fully tapped, and potentially a vast reservoir for large revenues. In addition to its increasing scope it has the great advantage of fluidity—the patterns of business in this market are not finally set—and the grave difficulties of theatrical distribution, including its high cost of operation, its multiple exchanges and its non-binding agreements are not established precedents. Many keen industry minds see the future of film in such areas rather than the more traditional forms.

We are here talking about distribution other than to theatres which charge an admission to the public. Our reference is to the showing of film in colleges, clubs, schools, churches, museums and homes. While television and Community Antenna Television (CATV) are a form of non-theatrical distribution they deserve and receive separate treatment (see chapter 11). So do the other new technological developments presently arising and coming in the future, such as videotape recordings and cassettes. Here we limit ourselves to what has traditionally been called the non-theatrical area or, in even earlier times, "16mm. release."

The matter of film gauge, however, has become irrelevant. For many years 35mm. film was established as the format for theatrical distribution and 16mm. was only considered relevant elsewhere. This accounts for the many industry contracts referring to non-theatrical rights as "16mm. rights," while theatrical was referred to as "35mm. rights." These distinctions have now lost their significance and contracts may no longer be so phrased as serious ambiguities would thus be created. In fact, there is and has been litigation over such grants in past contracts.

The problem arises on both sides of the coin. In the traditional market we now have large numbers of theatres, frequently automated in nature, exhibiting 16mm. film. There is no difference in principle in these showings as opposed to the operation of a 35mm. film theatre. Both cater to the general public, both are open to whomever will pay for admission at the box office. Both must license film from a distributor on similar terms. A "non-theatrical engagement" today, however, may now occur on a college campus in a huge auditorium in the 35mm. gauge as well as in smaller rooms in the narrow gauge. Under these circumstances the width of film, whether it be 35, 16 or even 8mm or more or less, is clearly irrelevant as a criterion for the type of distribution involved.

In fact, the lines between theatrical and non-theatrical in today's context are becoming increasingly difficult to draw. Theatres are open to the public for a charge. Exhibition in schools, churches and clubs in theory is limited but in practice may not be. There may or may not be a fixed admission price—viewers may or may not be limited to students or club members. Where licenses for such engagements were once on a purely straight-fee basis (for example, $50 for one engagement) they may now be granted in certain situations by distributors on a percentage of gross, just as in the case of theatres. Some of the college auditoriums are equivalent in size to the nation's largest moviehouses.

A prominent "non-theatrical" distributor has, in addition to a flat cash rental system of licensing, six classifications of charges for a film's engagement. They cover the following types of showings:

NO ADMISSION CHARGE, SUBSCRIPTION FEE OR COLLECTION

Type 1. Audience under 200 enrolled members of class, museum or club. Not open to general school population except where total attendance will not exceed 200. Not open to general public.

Type 2. Audience over 200, restricted to campus, museum or other institution enrollment. Not open to the general public.

Type 3. Audience open to public, regardless of size.

WITH ADMISSION CHARGE, SUBSCRIPTION FEE, COLLECTION, DUES OR ANY OTHER FORM OF PAYMENT

Type 4. Audience under 300. Showings open to members of a class or club, to the campus or to the public.

Type 5. Audience over 300, but not in excess of 500. Open to members of a class or club, to the campus or to the public.

Type 6. Audience over 500.

Superimposed on these categories are four classifications of film specified in the distributor's catalogue. If a film is in group A (of modest importance) there is a flat charge for a Type 1 showing, which might be $22.50. A group B film (more significant in nature) is available for $32.50. If the film is a C (important feature), the fee rises to $45 and in the case of S (specials), $60.

The rates rise with the various types of showings until reaching a minimum fee of $125 applied against 50% of the total receipts to an S picture, in a situation where admission is charged and the audience is in excess of 500.

It is apparent that the concept of a sharing of gross revenues on a percentage basis at rates as high as 60% is a phenomenon to be anticipated. These developments signal the end of a buyer's market, at least for films of broad and successful appeal.

It should be clear from this outline why theatre owners, and particularly those near college campuses, are in a constant state of alarm about non-theatrical bookings. A vast number of these engagements do compete with local exhibitors and frequently do so at a reduced price to a general audience. Their costs of operation are generally lower and their use of tax monies may be regarded as subsidized competition. Exhibitors are also unhappy about the constantly reduced periods of clearance from theatrical to non-theatrical exhibition. Some features are now reaching the market well inside of two years from their initial release. In fact, many producers earn more revenues from their pictures from such engagements than from theatrical showings. While the exhibitors' cries of anguish are disturbing, if our aim is to see producers fairly reimbursed for their efforts we cannot, however, sanction the stifling of this market.

Many non-theatrical distributors also sell (or license on a long-term basis) copies of prints of various films. Frequently there are documentaries or shorts for which such rights have been granted but, on occasion, theatrical features are available for sale. A print of a feature recently sold, for example, for $795. Sale of prints may create various problems with regard to duplication or other improper use but it nonetheless can achieve substantial revenues. (Transfer of the print does not transfer the copyright in the material contained in it.)

It should be noted that similar problems are not necessarily avoidable where prints are leased on long- or short-term arrangements. Current technology is such that good quality duplicating prints or tapes can be manufactured by nefarious parties on very short notice. This poses a serious problem for the producer or distributor who is threatened by the existence of illegal and competitive "hot prints."

The contract for exhibition in a non-theatrical setting nearly invariably provides written assurances against such conduct. A rental or sale prohibits alteration, televising or reproducing the film in any manner without permission in writing of the licensor. But like so many other things in our society, it is one matter to specify these guarantees and another to enforce them, as unhappy producer-distributors have all too often discovered.

The essential terms of the contract include rental charges (either flat or percentage or guarantees against percentage), place and time of showings, number of exhibitions allowed and whether admission prices are to be charged by the licensee. Provision is made in percentage engagements for statements and accountings.

In some cases, there are limitations on how the licensee can advertise his showings including specific bans against advertising "off-campus," on radio, or television or in newspapers. The effort is to limit audience appeal to the particular group involved and is a response to exhibitor pressure. By no means, however, do all non-theatrical distributors require it.

The non-theatrical side of the business has gradually developed, with the rising interest in film, to important proportions. In particular, the development of "cinema" as an art form—including the sponsorship of many college courses, campus clubs and film societies—has speeded its growth. In the early 1960's, governmental support in the form of large subsidies to educational institutions provided an additional spark, which has since faded. Elsewhere non-theatrical interest has increased in private homes, churches and museums.

In the usual course, "entertainment" (as opposed to educational) pictures are licensed non-theatrically only after their initial release in theatres. A reasonable time of clearance (up to several years or more was generally accepted) was allowed to protect exhibitors. This also helped develop the necessary publicity and interest for other audiences. With the rise in selectivity in film viewing, however, the old policies are no longer axiomatic.

Reversing the usual roles entirely, the church-sponsored *Martin Luther* started non-theatrically and rolled up literally fantastic grosses for this type of distribution. While perhaps this was a "fluke," other films that have not fared well in theatres have done remarkably well in non-theatrical distribution. A leading illustration would be *War Games*—a British quasi-documentary on a third world war, with limited appeal for theatre audiences but vast impact in the colleges. Similarly, some college-oriented films such as La Comedie Française production of *Candide,* which had no theatrical run worthy of notice, have been highly successful in academic communities.

There is, of course, no rule that non-theatrical success will necesarily follow theatrical triumph. On the contrary the selective trend of intellectual audiences might well make a film of limited intellectual appeal successful in the mass audience but unsuccessful in the latter market. It usually, however, is helpful for a film to have at least played off a limited number of theatrical engagements. The list of films that have succeeded non-theatrically after difficulties in general exhibition would include efforts of Britain's "angry young men" (*The Loneliness of the Long Distance Runner, This Sporting Life, Saturday Night and Sunday Morning, A Taste of Honey*). Films such as these in many cases found their true market in the non-theatrical area. Similarly, *War Games,* which we have already mentioned, ran up unprecedented grosses in the school-church market. French "new wave" directors, such as Godard, Truffaut, Resnais and Vadim, have found a strong response. So, of course, did Fellini, Antonioni, DeSica and Visconti. We should not omit Bergman, Ray and Kurosawa.

A list of leading non-theatrical grossers would include: *Children of Paradise, Breathless, Hiroshima, Mon Amour, Michelangelo, The Titan, A Nous la Liberté, Nanook of the North, Picasso.*

Some "current" favorites might include *Macbeth, The Private Life of Henry VIII, Oedipus, The King, Cyrano de Bergerac, Hellstrom Chronicle* and *All Quiet on the Western Front*.

In earlier years most of the major film distributors, following theatrical release, simply turned over their films on a nominal basis to a non-theatrical distributor. Several companies licensed on a non-exclusive basis to various such organizations. The market was regarded and treated as a modest source of revenue. Prices to licensees were generally flat and the income quite limited. This has changed in the modern era. The producer-distributors have found that there is "gold in them thar hills." This has occurred at a time when revenues have become quite difficult to find elsewhere. The distributors now demand substantial guarantees for their important films. As we have seen, the price to the consumer as well has risen sharply and the practice of percentage licensing has gained a foothold. Based on their vast appeal and with huge catalogues of distinguished foreign films, such leading companies as Contemporary, Brandon and Audio have now been absorbed by major conglomerates (McGraw-Hill and Macmillan). Other large companies have developed as competitors. In addition, many producer-distributors have now formed their own subsidiaries to earn a fair return in this particular marketplace distributing their own (and other) selected films.

Unfortunately, the rise in rental prices has moved swiftly and discouraged some of the collegiate "film buffs" who brought on the non-theatrical excitement in the first place. Having licensed films for pennies, whether they can stand such rates as a $500 guarantee against half the house is questionable. The high rental figures have also encouraged film bootleggers who secure stolen prints and undersell in the competitive market. Their illegal activities are difficult to control.

Hopefully these are but temporary problems. With a continued rise in interest in specialized films a substantial market in non-theatrical areas would seem assured. The careful and intelligent promotion of that market should prove a necessary and helpful aspect of the general film industry for years to come.

11

Non-Theatrical Markets 2
—TV and the New Media

A SECOND GENERAL CATEGORY of non-theatrical distribution of feature films lies in the area of television as well as an entire new species of related, if distinguishable, modern visual techniques. As the rate of technical improvement is intense, it cannot be doubted that other innovations may be coming along even before this book is published. Your author has neither the experience nor technical ability to engage in conjecture on such topics of future impact. But it should be pointed out that there is invariably a "time lag" between the development of new media and their profitable commercial utilization. Fortunes can be lost while waiting for the promise of tomorrow. They also can be made if the parties involved have the financial strength and staying power to back up their convictions until the anticipated "time has come." Certainly this was the experience in the early years of commercial television.

Our first problem is one of definitions within the area. There follows an effort to break down categories so at least we can specify the topics of our concern.

"Free television" is the ordinary, everyday common variety of American television present in the vast majority of homes, as well as in bars and other places of dining and entertainment. Except for a limited amount of public and foundation-sponsored broadcasting, advertising revenues, as in radio, have financed free television. Broadcasts are over the air and are received where reception is practical without charge. Over the past 25 years free television, while sharply reducing theatrical attendance, has provided huge audiences, and vast financial benefits to producers and distributors who have licensed films to this truly mass-media.

"Community antenna television" (CATV) initially developed in those areas where free television, due to technical problems, could not properly be seen. Where, for example, mountains blocked the television signals, high towers were built to catch the waves which were then re-transmitted by wire to the homes of subscribing customers. It was, in brief, originally a method of bringing television to areas where it was theretofore unavailable for a connecting fee and monthly charge. Since that beginning, CATV has had a fantastic development premised on extended uses of the wire re-transmitting cable, including numerous new channels, otherwise unavailable, exclusive programming and improved reception. The extraordinary growth of CATV has contained the promise, thus far unfulfilled, of huge treasures for the licensing of motion pictures. As in the case of free television, its omens for exhibitors are not favorable.

The term "pay television" (Pay TV), as distinguished from present forms of CATV, has involved direct "per program" payment or billing rather than a general monthly programming fee. Pay TV has been utilized in conjunction with a scrambled TV signal broadcast over the air which is decoded by a coin, card or similar device. The viewer selects and pays for only the program he wishes to see. To date Pay TV has failed to fulfill its promise in either audience appeal or revenue creation for theatrical films or otherwise. A variation on Pay TV is "pay cable" which would allow direct charge for use of a particular program on cable TV.

"Hotel television" is a special mixed breed of CATV and Pay TV for hotel, motel or apartment dwellers who, for a direct charge, may view a selected film or other program. The system is a new development and holds high hopes for an obviously narrow but significant paying audience.

"Cassettes" are really a new projection technique readily usable in conjunction with television receivers for viewing purposes. Their appeal lies in their convenience and flexibility. The distribution of cassettes opens the door to delivery to the viewer in his home or elsewhere, on a rental or sale basis, of the precise programming he seeks at the very time he wants it.

Other forms of non-theatrical distribution more easily defined include exhibition on airplanes, ships, trains and other vehicles. The former, particularly, has proved a significant source of revenue not only for air lines but for those specialized distributors that have developed effective exhibition techniques in difficult circumstances.

Free Television

Free television entered the American scene, after a long preparatory period in the late 1940's, with devastating effects on theatre attendance. Its impact, coupled with the consequences of the anti-trust decrees and the changes in public taste in the post-World War II era, have had decisive effects on the nation in general and the motion picture industry in particular. Less pictures, more selective production, the end of the "B" film or programmer, emphasis on novelty, thrill and specialty—all can be traced at least in part to the rise of free TV.

The original failure of the film distributors, influenced by their theatrical customers, to participate in and ride the television crest, was a disastrous mistake. Imagine what a commanding position the established purveyors of filmed entertainment could have achieved had they moved directly into the television media at its origin. Perhaps they would have been stopped by the anti-trust laws, but in any event the opportunity was missed.

A second opportunity, however, arose with free television's shortage of successful entertainment packages to fill the screen that developed in the 1950's. This time the film companies did not fail to participate. They unloaded vast numbers of early films to the medium, either by sale or licensing, garnering what were then considered large revenues to balance their losses in the theatrical markets. A new business of TV distribution arose. Either independents or major affiliates entered the field to meet the requirements for national sale and local station by station syndication. More than one major film company was saved from bankruptcy or receivership by the television revenues of this period.

By the mid 1960's licensing fees for recent American features for national television had skyrocketed to unprecedented prices which, in rare instances, exceeded $1 million for several showings of a film. Motion picture ratings for top films were extraordinarily high in audience appeal, and network competition for these pictures was intense. Packages of film were licensed to networks for average sums in excess of several hundred-thousand dollars per film. Syndicators or licensing organizations, dealing directly with stations rather than networks, piled up large grosses and the future looked promising.

The bubble burst in the late 1960's and the price of film paid by free television sharply declined. Several factors played a role in this. The development of TV talk and other live-shows precluded a substantial amount of time that had been allotted to feature films. An entirely new industry of producing features primarily for television and not theatres developed, which further limited the market. These pictures, despite modest budgets and hackneyed plots, have found their place in the medium and proved their ability to compete.

Thirdly, a growing selectivity, even among television audiences, may diminish the appeal of many older films. The trend of new theatrical films toward maturity of approach ("R" and "X" ratings) eliminated many films from consideration for television where censorship standards, though increasingly lenient, have not reached the point of permitting nudity and open sex play on the home screen. For all of these reasons and others only the extraordinary can today achieve huge licensing fees from television, and syndication revenues have declined.

Will the market firm again? Despite all the negatives we have listed above, this remains more than a vibrant possibility. The amazing demand for outstanding films on television was illustrated by the licensing in 1972 of outstanding features at collosal prices. These included *Love Story, Patton* and *Goldfinger,* all in the multi-million classification for limited showings. Other large packages have also been licensed.

In addition, the ratings and market "shares" of movie series continue at a high rate on domestic television listings. It appears that film has a vast national audience that simply cannot be underestimated and that many audiences will enjoy at home that which they will not pay for in theatres. Despite every obstacle, and there is no shortage of them, (talk shows, T.V. specials, created film for T.V., censorship problems, and a degree of audience selectivity), there is every liklihood that there will remain a strong and vital market for film on free television.

While free television will accept more mature films, particularly where judicious cutting of "objectionable" sequences occurs, acceptance of "X" and "R" rated films as shown in theatres is still over the horizon. Late night showings as practiced in Toronto, remain a possibility. Product with "problems" will frequently have to be licensed for smaller sums than equivalent films lacking such considerations.

It should be pointed out that foreign films (apart from English language pictures made abroad) have always had a difficult time in the free television market. They did not share in the great prosperity and have never had large revenues from television. In the case of subtitled films, their appeal has been negligible as the dialogue is frequently illegible on the screen and dubbing into English of foreign sound tracks has not been well received.

Purists, in fact, find any popularity of film on free television surprising. Cutting of scenes, adjustments for commercials and rigid time-limitations all interfere with entertainment values. Surprisingly, there has been no large scale audience revolt against such practices and, apart from the extraordinary case, they continue unabated. Efforts by a few prominent directors to prevent cuts in their films by free television have generally been in vain except where their contracts are precise and explicit on the point.[1]

Free television will remain an important market, although it cannot be considered a panacea to cover all theatrical losses. Technical improvements, such as large wall screens and improved color can help, but the rise of CATV or pay television should eventually create limits.

Community Antenna Television (CATV)

CATV is a question mark with a high-looming potential. Unfortunately, its pick-ups of signals from free television, which were thereafter re-transmitted to paying subscribers, were immunized from legal liability in a disastrous opinion of the United States Supreme Court in 1968.[2] The Court in its infinite wisdom, reversing both the District Court and the Circuit Court of Appeals, held that the re-broadcast by CATV of films seized off the air from licensed television stations without anyone's permission, was not an infringement and

---

[1] See *Preminger* v. *Columbia Pict. Corp.* 49 Misc. 2d 263 (1966) aff'd 25 A.D. 2d 830; 18 N.Y. 2d 659; *Stevens* v. *NBC,* 148 U.S. P. Q 755 (Calif. 1966).

[2] *Fortnightly Corp.* v. *United Artists* 392 U.S. 390 (1968).

payment for rights to the copyright holder could not be enforced. A more flagrant miscarriage of justice is hard to imagine. Here was a new and successful medium capitalizing on the creativity of others, charging a fee to its customers for viewing someone else's property, refusing to pay for it and convincing the court that CATV was in reality simply a receiver of programming and not a broadcaster. Accordingly, it had no responsibility to the copyright holder or owner of the property it showed for hire. Only the lamented Justice Fortas found the truth of the situation in a cogent dissent. A recent case in the Federal Court of Appeals indicates a possible modification of this doctrine but this remains in doubt.

Developments in CATV since 1968, however, have shown promise. The thrust of Federal Communications Commission (FCC) policy has been toward a high degree of program origination by local CATV stations, coupled with strong limitations on the use of film siphoned from free television outlets. Origination must mean some film programming which must be paid for to be acquired. Responsible elements in CATV have also met with film industry and free television people in an effort to work out the problem of fair compensation for copyright proprietors and licensors. A new copyright bill or other legislation remains on the horizon, quite possibly involving some type of solution to the problem of payment for programs taken from regular television stations. Proposals have been made and considered for the setting of different types of fees for different types of transmissions, the possibility of an agency to monitor and compensate property owners, or an agreement that involves direct negotiations and licensing to CATV stations—all are within the ambit of possible solutions. By opening the door to CATV transmissions without payment the Supreme Court complicated and delayed solution of the problem, but in time it must of necessity be determined.

Can CATV afford substantial rentals for films? The eventual answer must be affirmative. The medium has had a fantastic growth and is already present in millions of homes. The number of channels available on the cable is large and can encompass all kinds of programming. Huge revenues per channel are possible, but even modest revenues would suffice. Already professional sports, such as hockey, are moving toward CATV with an eye on a large paying audience. The use of motion pictures will clearly be necessary where stations originate. In the future CATV may produce its own or outbid the free television stations for film. For the present, theatrical film is available to the medium in quantity and can provide usable entertainment values to the audience. A substantial market appears imminent where CATV originates programming. Where it utilizes other programming it should, of course, the Supreme Court to the contrary notwithstanding, pick up the check for what it does. One should not reap where one has not sown.

The FCC, while restrictive in the past towards CATV, now shows signs of letting the medium have its head. The restrictions against use of motion pictures may well go or be modified. The consequences for free television can be significant and harmful. But if a workable plan of compensation for copyright holders is developed, the possibilities for film distributors can be substantive in this area as well as origination. Accordingly, as we view it, CATV with its possibilities for revenue on a per-channel or monthly-service basis provides an imminent possibility for large revenues for theatrical features. It should not be limited by anti-competitive forces or vested interests.

Pay TV

Pay TV, or scrambled air-signals subject to unscrambling devices with program charges, appears to have been pre-empted by CATV. Various tests of this new medium in Oklahoma, Connecticut and Ontario have failed, to date, to show a substantive response. It is a complex method of televising, probably less than foolproof against "purloining" and too weak to bid for the best in programming. Like CATV, it has been subjected to FCC regulation which has limited its right to use regular TV programming in an effort to avoid siphoning of material. Under these circumstances, as well as overt public hostility such as witnessed in a California referendum, the industry has not thrived and, in view of competition, seems to face a most uncertain future.

Hotel Television

Hotel television is a wired TV experiment with charges per program in a limited area which appears to offer significant possibilities for audiences and revenues. Early experience indicates that, for the privilege of seeing a new or reasonably new film, hotel residents in quantity are prepared to pay a normal charge either directly or as a part of their bill. The system, being entirely wired and local, is not subject to FCC regulation so it avoids the restrictive policies previously indicated for Pay TV and CATV (although there is the danger of municipal regulation). The essential question now is whether the paying public will justify the large expenditures necessary for installation, as well as recoup any losses that may be suffered in the theatrical market by virture of the new system. On the basis of successful tests, a number of hotels are proceeding with the service and it seems likely that within a brief period the programming will be available on a large-scale basis. Film companies will no doubt utilize the service despite wails and howls from anguished exhibitors. The market has real possibilities.

Cassettes

Cassettes, as a method of distribution, also avoid the FCC regulation problem as they do not come in over the air. They are, of course, attachable to various devices which by virtue of modern technology make them viewable on a television or other screen at home or elsewhere. The commercial concept here is the sale or renting of films and other materials to those who have purchased the requisite hardware which, incidentally, does not presently come cheap. Programming can be current and competitive with free television.

The distribution of cassettes may well also avoid obscenity and rating problems incurred by other media. Pornographic cassettes are already available and their use at home (if not their sale) appears immune to prosecution. Anything that can be put on film or tape can be included in the cassette.

While the possibilities of this medium are significant, the high cost of the hardware to utilize it, as well as the many incompatible systems of exhibition, have discouraged progress. It is not for your author to say which of the many systems is technically best or has the most promise. Several have unique advantages including the ability to tape and replay at one's convenience existing TV programs and home movies. Others are more limited in scope. Which system the public will choose remains an open question.

Can feature films be sold or licensed in large quantities through the medium of cassettes. Present trends indicate that their effectiveness will, initially at least, be most significant in other areas. Their use for teaching, at home or in school, instruction in the use of products, convention relays and other commercial usages will precede any large-scale market for entertainment features.

The price of the equipment, and the price of the cassette for license or purchase, must be reasonable if the experiment is to succeed. The various techniques must be made compatible so that any cassette can be used to be projected through any television set. It seems doubtful that many people, other than true film buffs, will want to create their own library of films—and this will not, in my judgment provide a significant sales market for theatrical features. Licensing is another matter. That is not to say that it should not be tried, used and exploited in every possible manner. It is merely to post a *caveat* to the many high hopes repeatedly expressed.

TV on Airplanes, Ships, Trains

In the world of communications there lies an entirely distinctive non-theatrical market that is now being effectively tapped for features. In particular, the remarkable leadership of In Flight Movies which developed both the techniques of exhibition and distribution on the airlines is to be commended for ingenuity and courage. The successful development of this industry shows again the power of positive thinking backed by the willingness to put one's money where his mouth is. Films are in airplanes, they are enjoyable and useful in flight, and their exhibition is important to both airlines and film distributors. For a limited group of features they are an excellent, if small, market. Again, foreign and "X"-rated films are relegated to a relatively minor role, but the tendency of some of the airlines to run two films (one for adults and one for family) may mitigate this problem.

Ships and even trains can also use feature films as an entertainment medium. The shipping market is even now significant. So long as there remain viable modes of transportation requiring more than brief passage these systems should prove reasonable sources of revenue for feature films.

The non-theatrical markets are presently important and will grow in importance in the future. In some way, in one way or another, vast quantities of theatrical film and dollars flowing in opposite directions will come to producers and distributors from markets other than theatres. Theatre organizations would be wise to move with these trends rather than against them in the days ahead. Guessing which technique will prosper must be the name of the game for the entertainment entrepreneur in the years ahead.

12

Print Piracy

THE PROBLEM OF print piracy is a substantial and growing one in all the entertainment industries, and modern technology promises more rather than less of the same. In essence, we are talking about the use of one man's print or tape by another without the faintest shred of legal authority. We are concerned with the dilution and destruction of vast productive efforts, of unrecouped investments in time and money, and the literal "reaping" where one has *not* "sowed".

There are any number of facets to this difficulty. Loss may be suffered when a distributor in South Africa discovers that he cannot book his film because a pirate has already performed it publicly in private homes to numerous people. Or when an American distributor discovers that a print has been "bicycled" from a theatre holding a legitimate license to exhibit at a different theatre with no such authorization from the legitimate owner. A 16mm. non-theatrical licensor may well find his college market saturated with unauthorized copies of his film. And an owner of television rights lawfully acquired may discover to his dismay that the properties he purchased or licensed exclusively are by no means exclusively in his possession.

In a case within your author's experience, an enterprising individual with several video tape recorders took the trouble to record all material including copyrighted films being played over free television in a northwest city. He, thereafter, flew the recordings to a group of small Alaskan towns which receive their television via the wired cable. The programs were exhibited as received to local paying audiences in Kodiak, Cordova, Skagway, and the like, until the entire procedure was enjoined by a Federal Court.

Illegal larceny must, of course, be distinguished from the legal variety. That which is in the public domain is free for all to utilize, although this does not justify the pilfering of physical properties such as prints. If there is no copyright in the jurisdiction involved, there may be no remedy. And even if there is a copyright, there may be no guaranty of protection. The problem is illustrated by the unhappy Fortnightly decision growing out of the development of Community Antenna Television (CATV).

This procedure originated as a service in areas where television reception was inadequate due to geographical or other factors. By creation of a separate antenna and the transmission of signals over wires or by microwave, televised programs were taken off the air as broadcast by regular TV stations and forwarded by CATV to its subscribing public. The practice spread far and wide, beyond its creators' dreams, and has become a major source of television usage.

There was nothing eleemosynary about the procedure. Televised film programming, subject to exclusive contracts in particular areas, was seized by noncontributing CATV stations and vended to customers for a high tariff. Consent of the original licensor was never sought. In brief, the CATV system took the copyrighted product, produced, licensed and distributed by others and sold it for a price without compensation to owners, licensors or creators.

A film distributor (United Artists Corp.) justifiably took exception to these practices and instituted suit against what one might ordinarily consider a clear breach of copyright interests. It premised its position on older cases, holding that rebroadcasts by separate wire to hotel patrons of copyrighted radio programs was a violation of the sender's rights. In well considered opinions, the District Court and the Circuit Court of Appeals upheld these contentions and labeled CATV's practice an infringement of the owner's rights.[1]

But the United States Supreme Court, to the dismay and astonishment of close to a unanimous copyright bar and entertainment industry, concluded that the acts of CATV in receiving, amplifying and transmitting signals to paying customers was not a "performance" of

[1] *United Artists* v. *Fortnightly* 255 F. Supp. 177 (1966), aff'd 377 F. 2d 872.

United Artists copyrighted works. In a simplistic opinion, the CATV
operators were held legally entitled to nothing other than a pure wind-
fall at the expense of copyright proprietors.[2]

The net effect was to legitimize piracy of copyrighted material
over the airwaves. An incidental, unfortunate result was to delay
revision of the long obsolete 1909 Copyright Law as the CATV—
Free TV—motion picture dispute was one of the major items in
question, and the decision torpedoed the negotiations of the conflicting
groups.

Owners of literary and other rights were also adversely effected
in their efforts to protect themselves by another pronunciamento of
the Supreme Court in the related patent field. Here the august tribunal
had held that despite precedents, an unpatented lamp could not be
protected against direct copying under State law by the doctrine of
unfair competition.[3] Without patenting his invention the court found
that the plaintiff proprietor had no means whatsoever of legally enforc-
ing his rights against even a precise duplicate. This was held to be
Congressional intent enforced by the supremacy clause of the Con-
stitution, leaving only a handful of exceptions such as restraint on
"palming off" one's product as that of another, or the mislabeling of
products under the trademark law. Patent legislation was thereby held
final and binding as to matters of protection within its scope. Unfortunately, the identical reasoning was also applied by the Justices to the
copyright area. In the Supreme Court's view, it would now appear
that as to matters uncopyrighted (or perhaps even uncopyrightable)
there can be little or no protection against infringement.

The effect of these decisions has been to open wide loopholes
for pernicious practices not only in the areas of print and material
piracy, but in the prevention of unfair competitive practices in a host
of other areas beyond the scope of this chapter.

Despite these difficulties and others, however, certain aspects of
piracy remain quite clear and beyond dispute. Where filmed material
is copyrighted, the right of performance belongs to the owner or his
licensee. It does not belong to a third party, unless he has legitimately
acquired a right to use the same from the owner, and even then, only
for the specified purpose licensed. Under the law, in theory at least,
he can be stopped.

---

[2] *Fortnightly Corp.* v. *United Artists* 392 U.S. 390 (1968).
[3] See *Sears, Roebuck & Co.* v. *Stiffel Company* 376 U.S. 225 (1964); *Compeco Company* v. *Day-Brite Lighting, Inc.* 376 U.S. 234 (1964).

How Piracy Operates

The techniques of acquisition by the print pirates are numerous. Some of the methods of direct acquisition follow. Usually seizure or creation is in 16mm. or the smaller gauges, as these are easier to handle and less conspicuous than the larger sizes of film.

1. Positive prints are processed at laboratories from orders of owners and licensees. A dishonest lab employee can, with relative ease, run off an additional copy for himself.

2. At theatres and other places of exhibition, a dishonest theatre owner or his employee possessed of the proper facilities may remove a print from the theatre or hall, after exhibition, for a modest period of time and create from the print duplicating material from which new prints can thereafter be made. The original print may thereby be briefly delayed in its return trip to its rightful owner.

3. The same possibilities as specified for exhibitors are readily available to those involved in shipment, transfer and storage of prints. New printing materials can be created from which in turn prints may be manufactured only slightly inferior in quality to the print in possession.

4. The Army, Navy and Air Force order narrow-gauge prints in quantity of many films for showing to servicemen. These are frequently subject to direct pilferage at bases or in transit, in addition to the possibilities for duplication listed above.

5. Hotels, airlines and transportation systems (boats, trains) are now heavily in film exhibition. The prints in their possession can similarly be seized or subjected to duplicating procedures.

6. Non-theatrical users are some of the worst offenders. Prints may be left around schoolrooms or clubs available to members and others with nefarious motives. Museums and lending institutions are still another source for illegal duplication.

7. Television uses motion pictures in an atmosphere of advanced technology where pirated tapes can be easily manufactured for use or duplication.

8. With reference to broadcasting, the newly developed videotape recorder opens up the possibility of the creation of large libraries of films on tape in homes as elsewhere—all subject to the same uses and abuses we have noted. No doubt more efficient devices are on the way, and it can only be a matter of time until first class recording and duplicating facilities are generally available to the public at reasonable prices. The prospect is alarming!

9. In earlier times, and even currently, some film companies sold copies of 16mm. prints of their older films to customers directly and outright. Although only the print was purchased for home exhibition under explicit restrictions, it was and remains difficult to police the unscrupulous purchaser who may have more material pleasures in mind.

10. Frequently, at the end of a license term, aging prints are "junked" by an agent or sub-distributor. Abuses are quite possible in the junking procedures. A theoretically junked print may easily pop up in distribution despite affidavits and certifications that it is destroyed. Sometimes such notarized documents are not, as Sam Goldwyn eloquently said of oral agreements, "worth the paper they are written on."

Pirates come in all breeds and shapes and not invariably with the worst of motives (whatever the results of their actions). There are collectors who start with the assumption they are only building a home library, but wind up in business when the rewards become too promising. The rising trend of pricing policies in the market of 16mm. prints to schools, clubs and other institutions has created some modern "Robin Hoods" who, in the interest of better informed film lovers, have decided to market ill-received prints at lower charges to the suffering institutions. While their motives may be of the best, the results are nonetheless disastrous to those who invest time, money and effort in creating and distributing worthwhile (or even not so worthwhile) film. There must be better ways of controlling pricing policies of licensors.

Of course, the normal pirate is no model of idealistic altruism. His interest is in using someone else's property to earn dollars or pesos for himself. He gets his prints in one of the manners we have specified, and proceeds to market the film ware. He may do it by modest "box" advertising in exhibitor or film buff publications, indicating availabilities through a post office box. Others with more gall, issue their own brochures, listing films on hand. Frequently, the brochure fails to indicate any address or source, but is based on word-of-mouth as to the pirate's identity. And then there are those who go all out and publish their lists with names and addresses attached, daring their victims to bring on a judicial challenge.

In a recent situation in the Southeast, a distributor with literally hundreds of hot prints operated openly in the Caribbean and Latin America and through agents in other parts of the world. Theatres, homes and other establishments were illegally licensed. A tremendous business, primarily outside the United States, was built on possession of unauthorized prints and materials. The instance referred to was not singular, and businesses of like nature are operative elsewhere.

In the parallel field of record piracy, a truly gigantic industry was developed in the United States, based on the re-recording and illicit publishing of musical works. Here the perpetrators were aided by anomalies in the ancient copyright law which prevented the copyright of recordings as such and created other significant loopholes for copiers. Fortunately, that condition has at least been cured in part by an amendment to the law making new recordings after a date in 1972 copyrightable, as well as prompt, vigorous and imaginative action by legitimate recorders, their associations and attorneys. But despite all a significant record piracy industry still remains.

Protection against piratical practices is a tall order calling for a host of measures. In an era of excessive materialism, rising crime rates, disrespect for existing authority and fantastic opportunity for ill-gotten gains, there are no magic remedies. Furthermore, legal loopholes in copyright protection and otherwise in the U.S., and particularly elsewhere in the world, make the job doubly difficult. Criminally minded, imaginative individuals who have the will are likely to find a way. The film and entertainment industries must bring to bear all their unified powers of force and control to limit or hopefully destroy these practices.

Piracy Controls

The job is formidable. Nonetheless, it has been shown that it can be done. It involves such techniques as:

1. Rigorous controls on laboratories to see that only the prints ordered are produced and delivered. There are available numbering techniques and other methods that will reveal or signal improperly produced prints. Personnel practices of the processors must be controlled as well to guard against the corrupt apple in the printing barrel.

2. Print controls in distribution must be vigorously enforced. Every distributor must know at all times where every numbered print is located. There should be insistence, with enforceable penalty provisions, on the immediate return of prints from specified engagements. This applies not only to exhibitions, but to those who ship, transfer, and store prints. Each print must be frequently accounted for to a

responsible individual—regular reports of prints on hand should be backed up by spot checks and surprise audits to insure their presence and availability. The looseness of operations in many of these areas is legendary. It must be a first victim.

3. Users of film such as the military and airlines and all forms of television should be subject to rigid penalties on their failure to immediately return available prints. If not in use, prints must be securely stored.

4. Prints which properly belong in the exhibitor's hands for a period of time must be secured by them so they are unavailable to third persons. If the exhibitor will not enforce this, the distributor should impose penalties to prevent the leakage.

5. A code of procedures within the videotape recording area must be worked out, limiting insofar as possible abuses within this field. Obviously, the sina quo non of video taping is the recording of events and programs, but this cannot mean that any and all copyrighted material can be taken or used with impunity. A code of ethics and procedures must be set forth in detail to limit use and reuse of materials and prevent wholesale manufacture of unauthorized prints. The area is complicated and difficult, but with good faith on both sides, reasonable limitations should be achievable and enforceable.

6. The outright sale of prints must be halted or much more vigorously controlled to prevent impermissable uses or duplication. Contractual terms with stipulated damages for misuse could be one answer. The rights granted should be explicitly set forth in the license and none others permitted with serious economic loss to the violator.

7. "Junking of prints" should be rigidly supervised or performed only by the authorized holder of rights. Too many contracts contain loose terminology permitting the licensee to dispose of "old" prints on his own certification or that of a dealer. This is a fertile area for illegal prints and far from impossible to secure. Decisive steps can and should be taken.

8. All new films produced should be copyrighted pursuant to law to take full advantage of the statute and international protection granted. The procedure is simple and inexpensive, and the Copyright Office is most cooperative in the matter of print presentation. Reliance on "common law" copyright or non-publication is ill-conceived and likely to wind up legitimizing print piracy. Regardless of other ambiguities, the copyright law is completely clear in that it confines to the copyright owner for his term, the exclusive right to make copies and

reproduce films. It has been held explicitly to bar the making of "unauthorized prints" which is precisely what we are talking about. In view of the Supreme Court's ambivalence about protecting literary or other materials where there is no copyright of the property involved, the issue of whether or not to copyright (and renew) is now obsolete. Copyright your film to protect it!

9. The value of joint action by distributors against clear and open offenders has long been apparent. Fear of antitrust claims by offenders should no longer be a prime consideration. This has long been an industry neurosis limiting and holding back the necessary unified moves which can really hurt the piracy culprits. There is already of record clear proof of what simultaneous response of certain companies can accomplish. Pirates have been halted, prints returned, bonds posted against future misconduct—all by unified response. The costs of joint action are far smaller than those involved if each company must move individually. The organizational means are at hand, and in use, and must be prosecuted vigorously to reduce this problem so common to all.

The American copyright law, even as presently written and construed, does not lack for remedies. The law permits monetary relief when rights are infringed. Damages can be recovered for losses suffered. Alternatively, an accounting of profits improperly gained is available. A wrongdoer can be punished as well with punitive damages unrelated to losses, where his conduct is outrageous and shocking to the court.

If damages or profits are not clear, statutory damages in lieu of other losses may be granted. These are limited sums set up by the law to measure losses where their amount is imprecise. Although the statutory damage provisions of the old copyright law were poorly drafted and the case law has not cleared up the many resulting ambiguities, they remain a potentially potent weapon against infringers. Despite all, large grants of statutory damages have been made and will continue to be made.

Beyond its damage provisions, the copyright law authorizes injunctions (preliminarily as well as permanently) to restrain continued violations. Such a remedy can literally put an infringer out of business. While not easily granted, injunctions are a grave threat, and their very possibility may dissuade a violator from continuing his practices.

If copyright infringement is established, the law further authorizes a court order to the defendant to deliver for destruction copies (i.e. illegal prints) as well as other materials and means of duplication. A pirate faced with such an order confronts a devastating blow.

In addition to these remedies, there are mandatory court costs against a proved infringer, and he may as well be confronted with a bill for his adversary's legal fees. Unlike most fields of law, in copyright the court has authority to grant a counsel fee payable by the loser to the prevailing party. Unfortunately, this power has been sparingly used, but its potential remains vast.

Criminal actions against willful pirates are also authorized, although infrequently utilized. Unfortunately, U.S. District Attorneys have too many other offenses on their minds these days to play an active role in the copyright area. The possibility of such action, however, should not be neglected.

International problems are implicit in piracy prevention but unfortunately legal authorities in many jurisdictions seem unable or unwilling to deal with the matter. While there are international conventions, they are not executed by all states, and where they are applicable, they apply local rather than international rules. Strengthening of international procedures would aid the attack on film piracy, but it is no panacea. The emphasis should be on meeting local problems where they exist by generating when possible strong local laws or administrative actions. Protection now varies substantially from country to country. Joint action to retain top attorneys and advisors in those areas where pilferage is ripe and to find remedies for such wrongs seems essential.

It is not only copyright law that may be related to piracy. Larceny of a legally owned print is a local offense. Replevin or return by court order of duly owned materials may be available. Many other laws seem related and all must be used.

Beyond law, however, is the necessity of a definitive policy to remedy this wrong. The will and determination to seek and root out piracy practices is essential. It will cost money, but it is money well spent. For if these acts continue unmitigated, they constitute not only a revenue drain, but a definitive threat to all who legitimately produce, process, distribute and exhibit motion pictures.

13

The Impact of the Antitrust Laws

THE FEDERAL ANTITRUST LAW is aimed at the prevention of monopolies and monopolistic practices. Although enforcement is primarily a function of the Justice Department, the law also permits private damage actions premised on such violations. As a practical matter, however, private actions frequently require a substantial investment in legal and investigatory services, not to mention difficult trade relations arising from their institution. Consequently, they are unusual as a general rule except in those conditions when the Government has already secured a decree against the defendants on which proof of violations can be based. State antimonopoly statutes have been of infrequent use as they apply only to activities within a state and are generally weaker than national law.

A second legal brake on unfair competitive practices is the Federal Trade Commission which holds power in regards business activities tending toward monopolies or trade restriction. Its importance as in the case of the Justice Department, depends greatly on the enthusiasm and drive it engenders towards meeting its mandate. This has varied with time, appropriations and political appointments.

The motion picture industry has long been a key area for action by both the Justice Department and the Federal Trade Commission. Its history has been replete with examples of monopolistic practices under attack from both Government and private sources. In perhaps no other industry has there been such a high degree of regulatory and judicial activities aimed at creating fair conditions of trade.

The basis of this phenomenon has been the history and structure of the business. The origins of film as commerce have been well stated elsewhere. Following the development of the medium near the turn of the century, stores (theatres) emerged as the showplace for the unique spectacle of pictures that moved. Films (generally shown in a theatre) were licensed by distributors to these establishments on agreed terms. As the popularity of the new medium increased, production companies became organized as did groups in exhibition.

The circumstances calling for combination and restraint of trade were compelling. On one side theatres required a flow of film at reasonable license fees. On the other, producer-distributors saw their market controlled or threatened by the bargaining power of strong exhibition groups. Each moved to protect its interests.

The thrust of production-distribution was to acquire or control the nation's key theatre outlets. This was accomplished, to a substantial extent, by the purchase, acquisition and building of exhibition houses throughout the country. Paramount, in the 1920's, for example, built a mighty circuit of theatres which even today remains as part of the vast ABC television-theatre empire. Similarly Fox (later 20th Century-Fox) and Loew's (MGM) established great empires of retail outlets for their films.

Conversely, First National—an exhibition group—seeking to control its source of supply, became a producer-distributor (Warner Bros. First National Pictures). Its exhibition chain was combined with powerful production-distribution forces to create a significant business entity.

Integrating up from theatres and down from production, vast vertical concentrations were formed which, by the mid-1930's, had a powerful grip on the American film industry. In addition, strong non-theatre holding producers and powerful independent exhibition chains added to the squeeze on the small individual threatre owner. His cries of anguish were loud and to a great extent justified.

Questionable Trade Practices

A collection of questionable trade practices developed to strengthen the hands of the strong producers, distributors and exhibitors. Foremost among them was the policy of block booking or the insistence that theatres license all (with limited exceptions) of a particular distributor's annual production of films if he wished to play any of them. As early as 1916, the redoubtable Adolf Zucker was telling licensees that they must take "all or none" of the Paramount line. Keeping in mind that production thereafter rose to nearly 60 films a year from Paramount, this was a substantive diet. The major integrated companies (whose names occasionally changed) including such powers as MGM, RKO, Fox, Warner's, all known as "majors," as well as the production-distribution independents (Columbia, Universal and United Artists) followed suit. The block-booking provision requiring licensing of the entire production line with only a modest cancellation privilege (10-20%) became a standard in the industry.

Block booking also involved "blind buying," or the licensing of films by exhibitors before they were screened. Exhibitors complained that this practice, as well, left them at the mercy of the distributors.

Other ominous techniques were also developed to increase monopoly, or more accurately, oligopoly (partial monopolies of several companies) control of the business. To acquire theatres the majors threatened independent owners with a loss of their films. If that did not work, they indicated that they might build competitive houses across the street. Secret offers were made to landlords to acquire theatre leaseholds on termination. Where controlled theatres competed with independents, favorable terms for licensing were granted the subsidiary as opposed to the victim. When all else failed, competitive theatres could be and were built regardless of need or even losses suffered in order to prove that the major companies meant business and could pay the price.

By these tactics, control of the vast majority of the most important theatres was attained by the majors and their associates. These houses received the Class A, first-run films, not only from their integrated owners but under special arrangements as well with the other leading producer-distributors.

The game of "backscratching" developed. Where company A controlled the leading theatres in one town, it received preferential treatment over its competitors, as did company B reciprocally in the communities dominated by it. By cooperative theatre arrangements and a pooling of interests, many theatres were operated jointly for the benefit of the combined monopolists. Strong unaffiliated circuits, such as Interstate and Crescent, were also able to enforce preferential arrangements with the distributors in their territories. The small independent theatre owner was all but frozen out of first-run exhibition in important areas.

In all but single-theatre communities films were generally exhibited, until quite recently, on a series of runs—first, second and subsequent. To protect the first-run house from competition, a clearance or time-lag was established during which the film was not available for booking to others. This encouraged customers to come downtown and pay a higher price to see a film initially instead of waiting for his local neighborhood engagement. The longer the clearance period, the greater the protection. Although clearance itself was justifiable under such a structure (now generally obsolete), the dominant industry forces abused it. They granted arbitrary amounts of such time to protect their own and affiliated theatres but ignored or minimized the similar requirements of independents.

Another improper tactic of distributors involved preferential treatment of terms to the strong independent circuits. Deals were made across the boards for most or all of the theatres involved on conditions far more favorable than those granted to competitors. Again the independent was disadvantaged, if not actually driven out of business.

Finally distributors, by their contracts, frequently dictated the box-office price which the public could be charged by exhibitors. They thus prevented natural price competition in the market and assumed functions properly belonging to the theatre owner.

Exhibition licenses at most theatres is, and has been, based on a percentage of gross receipts of the film being displayed. The bargaining strength of the majors in this respect was too much for most exhibitors, who either acceded to the terms offered them or attempted to renegotiate after exhibition to keep the film rental reasonable. An alternative way out, still not uncommon albeit reprehensible, was to cheat or distort in reporting grosses and thereby reduce the distributor's share of receipts. All along the line, monopoly power and unfair practices created an intolerable situation in the trade.

Exhibitor groups and organizations led the assault on these conditions. As early as 1919, at their instance, the Federal Trade Commission condemned a host of theatre acquisition tactics of the majors and attempted to limit their impact. The administrative machinery, however, proved ineffective and the growth of monopoly-oligopoly conditions continued into the 1930's.

At the instance of independent exhibitors, in 1938 the Justice

Department Antitrust Division brought a formal action against the majors as well as several suits against large independent theatre circuits. Premised on the practices we have described and seeking to alter the competitive scene, a temporary decree in 1940 limited block-booking licenses to groups of no more than five films at a time. The legal struggle, however, continued until 1948 when the Government won a sweeping judicial victory, thereafter confirmed by "consent decrees' accepted by the defendants.[1]

The "Consent Decrees"

The thrust of these and subsequent holdings was:

(1) Full and complete divorcement of the major producer-distributors from their exhibition outlets. In essence, this spelled the end of the defendants' theatre holdings throughout the country—which was the key to the monopoly conditions then existing. Although the rule still holds, it only binds the defendants and their successors and does not prevent other production-distribution companies from owning theatres. Nor does it seem to have precluded distributors from casually leasing theatres or acquiring periods of playing time on a "four-wall basis" where they, in effect, operate the theatre. This has been permitted in a number of situations. These and the other terms of the decrees are at all times subject to exceptions or modifications as permitted by a Federal Court in New York retaining jurisdiction.

(2) Similarly the decrees barred the pooling of intercorporate operations in controlled theatres. If one company could not own theatres individually, then a group certainly could not own or operate collectively.

(3) The practice of block booking of copyrighted films by the defendants was terminated. In brief, the licensing of one film conditioned upon the licensing of another was banned, dooming the pre-sale of an entire annual line of product or in fact any conditioned group license. It remains quite permissible to license films simultaneously provided they are not conditioned on the licensing of each other. While charges of such practices still continue to be made, this provision went a long way toward ending the assured market. It also

---

[1] See *U.S.* v. *Paramount Pictures, Inc.* et al 66 F. Supp. 323 (1946), modified 70 F. Supp. 53; remanded 85 F. Supp. 881; aff'd 339 U.S. 974 (1950); see also Cassady: "Impact of the Paramount Decision," 31 S. Calif. Law Review 150 (1958).

prevented the freezing-out of independent distributors from playing time at theatres.

(4) The practice of "blind buying," which involved licensing agreements executed without an exhibitor's opportunity to see the film first, was also condemned. Subject to a few reasonable exceptions, leasing sight-unseen was eliminated. Presently up to five films may, however, be offered by any defendant prior to screenings.

(5) The fixing by distributors of admission prices to be charged by an exhibitor was found a *per se* violation of the Antitrust Laws. Nonetheless, it remains possible, by setting film rentals in such terms as per-person charges at a fixed rate (i.e. for each adult customer the distributor shall receive $1), to avoid the rule. As a matter of practice, however, distribution control of retail pricing practices was generally eliminated. This is a responsibility of the exhibitor.

(6) The arbitrary granting of "priority of run" as well as periods of "clearance" to favored customers were prevented by the decrees. No clearance was allowed over operations not found in a competitive area or where not reasonably necessary to protect the prior runs. Under the old system of a tier of runs these were vital matters of concern. In today's context, with multiple openings of many films in large groups of theatres, at least in the major metropolitan areas, this aspect of the decree seems of declining importance. In smaller communities, however, the provisions are still pertinent and they have, in any event, had the effect of promoting much private litigation against the defendants in the 1950's and 1960's based on past condemned practices.

(7) Discriminatory pricing arrangements with major independent circuits, granting advantages for bookings covering groups of theatres, were condemned. Dealings were presumably to be made theatre-by-theatre, without regard to bargaining strength, to permit local independents to license strong films on their own merits. Obviously, if a circuit's entire bargaining power was brought into play, it could outbid individual local competitors unless some restraint was granted.

After much controversy, a proposed mandate to require "competitive bidding" in all situations was rejected by the various decrees. Under this system, each theatre would have had to bid against each other to acquire films. This would have meant a completely regulated market and a mountain of paperwork to complete licensing arrangements in practically all cases. Although not a required remedy, com-

petitive bidding was permitted on a discretionary basis and has been
utilized by distributors in a limited number of situations where choices
are difficult and there are fears of private antitrust actions in the event
a theatre is denied a run that it wishes.

There are obviously grave difficulties in determining winning
bids where the technique is utilized. Offers of competing theatres may
not be truly comparable as to the period of a run, by virtue of location
or as to the nature of advance guarantees and other related terms. In
addition, of course, there is the constant danger of charges of bid-
rigging, including premature circulation of information as to offers
before the appropriate date. Strangely, exhibitor agreements as to how
to bid (if at all) made with distributor "concurrence" have been held
valid. This amounts to a "splitting of product" and hardly seems
consistent with fair trade practices. All of these matters would seem to
diminish the value of competitive bidding as a proper technique to
determine film licenses.

The various consent decrees were followed by a flood of litigation by theatre owners against the majors.[2] Taking advantage of the
damage provisions of the antitrust laws (actual damages are tripled
if found by the court, and attorneys's fees may be added for successful
plaintiffs), a host of exhibitors brought suits premised on the practices
found wrongful by the courts in the prior period. Although initially
there were a handful of spectacular damage verdicts, most cases were
settled on moderate terms and many dismissed or dropped for lack of
merit. Still others were successfully resisted. With the expiration of
a shortened statute of limitations the cases have gradually dwindled
from many hundreds to a present handful.

Under the new dispensation most licenses are negotiated with
individual theatres. The trend in rental fees has been up but the policy
of adjustment of terms after the contract, based on the final gross, has
reduced the significance of the licensed terms. In view of these rene-
gotiations now customary in the industry the exhibit contract has
diminished in importance.

With the loss of the assured market by virtue of the decree as
well as a host of other unfavorable competitive factors—television,
foreign production, competition from other leisure-time activities and
a rise in selective tastes—production of American features has been

[2] See for example, *Bigelow* v. *RKO Radio Pictures* 78 F. Supp. 250 (1948), aff'd
170 F2d 783.

sharply reduced. Companies that once produced 60 films a year now produce 12, and the unhappiness of union labor with the limited output of Hollywood is endemic. The industry entered an era of higher budgets, reduced schedules and a selective market.

Developments in the 1970's

Controversies about trade practices still persist and it is safe to say that they will continue in this country and elsewhere. Exhibitors object to high rental terms, to the bunching of important releases at special times during the theatrical seasons (rather than an even flow of releases throughout the year) and a chronic shortage of "important" films. They also oppose the quick release of films to television and other nontheatrical markets and the development of new competitive media—CATV, pay television, hotel exhibition, cassettes, etc. Distributors equally and firmly point to their large losses, not only on numerous films but over-all during considerable periods, and insist that they must secure high revenues with their successful pictures as well as new sources of exploitation. No end of conflict is in sight.

It is not unusual to find theatre owners who now grieve for the "good old days" before the Government action initiated at their instigation. Such are the ironies of history!

A curious development occurred in 1970 with a group of major film distributors instituting suit against two major television networks on grounds remotely resembling the Governmental actions against the majors of 30 years ago. The thrust of the charge was that, by entering film production as competitors, the networks assured themselves a television market and to an extent froze out other producers from their screens. While there seemed to be some evidence of network discrimination in favor of their own film shows over their competitors', the situation hardly resembled theatrical distribution in the 1930's as many of the plaintiff's films were and continue to be licensed to television on prime time for vast sums. The majors were hardly "frozen out" as were the independent theatre owners as of another time. The action, consequently, seemed more in the nature of a move to prevent network competition in production. Since its initiation, new FCC rules have reduced the time available for network-produced entertainment, and at least one of the new production companies has ceased activities for economic reasons not apparently connected with the suit.

In another surprise move in 1972, a Government Suit was filed under the antitrust laws aimed at making the networks give up their financial interests in all entertainment programs. While other rights were involved including syndication and foreign revenues, the thrust again was control of prime time network programming through production and/or ownership of entertainment formats. The net effect of this ownership was allegedly to the detriment of "independent" producers. The suit came at a strange time following charges of maladministration of the antitrust laws in the ITT controversy and may not be unrelated to other disputes between the Nixon Administration and the television networks. In fairness, however, it should be said that independent television producers as well as film companies have, for years, charged the networks with discriminatory treatment in entertainment programming and the complaint had been in consideration in the Justice Department over a long period.

It seems unlikely that there will be substantial results from these actions. Network privileges have already been sharply reduced and the days of their large-scale abuse appear limited. Governmental and private actions are but one more push down the same old road. New competitive factors such as CATV, cassettes and pay television are shaking and threatening television as other factors did in the case of motion pictures. Whether the networks can hold their strength against these developments is a matter of grave and serious doubt.

14

Films and Conglomerates

THE MOTION PICTURE INDUSTRY has been very much involved in the process of conglomeration so significant in the American economy since the early 1960's. This is to be distinguished, of course, from the development of integrated companies with related film interests such as occurred in the earlier part of the century. A film monopoly or oligopoly group is generally limited to companies with similar spheres of operation. The rise of such film giants in production-distributon and exhibition is described elsewhere as an aspect of antitrust in the industry. Here, however, we are talking about motion picture companies as one aspect of a heterogeneous rather than homogeneous organization of companies. A conglomerate may involve such diverse interests as banking, insurance, auto accessories, zinc manufacture or any other activity as well as film production. It differs in kind from a horizontal or vertical large-scale film enterprise.

To the entrepreneurs of such large enterprises, the motion picture field has indicated great allure. Several of the major producers and distributors have joined their ranks and others may well do so in the immediate future. What considerations have prompted this development, and what have been its consequences?

The vulnerability of many film companies to expansionist efforts has long been apparent. This could be predicated on a number of factors. The broad distribution of equity shares of companies with but

106

iimited participation in ownership by management always opens inviting opportunities. Shares can be covertly or openly purchased, or tender offers may be made to stockholders at a price well in excess of current market evaluation. The opportunity to secure control is present in such situations which are not unusual in motion picture companies or elsewhere.

Vulnerability is, however, but one consideration to the "conglomerateur". In addition to availability, there must be attractiveness. For a variety of reasons, motion picture companies appear to have attained this quality. Some of the factors follow:

Why Conglomerates Are Attracted

1. Film stocks have tended to be undervalued due to their poor or erratic earning records. Their shares were, therefore, frequently available at prices regarded as minimal in view of their long-term assets.

2. Despite irregular earnings, these basic assets were frequently substantial. Such values might include strategically located real estate, foreign theatre holdings, or controlled subsidiaries in music publishing or related leisure-time activities.

3. The immense potential of existing film negatives in all of the new media lured the speculative urge. Huge libraries licensed to television had earned life-saving revenues before—the same thing could happen on the cable, in pay television, in the sale or licensing of cassettes or by some entirely new phenomena of exhibition.

4. A potential resurgence of theatrical audiences based on increased leisure time, a prospective 4-day work week, new theatres and other affirmative factors referred to elsewhere.

5. There is no underestimating the glamour appeal of film as an industry. As Irving Berlin wrote—and he may have had financial wizards in mind—"There's No Business Like Show Business." There are publicity, bright lights, film festivals and festivities, credits to "Executive Producers" and, inevitably, beautiful women. What other field of endeavor can offer such embellishments? This element of mystique, of glamour, as an inducement is not to be minimized.

For all these reasons and perhaps for others as well, the empire builders of the 1960's found themselves attracted to film.

Their efforts to secure control of various companies have by no means been universally successful. Several attempts at ascendancy were blocked by vigilant managements, proxy campaigns or litigation. But in other cases, new conglomerate interests have prevailed with or without opposition, and such companies as United Artists, Paramount and Warner Bros., have now become affiliates of such groups.

Concern About Conglomerates' Impact

Fears have long been expressed as to the impact of conglomeration on films. These included such prospective concerns as:

(1) Production by "committee" rather than responsible individuals. The assumption behind this concern is that, in large units, inevitably the individual is subordinate to some group rule which would prove inimical to effective film-making. The "one man" thesis of film production is well expressed in the writings of David O. Selznick and others.

(2) "Banker control" as opposed to producer-director control of film content (this objection ignored the high degree of financing control inherent in independent picture-making which nearly always requires some kind of outside financing). Bankers, or in any event non-film makers, were considered likely to impose rigid and impractical limitations on creative film artists.

(3) "Computerization" or the fear that creative functions would be turned over to some machine which would, for example, attempt to predetermine the subject material for films.

(4) "Minimization" or the gradual reduction of interest in filmmaking in view of other more profitable aspects of the conglomerates' activities. If, for example, automotive leasing services were more lucrative than film production or distribution, might not the new organization maximize their efforts in that direction and reduce the production of pictures?

Although the future is, of course, quite unpredictable, few of these fears appear so far to have been realized. A comparison of the conglomerate-dominated film companies with other majors does not appear to indicate any particular relevancy to this "chamber of horrors." The conglomerates certainly have proved so far as capable, as responsible and as willing as others to grant autonomy, allow individual expression, and adequately finance the making of significant motion pictures. Their record in this respect over the past few years is, if anything, somewhat better than that of their competitors. In brief, the dread conditions that were feared, do not appear to have come to pass.

This is not to say that budgetary limitations are not now vigorously imposed on creative personnel. They are and, in fact, they must be. In an industry so wildely unpredictable as film, such controls are essential and must be practiced by any organization intending to stay in business. That is the lesson of the 1960's to all film-makers and distributors-financiers—conglomerates and independents alike. The economic disasters of repeated multi-million dollar fiascos make production selectivity and rigid budgeting an essential "must."

Positive Effects

Conversely, the conglomerates have had positive effects on film-making in several areas which should not be overlooked.

(1) They have, in general, the financial strength to assure, if desired, a definite production program on a continuing basis. The independent producing company can rarely be certain of its resources and, in the face of set-backs, may have to limit or terminate its activities. The conglomerate's outside strength should be sufficient to avoid this, at least on economic grounds. This is not to say that, for a multitude of reasons, a conglomerate will not abandon planned pictures, reduce budgets or take other similar steps.

(2) The borrowing power of the conglomerates is such that they can self-finance or secure bank financing for films on terms frequently unavailable to the unaffiliated. The cost of money comes very high in the hazardous business of independent film production. Loans, if secured at all, frequently require personally signed notes, substantial collateral, completion guarantees, high interest rates and even over-riding profit participations to some lenders. A conglomerate can borrow from the bank in its own credit line on normal or near-normal terms, and need not be subjected to the rigid requirements of other lenders. Nor must there be a completion guaranty by a responsible third person to assure the lender. He is willing to rely on the conglomerate's general credit.

(3) Conglomerates have shown powerful political weight in moving government toward more favorable treatment of the film industry. Films for foreign markets are subject to specialized favorable tax treatment, and investment tax credits are available for producers—

at least in part, as a result of such influences. Some day, perhaps, a form of governmental subsidy for films will come to pass as a consequence of this political power.

The advantages of conglomerates in the film industry, then, appear substantive. Where properly administered, they permit the same delegation of power (within prescribed limits) to producers and directors as their competitors. The record shows that their companies have produced films of equally high artistic and box office performance as their competitors. Their financial strength and political "clout" enable them to plan and perform their activities on terms generally superior to others lacking their resources.

The subject of conglomeration as a social phenomenon on the American scene—with multiple impact in economics, monopoly conditions and ways of personal life—is beyond the scope of this effort and is not here considered. Confining ourselves to motion pictures, we find their alleged evils exaggerated and their positive results minimized.

There are, of course, no rules for the future. The conglomerates or their competitors may "pull in their horns" and abandon the risks of film production and distribution. They may substitute computers for human beings in the selection of film projects. They may deny autonomy and impose controls on responsible individuals. Our point is that to date they have not performed in this manner any worse than their non-affiliated competitors, and there is little in their record to indicate that they will.

15

Publicity and Advertising

TREMENDOUS EFFORT has traditionally gone into the publicizing and advertising of feature films. Obviously, it is essential that the public know when and where it can see a film if it is to lavish its patronage. But it seems critical that, with but a handful of exceptions, the greatest budgets and expenditures for promotion and advertising will accomplish little unless the public likes the picture once it attends. Consequently, the tendency has been to reduce expenditures sharply if "word of mouth" reaction is weak, and to push and promote where this reaction is strong. It is the rare film indeed that can be made successful by promotion alone.

Publicity may well start with the acquisition of a property. The purchase of the motion picture rights in a famous novel or play is frequently a good point of first release. While such a property may be considered pre-sold, the woods are littered with outstanding properties that have failed on the screen. Nothing can be assured and efforts should not be relaxed just because the general project or author is well-known. Other significant points for publicity impact would appear in the retention of a well-known script writer, the hiring of a director, certain stars and the first day of photography. Sometimes such events are accompanied by advertising, but the expenditure of large monies at such an early point seems a dubious investment. Experience tells us it will be many months, or even years, before the film is ready for public or even exhibitor showings. No one can buy tickets and few will remember what was said a year earlier.

For reasons not entirely clear, the practice of trade advertising, both pre-release and simultaneous with release, in the specialized motion picture press appears to have fallen on evil days. Certainly, one would think that early advertising, if justified at all, would be most effective here where the first customers (theatres) are concerned. But the trend has been contrary—not only pre-release but, amazingly, post-release as well. Trade advertising has sharply diminished, with considerable harmful results to producers and distributors. In an economy wave advertising budgets are, illogically, early sufferers and trade paper advertising one of the earliest.

On a major film, there are frequently opportunities for publicity stories during the course of production. There may be location shooting at an important place, stunt photography or even personal romances (shades of Burton-Taylor) justifying important news reports. Surprisingly, here too, publicity staffs have been cut and press releases are infrequent. Hollywood was a former publicity center, but on economy grounds it too has de-emphasized the function.

During production, still photos should be acquired for use in advertising and posters. Campaigns are developed to sell the film based on its potential audience. An initial effort should be engendered to develop a "press book" of prospective advertising and publicity material for the film to be furnished to exhibitors.

As the film nears completion, frequently the theme of the advertising campaign will be developed. Sketches as well as general copy and the prospective audience will be determined. It is important to know early to what segment of the audience (and there are many audiences) the film will appeal. The strategy of the campaign will be, for example, to catch the youth-oriented (*Easy Rider*) or the minorities (*Super Fly* and *Shaft*), or children (Disney), or such other division of the public as may respond.

Certainly the "trailer" campaign of a new feature is of vital import. Here an actual money-paying film audience is the direct target of an advertising film consisting of a few significant live segments of the coming attraction (200-odd feet of material with promotion copy). Unlike newspapers, radio or television, there is no wastage of effort or dollars on non-moviegoers. The trailer strikes right at the heart of a segment of the prospective audience and is a critical method of film promotion. That the trailer be carefully and effectively produced by experts in their trade, and broadly circulated, appears of obvious importance.

Less important than the live-action trailer, but still significant, are other forms of film announcements such as advance trailers utilizing stills and promotion material for earlier exhibition and one-frame screened announcements of films at affiliated theatres. Advertising spots for other non-film products are irrelevant to this discussion, but should be noted as an audience antagonizer with negative implications for business as well as an undignified reflection on theatres as a place of entertainment. At the very least, major theaters should avoid these overt manifestations of commercialism.

Under present trade circumstances, where films are usually distributed initially either with a limited number of prints at selected locations or on a mass scale in particular communities, national magazine advertising seems inappropriate. The bulk of the audience can have little idea from the copy where or when it will see a film, except in the rare case of a simultaneous national release. A local magazine or community newspaper is, of course, distinguishable and may be utilized just before a local engagement. It may also provide a readership with a special interest in the film in question.

Magazine or newspaper advertising to popularize a "brand," such as the name of a producer-distributor, appears utterly fruitless. Most people clearly attend films on the basis of their particular content, and not because they know and desire the films of Columbia, Paramount or Warners. Efforts to promote a general line of product by stressing the name brand have never succeeded in the past for film companies and hold little promise for future results.

The vital thrust of advertising and promotion is immediately before or following opening of a single or multiple date engagement of a new or revived film. The public must be told explicitly the theatre or theatres involved and the dates of the engagements. Beyond this, the advertising must encourage by skillful use of pictures and copy the broadest market available to the film. The creation of successful advertising is beyond the scope of this work, as well as its author's capabilities, but there are those with the skills and tastes adequate to this fantastically difficult task.

The choice of media, when confronted with today's limited advertising budgets and high costs, is a serious problem. In your author's view, the theatrical page of local newspapers is generally the most effective place to advertise and publicize the film. This is where an interested, attentive audience is ready to test the advertiser's message. An appealing campaign should succeed in drawing customers at least for a few days.

Alternative choices for expenditure are television and radio. Television is a magnificent advertising medium as it can show a specialized trailer or segments of it with live action on the screen. Not all film, however, can be effectively presented, and the medium is also extremely costly and diffuse. Many thousands may see the message, but they may well range far beyond the film's audience with total costs well in excess of other means of communication. Television advertising seems limited to major films with a large potential audience, opening in many theatres in the community, so that the cost may be broadly allocated. It must also be the type of film that can be effectively presented in a brief announcement, as longer uses appear uneconomic.

Radio may lack television's obvious visual advantages, but it is cheaper and has its own broad audience. It also allows, to a higher degree, a selective audience appeal to groups such as commuters, housewives and music buffs. Effective radio spots can clearly prove a significant means of promotion. Here again, the preparation of such material is for specialists.

In recent years, film advertising has been plagued with many problems of local media censorship. Independent and even major distributors handling X and R rated films with various types of advertising campaigns have met serious resistance from publishers and other media owners who are unhappy with the nature of both candid advertisements and candid films. In some cases, they have gone so far as to ban all advertising of X rated films from their pages. In others, they have altered copy, limited announcements and art work. When such a publication controls a one TV-station "newspaper" town, the results may be dire. As yet, no legal technique has been developed to thwart these barriers as the courts have consistently permitted newspapers and other media broad discretion in the advertising material they accept, despite their quasi-utility status. While the practice of newspaper censorship has been condemned, it is likely to remain or even grow in size in a conservative-oriented society. Code-approved advertising in the motion picture field is more a palliative than remedy, but does protect a good deal of major company advertising. The prime sufferers are independents with "X" or "R" or un-rated films with appeal based on strong copy and sketches.

While "point of sale" advertising is obviously the vital thrust, other techniques may also prove effective. Teaser campaigns may be used in newspapers or on the air to excite interest prior to opening. As indicated, they are aimed at enticing an audience without the particulars of broader coverage. Their success has been limited. Similarly, billboards and other outdoor advertising are still used, but apparently with declining effectiveness.

In prime theatres in important markets, distributors share with theatres or may pay the entire cost of advertising their films. This is known as cooperative advertising and is a major expense of most distributing companies. The theory behind such advertising is that the film is being established for subsequent markets and accordingly distributor support has a *quid pro quo*. He will earn monies elsewhere on his own sponsored advertising. In addition, in many situations, such as New York, the distributor will be netting 90% of exhibitor's gross over his house expense as part of his licensing deal—and with a successful film, may recoup a large part of his advertising expense.

On the other side of the coin, the exhibitor, where he does not share, gets a free ride on advertising, while guaranteed his house expense plus a 10% share of gross. Frequently he has the additional advantage of a rate discount from an advertising source where "his" annual use of lineage runs over a certain figure. Cooperative advertising then, while fair in principle, has certain built-in abuses to the advantage of the exhibitor.

A New York or Los Angeles opening campaign, even at only one or two theatres, is an expensive matter running into many thousands of dollars. To reduce the burden and amortize the cost over a larger number of engagements, frequently a multiple first or second run is utilized. There the advertising cost can be shared by the distributor with many theatres or at least collected from a heavier distributor's share of gross from the playing group. Of course, this may not be the only motive for a multiple date as there can be other favorable consequences, as well, for particular films.

There are many formulas for sharing cooperative advertising. If the distributor pays it all, no formula is necessary—but when he does not, the exhibitor may contribute a flat sum or share on a percentage based on his retained gross as applied to distributor's participation. In other words, the distributor pays advertising to the same extent he shares in gross proceeds.

Cooperative advertising is only for major engagements or

multiple runs. It has no application to the vast bulk of subsequent runs where the exhibitor determines his own advertising (usually from the distributor's press book), and must bear the cost. The exhibitor in this bracket is not likely to be one of the world's great spenders.

Experience shows that, with few exceptions, after its initial campaign a feature either takes off and performs on good audience reactions, or fails. Advertising and publicity may buy an opening, but if public reaction is negative, the film will not hold up at the box office for any length of time. Audiences appear to "smell" instinctively that which they want or dislike. If the response is favorable, additional or even massive advertising may well pay its way in new customers and spreaders of word-of-mouth. If unfavorable, it is extremely doubtful if changing or altering the campaign will improve the situation—it may well be a case of spending good money after bad.

The real choice arises with the frequent film that falls somewhere in between. Business following opening day is not strong, but word-of-mouth or audience cards or critical reaction seems to hold favorable promise. Does the film warrant a renewed or different campaign? As few exhibitors can finance the necessary effort, this is essentially a distributor problem. Some courageous companies have fought the battle to at least moderate success—others have gone down with their banners flying.

Favorable critical reaction, particularly for the intellectually stimulating film, can be very important. While it is no definitive assurance of success, it opens the door to a strong campaign based on quotation of the so-called authorities. The less intellectual the film— the less important this reaction seems. Needless to say, the successful exceptions to unfavorable critical reaction are legion—The *Love Storys* and *Airports* do not need the praise, while a host of "critical success-financial failures" mock the principle.

As usual, there are no rules. The public has its own special way of deciding what it wants. Advertising and publicity may create a good start or even an atmosphere, but without that intangible support of happy patrons telling their friends how much they liked the film, the road will be long and probably downhill.

Part Three

PROBLEMS OF CONTENT

16

Control of Film Content

MANY PEOPLE USE the term "censorship" loosely in connection with motion picture and other controls, so it is essential that terms be defined before there can be a serious discussion of the problems of film content. There are all types and kinds of "censorships" and their varying impacts and consequences are entirely different. Some types of controls fall entirely outside the scope of restraint and other methods are purely voluntary.

A list of the various categories of controls regarding film would run something like this:

1. *Industry self-censorship.* This is regulation of content by the motion picture industry itself. It was long a powerful force particularly with regard to American production. A code seal was or was not granted to motion pictures distributed by the industry's regulatory body. The granting of the code seal was an approval within the terms of a spelled-out written document, to wit, the obsolete motion picture code. This control is now obsolete and, although seals are still issued automatically to "G," "PG" and "R" rated films, they are of little practical significance in the exhibition business today.

2. *Industry classification.* As this chapter is written this is the prime method of motion picture control being utilized in the United States. Films are rated by an industry-controlled body within various classifications to be discussed hereafter. Their ratings are published

and publicized for general public knowledge, the essential aim of the system being parental guidance. In one category ("X"), however, children are not admitted regardless of parental wishes.

3. *Prior restraint censorship.* Long dominant in the United States, prior censorship involves the presentation in advance of films to a public body—be it federal, municipal or state—which determines the suitability of showing of a film. In a series of cases the doctrine of prior restraint has been sharply limited by the courts on constitutional grounds, and this is not presently an active system except in the State of Maryland. An additional special category of prior censorship is customs regulation, which can deny entry to an obscene film into the United States. Although the film may have been seen elsewhere, it is a prior restraint to American audiences.

4. *Obscenity law.* Under the police power of the states and various localities, obscenity laws may be passed which regulate the showing of motion pictures. They are criminal statutes and require a trial of the obscenity issue. These laws generally take effect following a showing rather than prior to one and should not be considered in the same category with prior censorship.

5. *Public classification.* There are also classification statutes established by various municipalities and state bodies. Here the locality itself, as opposed to the industry, makes a determination of the suitability of films for age categories. The Dallas ordinance, for example, put film into two categories: either approved or not approved for children under a specified age.

6. *Informal police power.* A gray area somewhat akin to prior censorship and obscenity regulation has been the exercise of police powers over film content on an informal basis. A policeman with or without authority may "request" that a theatre not play a particular film or films. His request may have effect. Licensing regulations having no relationship to the subject of the film may be used as a club to prevent their exhibition. Similar other irrelevant local rules may be suddenly invoked for varying purposes. This is a dangerous type of regulation because its exercise is arbitrary, unpredictable and frequently not subject to legal remedy. Recent efforts have been made to establish zoning and tax regulations in some localities to penalize the showing of "undesirable" films.

7. *Private controls.* In an entirely separate category, there have long been private influences brought to bear upon films. For many years the Catholic Legion of Decency (now renamed the National

Catholic Film Office) was a potent factor in this area. It rated films in various categories and moved vigorously to discourage the "condemned" group. Methods of action included the posting of lists in churches and schools, the reading of names of films from the pulpit (the famous *Baby Doll* case in New York is an example) and went so far as boycotts of individual theatres playing condemned films.

Other religious groups, although less active, occasionally performed similar functions. Similarly, on occasion, the American Legion took steps against those whom they regarded as politically "undesirable characters" (like Charlie Chaplin) by vigorous methods, including boycotts. Continuing to the present time, the National Organization for Decent Literature (NODL) has promulgated various lawsuits and taken other steps to bar what it considers to be obscene pictures. It is interesting to note, in this connection, that the National Catholic Film Office has in recent years adopted a much more affirmative stance supporting the pictures it believes in rather than taking a negative attitude about those which it "condemns." Nonetheless, the film classification supplement published by the National Catholic Film Office is still in effect and it contains the "C" (condemned) category.

8. *Parental restraint.* In addition to all the public and private controls we have mentioned, there has, of course, been a certain degree of family or parental control—frequently ineffective, but sometimes exercised by a dominant mother or father or guardian as to film content for children. In the author's family, at least, any rule against a particular film was usually accompanied by every devious effort to avoid the ban and undoubtedly succeeded in encouraging rather than discouraging attendance at prohibited films.

Is there a need for controls at all? This question was asked and answered by the report of the Presidential Commission appointed by President Johnson. The answer of the majority report of this body was that, for adults, there should indeed be no controls. No causal relationship was found between antisocial activity and film content in the adult category and it was felt that the dangers of rigid controls far outweighed any potential usefulness. A vigorous minority dissented on this and other aspects of the Commission's report, and both the President and the Congress have rejected it. Nonetheless, its reasoning appears sound to this author and its conclusions are recommended.

The Commission also split on the subject of controls for children's viewing but, here, a majority felt there might be some justification for restraints in the areas of obscenity and violence. Measured against the difficulties of determination and enforcement, this conclusion too might be questioned. But modern thinking has established different criteria for obscenity determination for children and this may well obviate the problem. The question of children's controls remains, however, an open one.

The Rating System

The motion picture industry, in order to meet the apparent problem arising from an increasing number of adult films, established in 1968 a code and rating administration aimed purely at the matter of parental information and children's attendance. The ostensible purpose of the program as stated by the sponsoring organizations is: "To give parents reliable information to enable them to make informed judgments in guiding the attendance of their children." This laudable objective which on its face does not actually involve any control of film content is established by a system of four ratings of the following nature:

G—*General audiences:* all ages admitted. This is a film which contains no material objectionable or embarrasing to any audience in the view of the rating administrator.

PG—*Parental guidance suggested.* Some material may not be suitable for pre-teenagers. By this symbol, parents are alerted to the need for inquiry before permitting their children to attend films. A similar category had previously been marked "M" (mature) and "GP" but it was felt that these symbols were confusing. (Whether "PG" will seem less confusing is a doubtful proposition.)

R—*Restricted:* under 17 requires accompanying parent or adult guardian. The "R" rating indicates a film which is adult in theme and treatment. Parents may wish to view the picture with their children. Schoolteachers are now considered qualified as "guardians" for purposes of this rating.

X—*No one under 17 admitted.* This is a serious control of content for those under 17 years of age. Films in this category are considered exclusively adult in theme and treatment. In some areas of the country the age may vary from 17.

The rating program has been the subject of great and serious dispute. Its major motivation, of course, was the prevention of other forms of controls such as prior restraint and obscenity law. It was, in fact, an entirely proper industry effort to avoid a resurgence of censorship or obscenity legislation by indicating that the industry controlled its own product.

The system, however, has public advantages as well. By breaking film down into categories, it encourages the production of all types of films rather than those addressed purely to a family audience. In so doing, the system meets the needs of a time when theatrical film is no longer a mass medium but primarily a selective form of entertainment. Different films can quite properly be aimed at different audiences and the rating system reflects this approach. All can be made and shown.

Finally, of course, the rating system is of aid in guiding parents as to the selection for children's film fare, except in category "X" where children are prohibited in any event. In the judgment of many, including this author, there should be no category "X" as the matter of children's attendance should be ultimately one of parental discretion. I do not wish the state or the industry to tell me that, if I wish to take my 16-year-old daughter to a particular motion picture, I may not do so.

While in theory the system seems quite appropriate, in practice many problems have, of course, arisen. It is by nature a voluntary system, particularly at the enforcement level, and a great many exhibitors (some of whom, in fact, openly or covertly oppose it) have not rigidly enforced the program. In the "R" category, children have at times been admitted in the company of others than parents, guardians or schoolteachers—or even alone. The same practices have also been charged in some instances in the "X" category.

Some distributors oppose the program in principle and refuse to submit films. Others object on the grounds of filing cost and do not comply. The pressure to participate on these parties comes from exhibitors and public response.

One interesting aspect of the program has been the availability of a self-rated "X." In this category no producer or distributor need present a film for classification or pay the requisite fee (unless pledged to do so.) If he wishes to rate his film "X," he may simply do so by self-rating and labeling the film in that category.

"X" however has proved a serious problem for many distributors and producers. In large numbers of theatres, "X" pictures simply will not be played except perhaps in the most extraordinary of circumstances (*A Clockwork Orange*). Elsewhere newspapers and television will not take advertising for "X"-rated pictures. The "X"-rated film unless sharply cut cannot play on television under present conditions even late at night. Under the circumstances many producers desperately seek to avoid the "X" despite the success of a handful of X-rated films. The vast bulk of "X" sexploiters are not successful.

There have also been grave difficulties in determining the criteria by which a film is rated. The sponsoring organizations for the program have received protests, for example, in the "G" area when a film that may merely imply sexual relations between unmarried partners has been so rated. More vociferous protests are heard when a "PG" film contains "undesirable" items such as explicit sex or violence. (See *The Getaway*.)

One of the major disputes before the Rating Authority was the case of David Lean's, *Ryan's Daughter*. Originally rated "R" the distributor refused to cut a foot and demanded a "GP" rating on appeal. The dispute centered on a bare bosom and a candid love scene between the British soldier and his willing Irish lass. Under great pressure the Appeals Board (also industry-appointed) reversed the administrator and granted a "GP" rating (now changed to "PG"). There was a fair-sized amount of public criticism but no avalanche.

There are several approaches to determining the categories. One is to lay down rigid lines of what can or cannot be seen or heard within each. On a recent appeal the rating administrator took the position that any showing of a bare breast required an "R" rating, even though the scene in question was one of mother, father and son innocently swimming in a river. The use of Anglo-Saxon expletives has been barred from "G" films although apparently not from "PG." Explicit sexual conduct can range from "PG" to "X" depending on form and substance. There seems to be no way to make the system entirely objective and satisfactory to all segments. The laying down of rigid rules is an unlikely solution. Nonetheless, to the present writing the rating procedure would appear to have achieved its major objective of holding back other statutory restraints while permitting the distribution of films of many themes and types. Its legality has also been upheld.

Other critics have attacked the rating system as censorship. This is erroneous because the rating system, in fact, permits the production of any type of film. It merely requires the labeling of audiences. Does anyone seriously argue that any and all films are right for any and all audiences regardless of age or maturity? The "R" rating establishes a perfectly proper criteria which will allow a parent, guardian or teacher to determine whether a film should be seen by a youngster under 17. Certainly there are films including scenes of excessive violence, lesbianism, homosexuality and aberrational sexual activity which should be subject to such guidance. Of course, there will be prior censorship and local obscenity regulations if the motion picture industry does not protect young people to this modest extent. We have already indicated that, insofar as the "X" category bans children from attendance without qualification, we regard it as inappropriate as this should be a matter within the discretion of parents, guardians and teachers.

Prior Restraint

The fact that films are modified by producers to achieve various ratings does not create censorship. The question is one of audience selection and whether a film is suitable for all (with or without guidance) or whether it is a film with an essentially adult appeal. It would be reckless and foolhardy and an invitation to the "bluenoses" to abandon such modest restrictions.

Religious leadership has also criticized the rating system as overemphasizing the visual and neglecting theme in determining categories. No doubt this is occasionally true. It has also been said by some that the system encourages "Xs," but this is a dubious proposition. The system arose because mature films were being produced. Were there no rating system it is predictable that many such films would be distributed. On balance, despite the merit of some criticisms the experiment appears to your author to be a "noble one" which, despite difficulties particularly in administration, should be continued.

Censorship

Turning to prior censorship, in a series of cases in the mid-1960's the United States Supreme Court sharply limited this traditional power on constitutional grounds. The key cases were *Times Films* v. *Chicago* and *Freedman* v. *Maryland*.[1] In the former an attempt to declare all prior restraint unconstitutional lost by one vote in the Supreme Court. In the latter a Baltimore exhibitor showed the film *Revenge At Daybreak* (a French-made story of the Irish Revolution of a totally in-

[1] *Times Films* v. *Chicago* 365 U.S. 43 (1960); *Freedman* v. *Maryland* 380 *U.S.* 51 (1965).

offensive character) without the necessary license from the Maryland State Board of Censors. The action was willful and the Board was informed of the act. The case was brought as a test of the legality of the statute.

A criminal action was thereafter brought, the exhibitor was convicted of violating the law and this decision was affirmed in the Maryland Appeals Court. In the U. S. Supreme Court, however, the decision was reversed.

A limited status for prior restraint censorship in this country was established by this decision. In brief, the holding was: (1) that there is a heavy presumption against the constitutionality of any prior restraint of film; (2) that the burden of proof is on the state to prove a film repressible rather than on the exhibitor or distributor to prove the contrary; (3) that the state must move immediately in court after an administrative decision by a censor board against a film to have the issue determined; (4) that rigid time limitations must be established to prevent any abuse of the process by the state.

As the Maryland (and all other then existing censorship) statutes failed to meet the above criteria they were held unconstitutional. Mr. Freedman's conviction was accordingly reversed.

Since that time to this writing only Maryland has revised its censorship law to meet the Supreme Court's requirements. Its procedure is now in accordance with the *Freedman* case. Recently a Maryland ban on *I Am Curious—Yellow* was upheld in the U.S. Supreme Court. There is therefore no question at the present time that there can be prior censorship on the limited basis set forth.

A long list of other cases, all spelled-out elsewhere,[2] had previously limited the criteria for prior restraint censorship to the question of obscenity. "Sacrilege," "indecency" and "harmfulness" had all been found too vague. So had other words of restraint. Only on obscenity was a state or local board authorized to act. And here problems of definition have sharply limited the potential power of any public body. Very few films have been banned in Maryland under its new law and, unless the Supreme Court changes the rules and modifies the criteria to authorize actions in such matters as violence, the functions will remain limited. Short of sweeping constitutional change it would appear that pre-censorship as a control technique has a dubious future.

An area parallel to prior restraint censorship is customs censor-

[2] See Mayer: *Foreign Films on American Screens,* Arco Publishing Co. (1965), Chapter 9.

ship, under which the U. S. Customs has authority to ban films if they are found to be "obscene." There are other categories of undesirable aspects set up in the law but obscenity is nearly invariably the pretext.

Customs regulation is subject to similar rules that we have set forth for prior restraint censorship. The burden is on the Government, administrative rulings must be promptly taken before a court and rigid time limitations are impliedly in effect.

Early in the Nixon Administration there were signs that the Government intended to vigorously pursue this avenue of approach to ban "objectionable films" coming into the country. The courts, however, have not been sympathetic to this approach and in repeated cases the Government has been defeated where it attempted to bar the importation of allegedly obscene films. A key example is the case of *Without A Stitch* which went to a jury on the issue of obscenity and was admitted. Similarly in the case of *I Am Curious—Yellow*, a Federal Appeals Court reversed the Government verdict below and admitted the film.[3] Customs censorship may however, be revived by the Supreme Court decisions of June 1973 discussed hereafter.

In New York in 1972 a proposed Cuban Film Festival was closed down by Federal authority on unusual grounds. There the promoters were accused of "trading with the enemy" under a different law and not having applied for licenses to import Cuban films. This does not directly relate to customs censorship.

Obscenity Laws

It has long been the rule that under the "police power" there is authority to control film after it has been shown. This has frequently taken the form of prosecutions under local obscenity laws. (Violence is not considered "obscene" and is not an issue in this area.) These actions, usually instigated by pressure groups, through ambitious district attorneys, have frequently foundered on court rulings limiting the scope of obscenity as a definable term as well as other technical points of defense.

Until quite recently, the judicial test of obscenity was threefold and difficult to prove:

(a) Did the dominant theme of the material taken as a whole appeal to a prurient interest in sex?

(b) Was the material patently obscene because it affronted

---

[3] *U.S. v. A Motion Picture Film, I am Curious Yellow* 404 F2d 196 (1968).

contemporary community standards relating to the description
representation of sexual matters?

(c) Was the material utterly without redeeming social
value? [4]

Within these multi-faceted criteria, very few films, and practically no books were found impermissible under obscenity laws.

In June 1973, however, the United States Supreme Court radi-
cally changed the rules of the game with a series of 5-4 decisions
clearly intended to deal harshly with "objectionable" material both
cinematic and literary.[5] The definition of obscene content was
sharply revised to establish easier and more simplistic guidelines for
convictions. Now matter which the average person applying contemporary standards would find as a whole appeals to prurient interest, and which depicts or describes sexual conduct prohibited by law
in a patently offensive way, can be condemned unless the work as an
entirety has serious literary, artistic, political, or scientific value.
Purveyors of such material are subject to punishment.

These are not just empty words of distinction from past definitions. At one stroke, the "utterly without redeeming social value"
test has been obliterated. The standards involved now are specifically
those of the state or locality, and not the nation as prior decisions had
found. Judges and juries in each locality may find their own "hard
core" pornography and condemn it out of hand. There is no assurance that a film or book found non-obscene in one jurisdiction may
not well be condemned in another.

The implications of this, for film distribution at least, are clearly
mind boggling. Must there be one print of a film for San Francisco
and another for Atlanta? Can national advertising campaigns or
trailers for suspect features be used at all? Will exhibitors, distributors and producers be vulnerable to penal sanctions unpredictable in
nature and varying from state to state and locality to locality depending on whims of juries and district attorneys? The answers appear
affirmative and ominous.

---

[4] Memoirs v. Mass 383 U.S. 413 (1966); Ginsburg v. U.S. 383 U.S. 463 (1966).

[5] June 21, 1973, Supreme Court decisions include *Miller v. California* (advertisements for books); *Paris Adult Theatre I v. Slaton* (film case, Georgia); *Kaplan v.
California* (book case); *U.S. v. Orito* (transportation of obscene matter); *U.S. v.
12000' of film* (Paladini) (customs case involving film); *Heller v. New York* (print
seizure); *Roaden v. Kentucky* (print seizure); *Alexander v. Virginia* (same). For a
new and intelligent approach to problems involved, see dissent of Mr. Justice Brennan
in *Miller v. California* and *Paris Adult Theatre I v. Slaton*.

The court repeats the unfortunate doctrine that obscenity is unprotectable as free speech. While this has, in fact, long been the rule, rarely before has obscenity been so broadly defined or arbitrarily condemned. The states are specifically authorized to presume that obscenity is socially harmful if they so choose. The court majority obviously advises them so to choose. The purported rationale and excuse that the forbidden covers only "hard core" pornography will not wash.[6] It can confidently be predicted that there will be included under local standards all kinds of material never previously considered obscene. And it can also be safely assumed that a literal flood of new convictions will never be reviewed by the Supreme Court which does not sit merely to review this type of litigation. There is no "high court of obscenity."

Other variations from past practice will also prove harmful to film exhibitors and distributors. No longer will the burden be on the state to prove with expert testimony that a film lacks redeeming social value. Expert testimony, while permissable, is deprecated by the new holdings which finds that films or books are quite sufficient evidence in themselves. The burden thereby passes to the defendant to prove affirmatively literary or artistic value of his work through experts or otherwise. No conviction will be likely to be reversed hereafter for lack of expert testimonial support for the prosecution.

Furthermore, on the subject of print seizure while an engagement is in process, the court opens the floodgates by permitting "neutral" magistrates to issue enforcible warrants without a prior judicial adversary hearing, with both sides present. This had been required previously in many local courts before a print could be taken. Now seizure for evidentiary purposes is permitted subject only to a prompt judicial hearing thereafter. The print is returnable only if copies are not available to the exhibitor. This could play havoc with long-planned engagements of important films.

The entire concept of adult freedom to see or read, so convincingly presented by the earlier report of the Presidential Commission, is rejected. So is the doctrine of complete privacy of reading or viewing for consenting adults, which is now strictly limited to the home and not elsewhere.

Transportation by public or private carrier of objectionable obscene matter is condemned even if the material is purely for private

[6] Justice Burger's examples of "hard core" include such matter as "lewd" exhibition of genitals. Who is to say what is lewd or wholesome?

use at home. Similarly, the importation of such materials for personal purposes is also restricted.

Despite anguished dissents from Justices Douglas and Brennan, the new Nixon Court has imposed serious limitations on screen and literature. The states and localities have been given what amounts to a free hand to determine that which is or is not obscene and objectionable. That they will use it to sharply reduce the hard-won freedom of the screen is a foregone conclusion. Already there have been steps taken against such important films as *Carnal Knowledge* and *Last Tango in Paris*. At what point public resistance will develop is impossible presently to predict.

Prior to June 21, 1973, an understandable trend toward regulation of content for children had been developing. A distinction had been drawn between appropriate fare for minors and broad freedom for adults. Now presumably, this all goes by the board and we will all (adults and children alike) be limited by the new legal dispensation in what we can see and read.

A qualification is in order, however. There is a very interesting recent trend by juries against holding pictures obscene. For many years it was the assumption of attorneys active in this field that the last thing one wanted to do in an obscenity case, on behalf of a defendant, was to get before a jury. "Twelve good men and true" were considered most likely to regard themselves as paragons of civic virtue and to feel it incumbent upon themselves to render a verdict in favor of the benevolent state trying to protect its citizens from crass, materialistic evil. A good many cases have shaken this old assumption.

For example, in the parallel field of customs censorship, where the issue was purely one of obscenity, the Danish film *Without a Stitch* was found non-obscene by a jury despite some of the boldest and most explicit sexual activity ever witnessed on the screen to that time. A jury in Binghampton, New York, of all places, found the amazing *Deep Throat* nonobscene. Other films passing judicial tests on this issue include *The Stewardesses, Censorship in Denmark* and *The Vixens*.

While governmental attitudes are obviously going to be far more restrictive under the new rules, the public attitude may prove less demanding. This will certainly be true in such major cities as New York and San Francisco. What will happen in the "hinterlands" remains a question-mark. It may well be that after the initial shock of a number of prosecutions which will be followed by jury acquittals or judicial reversals the allure of obscenity prosecution will be greatly reduced. As and when this happens, there will be new opportunities for the making of more mature films. Pending that date, bonafide fears must be expressed of a regression in film content by virtue of the "chilling effects" of the decisions of June 21, 1973.

Public Classification Statutes

Another area of possible control lies in the field of public classification statutes as opposed to industry classification. This has, in effect, been held legal insofar as the Supreme Court has ruled that a properly drawn classification statute may stand. It did this while declaring unconstitutional as too vague the old Dallas classification law.[5]

Public classification would involve the setting of categories for attendance by children at films. Criteria could be established based on age and a classification body could be appointed to perform the function. Classification is in effect in several municipalities and is likely to come to many more if the industry system fails. It presents a grave danger for producers because the risk must be run that the classifiers will classify differently in different localities. This could seriously affect advertising and promotion of pictures. It could also mean numerous fees, licenses and extra screenings.

The dangers of having a public board do what should be done by a private organization are manifold. Litigation will be encouraged, the dangers of unfair interpretations are ever present and political appointments would likely lack the necessary qualities for child guidance. There are better places to waste the taxpayers' money. Nonetheless, if the industry system fails we might have good reason to anticipate a boom in this area.

A virulent aspect of the controls problem is in the quasi-legal area. In this category threats are made to theatre owners or distributors without relationship to any true regulatory approach. A theatre's electric wiring, long approved by city inspectors, may suddenly be deemed faulty. Zoning applications by theatres that play "X" pictures may find a difficult response. Police may inspect premises for loitering or prostitution.

By these and many other devious procedures efforts can be made to halt the showing of films considered undesirable. This is a

[5] *Interstate Circuit* v. *City of Dallas* 390 U.S. 676 (1968).

dangerous and unlawful approach, but it does exist and undoubtedly will continue. It takes a courageous exhibitor to stand up against such local harassment.

Similar difficulties may occur with purely private bodies. We have indicated that, in the past, the Legion of Decency went a long way in attacking exhibitors and distributors of pictures they disapproved of. The religious groups have now on the whole turned around and adopted a more affirmative attitude toward film.

This is not to say that private organizations should not act where they feel their interests are adversely affected by film. They should have the same right of free speech as the film-creator. When, however, the matter comes to boycotts or extralegal procedures aimed at putting people out of business, the line between valid and invalid conduct must be somewhere drawn.

Some new ideas have also been recently added to the control concepts. There are those who would tax an exhibitor at a different rate for playing "X" and "R" pictures (as opposed to "G" and "PG"). This seems entirely discriminatory and should be ruled invalid by the courts. Similarly, a "nuisance theory" has been expressed, particularly with regard to drive-in theatres where the scene on the screen can be viewed from an adjoining highway. Some local legislators seem to believe that the playing of certain films at these drive-ins comprises a "public nuisance" against which localities can legislate. This seems a most dubious proposition in view of the First Amendment rights that are affected. It is an attempt, of course, to avoid the limits placed on censorship and obscenity regulations by a progressive judiciary. High fences for drive ins or new-type screens may prove an answer.

The correct approach to the problem of mature films is one of parental control guided by relevant sources of information. There are magazines which rate pictures. There are critics whose views should be analyzed. The nature of advertising is a pertinent clue. The motion picture industry's classification system can prove an effective guide. If all these elements are utilized, and if the classification system is enforced at the theatre level, there would seem to be sufficient "control" of film content to satisfy most reasonable parents. As there will, however, always be unreasonable parents, publicity-seeking district attorneys, legislators, judges and other moral souls always anxious to guide the viewing habits of anyone other than themselves, I expect we shall continue to have censorship and related problems in film from here to eternity.

17

Trouble about Titles

THE SELECTION OF TITLES has been, and remains, a most significant problem in the entertainment industry. In the first place, there is substantial accord that the selection of a "good" title may make a success of a particular project while a "bad" title may spell disaster—how one distinguishes between good and bad titles for these purposes is a problem on which there is little illumination, and which is fortunately beyond the scope of this effort. In any event, a title-selection process is frequently considered vital to box office or other success.

Secondly, there is, after all, only a limited reservoir of titles available. The ingenious entrepreneur may come up with a catchy new one but he is a rare bird and, for the bulk of common folk, the general usage is a title previously utilized or something closely akin to it. Some titles have, in fact, become so familiar that future repetition may be freely predicted. In a case involving the name *High Treason*, your author came up with a host of prior usages on film and otherwise. Such titles as *Backlash, Gun Law, Love Affair, Drifter, Big City* with minor variations are habitual. Other examples are legend. There are simply not enough desirable titles to go around and re-usage appears inevitable.

The copyright laws have been found not to protect titles. Although on their face these are literary creations, presumably subject to the same protection as other developed concepts, the courts have found them *di minimis*, or too small or common to favor, and have looked at them as a special species outside the scope of copyright law. While this ignores the by-no-means nominal importance of titles, it may be a practical, if not a logical, answer because there are simply too many properties looking for these brief labels and monopolies cannot be stamped down upon all of them.

The expiration of copyright on a property also discourages title protection. It is not, however, a sole determinant. In a controversy over *Alice in Wonderland*, produced by both Walt Disney and a competitive organization at the same time, the Disney organization was not afforded protection despite huge expenditure on their screen version of the Carroll classic.

For the benefit of its members and other participants who choose to utilize its services, the Motion Picture Association runs a title registration plan performing important tasks within its area. The service grants priority of use favoring early registrants. In case of disputes, an arbitration system is established which has worked smoothly and effectively to handle problems between members and other participants. Difficulties, however, still arise as to titles involving non-members, as well as related issues concerning the use of such labels in media other than film.

A further distinction eliminates many titles from protection in any event. Descriptive, as opposed to arbitrarily selected, titles cannot belong to any user. To illustrate—"The Life of Napoleon" is clearly descriptive as opposed to arbitrary or fanciful, and is free for anyone to use. No monopoly could be countenanced where the title merely reflects a description of the subject matter. This distinction, however, is not always so easy to draw. What one man considers descriptive another may find arbitrary. In the DeSade case hereinafter discussed, it is questionable whether that title is descriptive or arbitrary. Has the word "DeSade" become such common English usage that its meaning is clear and available for all? Of, is the life of DeSade protectible under that label? The categorization of titles as descriptive or arbitrary may well be the determining factor in a dispute or litigation.

Within the area of non-descriptive titles, protectibility has only been permitted in a limited category of cases under the doctrine of unfair competition. These are where the plaintiff's title is considered to be so much in the public mind as to establish a "secondary meaning" for the label. This means, in theory at least, that the title is identifiable in the minds of a sufficiently large or important number of persons as the work of the author or producer and that, therefore, he should be granted a monopolistic status to protect the same. In other words, those who by their efforts have earned the right to a title should be entitled to exclude the rest of the world from its use.

The crux of the matter, then, is the criteria by which "secondary meaning" is or is not established.

The first issue would involve the precise "public" with whom the title must be identified. If this were to mean the general public at large, it is apparent that very few titles could earn such protection. For the vast bulk of the public sees few films, reads few books and attends ever fewer theatres. They are ill-informed, not only as to titles, authors and subjects, but frequently as to public officials representing them and other matters of vital interest. Obviously, we can only be talking about a *substantial* number of the *interested* public. In the case of a foreign film, for example, it would seem sufficient if a fair number of exhibitors, distributors and customers of such films are aware of the title rather than a large number of the general populace. Similar reasoning must be applied in other cases. The determination must be made within a limited audience or there can only be secondary meaning in the rarest of cases.

How is secondary meaning achieved? Essentially, this involves the degree of public appeal of the work (i.e., its popularity) as exemplified by its record. In addition, the energy, enthusiasm and funds that have been expended to popularize, advertise and promote are distinctly relevant. So title cases frequently come down to an analysis of popularity achieved, and that which the plaintiff seeking protection has done to promote and exploit his property. If he has done much and succeeded, he may be found to have earned protection—if he has performed little or failed, the contrary would usually be true.

This is not invariably so, however. In the surprising case of the title "Slightly Scandalous," an unsuccessful Broadway production with that label had lasted but seven performances with an average attendance of 100 persons per showing. Shortly after the play's collapse, Universal produced a film bearing that title without any other similarity to the play. A California court granted judgment to the unsuccessful play's producer for damages in the sum of $17,500 for the misuse of his title, despite the evident lack of success and the minimal efforts extended in popularizing the title.[1] This, however, is an extraordinary

[1] *Jackson* v. *Universal Pictures* 37 Cal. 2d 116 (1950).

case from a great state for plaintiff's verdicts (i.e. California) and is not likely to be accepted as a binding precedent elsewhere. There are, indeed, other cases quite to the contrary.

Another criterion sometimes overriding the customary rules, is the existence of conduct akin to fraud. Where the defendant's behavior is permeated with this evil characteristic, the court is not likely to be too demanding in determining degrees of popularity or secondary meaning. Injunctions are created for just such purposes. In a case, for example, where defendant, simultaneously with the release of United Artist's *Exodus,* retitled an aging Italian film with that precise name and threatened to reopen it in theatres, relief was so granted.[2] Similarily in California when a six-year-old German film was retitled *Grimm's Fairy Tales* and advertised in a Hollywood trade paper—"A wonderful world of the Grimms brothers is depicted in Grimms Brothers *Grimms Fairytales,* wide screen and color, soon to be released by Monte Lee Enterprises"—at the precise moment when MGM envisaged results for its new *Wonderful World of the Brothers Grimm,* the court enjoined defendant's use of the phraseology.[3] Fraud in the form of a willful intention to capitalize on someone else's title can simplify the legal problem and justify injunctions or damages in cases where they would otherwise be denied.

What type of success and what type of expenditure to create is necessary in a case of disputed titles? There are no unequivocal maxims. As usual in the law, "it depends on the facts and circumstances."

In the case of the film *De Sade* an effort to enjoin distribution of a competitive effort, titled *Juliette De Sade,* failed despite the expenditure by plaintiff, American International Pictures of approximately $250,000 to promote their biographical film. *De Sade* was a major production with negative costs close to $2-million, while *Juliette De Sade* was a relatively insignificant low-budget production from Italy. A New York court, on a motion for a temporary injunction, found the title "De Sade" generally descriptive and in any event lacking in secondary meaning. Other disputed issues such as priority of usage (neither film had opened at the time of the application), deception to the public and general confusion were left for a trial court to determine.[4]

[2] *United Artists* v. *Exodus* 207 NYS 465 (1960).
[3] *MGM* v. *Lee* 212 Cal. App. 2d 23 (1963).
[4] *American International Pictures* v. *Brandt,* New York Law Journal 10/8/1969.

Helen Gurley Brown's well-known work, *Sex and the Single Girl,* was held entitled to a restraint of motion picture rights in another effort titled *Sex and the Single Man.* While the latter publication was not restrained for general publication, the licensing of a film with that name appeared to the court too close in nature to the amply promoted, protectible title of Mrs. Brown's work, which was then in actual preparation for film production.[5] Vast expenditures for the promotion and advertising of the prospective film *Sex and the Single Girl* were shown.

An unsuccessful play by Ernest Hemingway, called the "Fifth Column," had a two-month run in New York. Defendants renamed their film *Spies in the Air* as *Fifth Column Squad.* The court found secondary meaning in the key phrase identifying Hemingway's play with the words "fifth column." [6] Since then the expression has become a common usage in the English language, referring to a group of internal traitors at the time of foreign war or strife. One would feel that it was now a descriptive use and would no longer be enjoinable.

Warner Brothers' *Golddiggers* was also found to have sufficient secondary meaning to interfere with a competitor's *Golddiggers of Paris.* The court granted a peculiar injunction requiring the offending *Golddiggers* to expressly state in their advertising that they were not the *Golddiggers* produced by Warner Brothers, based on a play by Avery Hopgood.[7]

A court has found that book titles were less entitled to protection than film titles because in the former case the public presumably pays greater attention to authors than in the case of film. Book titles are therefore less important to protect. The accuracy of this statement may be doubted in view of the *auteur* theory which credits many film directors with the creation of their works similar to the responsibility given authors for books. In fact, it might be argued that the public now looks more at directors of films as creators than it does at book authors, in view of the many pseudonyms and ghost writers who now practice their trade.

Priority of use, while sometimes important, is not a critical factor in the field of titles. An earlier user may or may not have achieved the required public prominence for his book or film or TV program. If he has failed to achieve fame or reasonable significance, the title is

[5] *Brown* v. *Lyle Stuart, Inc.* 141 U.S. P. Q 936 (1964).

[6] *Hemingway* v. *Film Alliance* 174 Misc. 725 (1940).

[7] *Warner Bros. Pictures, Inc.* v. *Majestic Pictures Corp.* 70 F2d 310 (1934).

unprotectible. To the contrary, however, a later user may have developed a broad interest and market for his work sufficient to be granted preferred status. It is *his* title and not the identical title of an earlier user that deserves the rewards of protection against a newcomer.

"Palming off" is a phrase frequently used, in unfair competition cases, given to individual effort by a defendant to present his product or services as that of another. The defendant is seeking by subterfuge to give the public the impression that his product is that of someone else. The essence of this conduct is imitation, false representation and essentially fraud. While important in the past, "palming off" has not recently been considered a vital aspect of title protection. The protection theory has been that, if there be true secondary meaning, it does not require offensive conduct on the part of the defendant to justify a remedy. If I have earned title protection for my book, I should not be required to prove that the defendant endeavored to sell his book as if it were mine. The courts have gone so far as to hold, in the past, that products need not be in competition where the plaintiff's rights are jeopardized. In one instance, a famous jewelry retailer, enjoined the use of its name and symbol by a film distributing company on the grounds that it owned the name. There seemed not the faintest possibility that anyone viewing a Tiffany film might think he was acquiring the plaintiff's jewelry, but the name protection stuck just the same. Other cases also support this doctrine.

Now, however, the entire development of title protection has been challenged by the *Sears-Compco* doctrine promulgated by the Supreme Court.[8] In an otherwise unrelated patent decision, the august tribunal took the position that any unpatented articles could not be protected by other doctrines in state or local courts. By *dicta,* the court went further and indicated that the same reasoning applies to uncopyrighted material. If the matter is not copyrighted (and titles are not copyrighted), it is presumably by this decision open to public use and not otherwise protected. If this be literally so, no title can be protected and open competition and usage would be mandated.

It seems hardly likely that the rule will go this far. Courts have indeed already found ways to avoid such harsh logic. One escape would be to hold that titles are not copyrightable and, therefore, not subject to copyright law in any event. Or it could be said that the

[8] *Sears, Roebuck & Co.* v. *Stiffel Co.* (Supra); *Compco Co.* v. *Day-Brite Lighting* (Supra).

Supreme Court's opinion is not applicable to situations where fraud exists or may be inferred. A footnote in the *Sears* litigation indicated that "mislabeling" or "palming off" might be exceptions to the general rule. Furthermore, titles could be regarded merely as a species of trade names inapplicable to the court's mischievous rule.

For all these reasons, it is felt that the *Sears-Compco* decision will not be applied so as to wipe out protection of titles. There may, however, be limitations to the situations of applicability and we may have a return to the ancient rules limiting protection to those situations where one person's title has been "palmed off" as that of another.

Title protection is not necessarily limited to unfair competition doctrines, although this has been the favorite judicial approach. It is still possible that, by re-interpretation, the law might permit the copyrighting of titles, although this seems unlikely. Normally, contracts between parties may regulate usage such as in the case of the Motion Picture Association system. As previously stated, fraud may justify relief even in the absence of "secondary meaning." The fertile legal mind will strive to find a way to protect a well-chosen and successful title.

So long as titles play such an important role, even if only in the minds of producers and artists, there must be grounds for protective action. Obviously the protection must be limited, as the English language cannot be the subject of unrestricted monopoly. The finding of the formula to protect that which is justifiably protectible is, as ever, the function and the role of law.

18

Film and Defamation

DEFAMATION IS THE PUBLICATION of words or images that hold one up to scorn, obloquy and contempt. Can motion pictures defame? The answer to that is a brief, unequivocal yes. Any method of presentation to the public or, in fact, to even one individual that can destroy or diminish someone else's reputation is defamatory. The only requirement is "publication."

Libel

Publication in the law of libel is a word of art. It does not mean merely publication in the form of a book or magazine, although, of course, it includes such acts. In the context, all that is required is the communication of defamatory matter to a third party or parties (the expression of such matter merely to the person defamed alone is, of course, insufficient to comprise the offense of libel or slander, because no one's reputation can be diminished by words addressed solely to him).

The law, then, makes no strict rule about the technique of publication. Illustrations of libel in the performing arts are frequent; instances of defamation in the course of radio programs have often occurred and, while hard to find, there is no doubt that characterization in the form of a play or ballet or recording can be equally defamatory. Standard definitions of the techniques of publication have for years included "acts, gestures and effigies" as well as other methods of dissemination.

In a striking illustration some years ago, a complaint by an alleged but unproven murderer was upheld against Madame Tussaud's Wax Works. The claim was that the plaintiff had been portrayed in wax as a criminal killer at the scene of his offense at the famous emporium owned by the lady defendant in London.[1]

Other instances of defamation in the sphere of "dramatic action" frequently occur. The most significant group are in the area of wrongful accusations of shoplifting. A case in this regard might involve a person, leaving a retail store with alleged unpaid acquisitions, being abused or upbraided by the local manager. Some courts have gone so far as to find defamatory such clearly innocuous expressions as "did you pay for that scarf?" in the dramatic context of a pursuit, search and/or seizure of such a victim. It is the performance rather than the oral charge that really causes harm to the reputation. Similarly, the acts of "watching, shadowing and eavesdropping" as forms of detection have been found defamatory.

In an unusual Nova Scotia situation the wife of an absent soldier returned to her rural home from a visit to a city with a local farmhand. She was greeted by a "charivari," which appears to be some kind of a local wedding celebration. She brought suit for libel against several participants and recovered a judgment.[2]

It therefore seems eminently clear that the performing arts, including motion pictures, may be the conduit of transmitting defamatory words, thoughts or images of a harmful and damaging character to the members of its audience.

Slander

An initial question arises, however, as to the character of such defamation. Logic to the contrary notwithstanding, there has been and remains a vast distinction between the legal concepts of libel and slander, even though each deals with the same general offense of harm to reputation. These differences are historically based and, in the view of many scholars, obsolete and anachronistic in character. Nonetheless, they survive and remain of vast significance. In brief, slander

[1] *Monson v. Tussaud* 10 Times L.R. 227 (1894).
[2] *Varner v. Morton* 53 Nova Scotia 180 (1922).

refers to the oral transmission of defamatory words and very few words at that. There are only four basic categories of words considered slanderous *per se,* that is, for which the defendant can be assessed presumed damages without proof of actual harm. These include words charging:

(1) Criminal conduct.
(2) Incompetency within a trade or profession.
(3) That a victim possesses a so-called loathsome disease.
(4) Lack of chastity (as to a female only).

Actually, from this enumeration it is clear that today there really are only two significant categories of slander because elements (3) and (4) have become obsolescent if not obsolete. It is fair to say that the concept of a "loathsome disease" no longer has the significance it might have had in Victorian society. "Loathsome diseases" are now more curable than they previously were and, while hardly a badge of honor, are presumably considerably less loathsome. There is serious doubt as to whether the charge of a person having such an affliction any longer will give rise to presumed damages in slander.

The fourth category named has an equally dubious future. A charge as to a woman's lack of chastity sounds prehistoric and ludicrous in modern context and one can even foresee the day when the opposite charge, i.e., that the woman is virtuous, might be considered slanderous *per se.* One need only read newspaper stories about the attitude of college girls toward their virginal classmates to get the present drift of things. Accordingly, if this thesis be correct, only two categories of slander (charges of crime and charges of incompetency in work or profession) seem presently significant.

Libel *per se* runs a far broader range. Here we are talking about writings, pictures, cartoons and the like that hold a person up to "scorn, ridicule and contempt." Instead of two categories, the areas of responsibility for libel are of a broad and divergent variety.

Distinction Between Libel and Slander

Why this broad distinction between responsibility in slander and in libel? Historically it is based on the concept that the spoken words were fleeting—here today and gone tomorrow—most likely the product of temporary passions and heated moments and not of lasting harm to anyone's reputation. Libel, on the other hand, was printed or put in some more permanent form—presumably well thought out—published in a lasting medium with probable intent to harm. As Benjamin Cardozo put it so well:

> The schism in the law of defamation between the older wrong of slander and the newer one of libel is not the product of mere accident. . . . It has its genesis in evils which the years have not erased. Many things that are defamatory may be said with impunity through the medium of speech. Not so, however, where speech is caught upon the wing and transmuted into print. What gives the sting to the writing is its permanence of form. The spoken word dissolves, but the written one abides and perpetuates the scandal.[3]

In the light of this vast distinction, the question is posed whether "publication" by the performing arts or film may be libel or slander. While the modern and well-considered trend has treated this type of publication as libel, there are contrary decisions in certain areas as well as state statutes and the issue is far from ultimate clarification.

This is particularly true in the area of radio (and in some jurisdiction, television). Let us assume a radio broadcast of a performance involving defamatory words. Is it libel or slander? The first question posed is whether there was a script for the broadcast.

In *Hartman* v. *Winchell*,[4] the New York Court of Appeals faced this specific issue: "Does the utterance of defamatory remarks read from a script into a radio microphone and thereafter broadcast constitute publication of libel or slander?"

If it were slander, the words used were in this instance not of a nature as to be considered *per se* defamatory. If libel were involved, however, they were quite sufficient for that purpose.

The court went back to ancient precedents in its treatment of a modern medium to determine that the "reading" was libelous. In John Lamb's case,[5] it had been held "that if a man read libel on another to himself and then read it aloud, that made him a libeller." Similar was an aging New York case [6] where the defendant read to his friends a defamatory letter and this was held libel and not slander.

[3] *Ostrowe* v. *Lee* 256 N.Y. 39 (1931).
[4] *Hartman* v. *Winchell* 296 N.Y. 296 (1947).
[5] *John Lamb's* case 9 CO. Rep. 60 (1610).
[6] *Snyder* v. *Andrews* 6 Barb 43 (1849).

Accordingly, the court majority found that reading from a script over radio constituted libel and not slander.

Concurring, the prescient Judge Stanley Fuld agreed, but went further to formulate future New York law. He found the words libelous, not because they were read from the script unknown to the listening public, but on the public policy grounds that radio like the written word reaches thousands, if not millions, and has a true "capacity to harm" that oral statements to a handful of onlookers lacked entirely. Judge Fuld's concurrence has now become New York law. It no longer matters in this state whether the words are read from the script or come direct from the tongue to the public via radio or television. In New York any such defamatory matter is now libel and not slander.

This was clarified in *Shor* v. *Billingsley,*[7] where in spontaneous oral conversation over the air (no script involved) Billingsley stated with reference to a picture of Shor on the TV screen, "I wish I had as much money as he owes." Citing numerous authorities, Justice Hecht found the opinion of Judge Fuld in the Winchell case compelling and specifically held the law of libel applicable. A complaint based on the above quotation was upheld against a motion to dismiss despite the ingenious argument that such a statement was not defamatory, as it merely indicated that Shor owed people money and that was a high compliment in our capitalist, debt-ridden society.

Again in television, in the case of *Landau* v. *CBS*[8] the issue involved the inadvertent portrayal of the plaintiff in the TV series entitled *Crime Photographer*. In the course of the segment, the "Easy Way," a young newspaperman-photographer, in the course of exposing a crime syndicate, comes upon a center of criminal mischief behind a certain door marked "Credit Consultants Inc." Twice this door was flashed on the screen. The plaintiff, Harry Landau, doing business in New York as Credit Consultants, took umbrage and brought suit for libel, claiming identification with the crooked malefactors. Following the Hartman case, Judge Martin Frank found the issue one of libel and not slander, but in view of the totally fictional nature of the play, the complete failure of identification with the plaintiff, and the mere accidental similarity of office titles the verdict was for the defendants.

It must be stated in this connection, however, that there are

[7] *Shor* v. *Billingsley* 158 N.Y.S. 2d 476 (1957).
[8] *Landau* v. *CBS* 128 N.Y.S. 2d 254 (1954).

numerous state statutes and holdings contrary to the New York rule indicating that the spoken word on radio or television is in the nature of slander and not libel. One court has even created a new offense called "Defamacast." [9] In any event, a powerful radio-TV lobby has won substantial victories in its efforts to protect broadcasters who may authorize or permit harmful matter over the air. Of course, in fairness, a case can be made for this relief where the broadcaster has no control or supervision over content.

Identification

Identification is, of course, a key issue in cases arising out of the performing arts as well as elsewhere. Here the question is one whether a party defamed can reasonably be identified by the public or part of it as the plaintiff. This can easily be a problem in the performing arts. Long ago in England, in the matter of Artemus Jones,[10] an imaginary character was portrayed in defandant's newspaper as gallivanting on the Continent with a lady not his wife. The fictional name Artemus Jones was given to him. There appeared, however, a real British solicitor born to the name who claimed that his reputation was injured by this piece. The court established what has become a troublesome rule in libel—"It is not who you aim at, it's who you hit"—and held in favor of plaintiff Jones. The decision has been causing difficulty ever since.

In the *Crime Photographer* case previously discussed, Judge Frank had an interesting and relevant observation on the hopelessness of trying to avoid common use of names applicable to all entertainment media:

> To avoid the charge of libel would compel the need to scan thousands of telephone directories and business indices, to comb voting lists and city rosters, to rake the census rolls and a myriad listings of names, individual, trade and corporate. With our population stemming from every national origin, bearing names of infinite variety, even to anagrammatize a name like Jones or to spell it backwards would be little protection, for somewhere in this wondrous land there must someone named Senoj.

[9] *American Broadcasting Company* v. *Simpson* 126 S.E. 2d 873 (1962).
[10] *Hulton* v. *Jones* 26 Times L.R. 128 (1910).

The rule remains, however, that name changes to the contrary notwithstanding, if the identification fits the plaintiff, there can be legal responsibility. Other cases in libel by fictional publication have indicated that changes of spelling, minor variations in personality and other such camouflage will be ineffective if the plaintiff's shoe really fits.

In motion pictures, in the classic case of Rasputin—"the Mad Monk," [11]—a princess was by implication either raped or seduced by the bearded advisor to the last of the Czars. Although her name in the film was Princess Natasha, a British jury found no difficulty in identifying her as Her Royal Highness Irina Alexandrova Yousoupoff and granted her £25,000 (pre-World War II valuation) for her diminished reputation. An upper court affirmed the ruling, holding, incidentally for the first time, that under English Law defamation by motion picture is libel, as opposed to slander, and that in fact this charge was libelous *per se*.

The doctrine that a motion picture may be libelous was also upheld at the start of the new century in the State of New York in *Merle* v. *Sociological Research*.[12] Here, in a premature sexploiter of an earlier day entitled *The Inside of the White Slave Traffic,* plaintiff's building was indicated as a center of certain iniquitous practices and headquarters for a depraved group of pimps, prostitutes and procurers. Mr. Merle's complaint that the portrayal of his building with his name on it in the middle of such a scene held him up to ridicule and contempt, was upheld against the traditional motion to dismiss the complaint for failure to state an offense.

In *Brown* v. *Paramount Publix*,[13] the libel doctrine was again applied as against a motion picture. In this instance, the case involved an attack on Theodore Dreiser's important novel, *An American Tragedy*, filmed initially by Paramount. The reader may remember this touching story of a young man "on the make," his complaisant sweetheart and the questionable accidental death of the pregnant girl on the lake. Here the plaintiff was the mother of one Grace Brown, who was the victim of similar circumstances at Big Moose Lake in upstate New York. Mrs. Brown pleaded that the film indicated that she was "illiterate, unkempt, slovenly, neglectful and low grade" and that in essence she had neglected her daughter, and permitted her

[11] *Yousoupoff* v. *MGM* 50 Times L.R. 581 (1934).
[12] *Merle* v. *Sociological Research* 166 A.D. 376 (1915).
[13] *Brown* v. *Paramount Publix* 240 AD 520 (1934).

daughter to carry on a clandestine affair with the young man in question. As a consequence, she claimed the film held her up to contempt and ridicule.

In upholding her claim, New York's Appellate Division found that such a production may be libelous and that the alleged portrayal of Mrs. Brown could expose her to public contempt. New York has not since changed its rule.

There was little problem of identification in the case of MGM's *They Were Expendable.* Here a movie version was made of Theodore White's famous work on the exploits of a naval torpedo squadron operating out of the Philippines in the disastrous days of early 1942. There could be no question that this was the story of true events that actually occurred, although the film was fictionalized for public consumption.

The defendants renamed a certain Commander Kelly as Ryan and made the traditional, if ineffectual, disclaimer, "All persons and events shown in this picture are fictional and any similarity to persons living or dead is purely coincidental." These arguments got short shrift from Judge Wyzanski. He found "Rusty Ryan" as a naval officer clearly a personification of the real Robert Kelly. The actual portrayal in the film was, in fact, rather favorable. It nonetheless indicated a sufficiently unprofessional and non-naval attitude on the part of the Commander so as to justify a $3,000 verdict on his behalf.[14]

Alterations of locale, names and other details from a novel proved sufficient to avoid liability in a suite for libel against the film *Primrose Path.* The court found the plaintiffs insufficiently identiable to support their charge.

More recently, in *American Broadcasting Company* v. *Simpson,*[15] an episode of the series *The Untouchables,* entitled "The Big Train," dealt with the transfer from Federal Prison in Atlanta of one Alphonse Capone to Alcatraz in San Francisco Bay. Certain aspects of the production were clearly historically accurate. These included:

1. The fact that Capone was transferred as between the two places.
2. The correct dates of transfer were used.
3. The real persons appeared in the teleplay, being said

[14] *Kelly* v. *Loew's* 76 F. Supp. 473 (1948).
[15] *American Broadcasting Co.* v. *Simpson* (Supra).

"Scarface Al" and the then Attorney General of the United States, Homer Cummings.

4. The correct number was used on Capone's uniform.

5. There were actual film clips from Atlanta Penitentiary and Alcatraz Prison inserted in the play.

6. The transfer from San Francisco to Alcatraz Island was properly portrayed as by a train on a barge.

Contrarywise, certain fictional things were also inserted into the script. These include:

1. The charge that an officer of the U.S. Bureau of Prisons accepted a $1,000 bribe from Al Capone for the purpose of aiding in his escape.

2. A second officer of the U.S. Bureau of Prisons thereafter threatened to expose the bribe unless he was "cut in."

3. The second officer was thereafter shot to death in a Capone-sponsored "trap" outside of prison.

4. One of the officers passed certain information to Capone as to the departure of the train for Alcatraz for the purpose of aiding his escape.

5. Capone actually is temporarily freed while on the barge to Alcatraz by the efforts of these officers.

Plaintiff in this case, brought before the Supreme Court of Georgia, was a retired officer of the U. S. Bureau of Prisons who had been one of the two guards who made the trip from Atlanta to Alcatraz with Capone. He claimed that this portrayal defamed him as a bribe-taker and as one unfaithful to his trust.

Apart from a novel holding that defamation by broadcast constitutes a new tort which the court labels "Defamacast," the most interesting aspect of this opinion concerns identification of the plaintiff. On two grounds his complaint is upheld: (1) that he may prove by extrinsic fact that he was actually the guard portrayed who allegedly accepted Capone's bribe, and (2) that, as one of two unidentified men charged with a crime, he is a member of a sufficiently small group of whom one is unquestionably being defamed and therefore authorized to sue. On both counts, the Supreme Court of Georgia accepted the plaintiff's view and permitted suit, although plaintiff was never identified by name nor did the guard in the teleplay resemble him. This is a logical holding, and a fair one insofar as plaintiff's reputation is involved. The mere fact that his name was not used should not bar all liability and he should be able to prove either that he was the specific man accused or that, as one of the two people charged, he is a member of a sufficiently small group. By being that particular one, he is inextricably caught in the meshes of the claim.

Failure of identification caused dismissal of actions in two other film cases involving alleged libel. In *Wheeler* v. *Dell*,[16] an attack by a widow and her daughter on the novel and movie *Anatomy of a Murder* failed. Mrs. Wheeler claimed to be characterized by the screenplay and fiction piece but the court said she could not be identified with the character, Janice Quill, for lack of her "unsavory characteristics." Similarly, her daughter's "innocuous role" and age differential from the victim in the film eliminated her as a litigant.

In *Levey* v. *Warner Bros.*,[17] the divorced wife of George M. Cohan was found nonidentifiable with the Joan Leslie role in *Yankee Doodle Dandy*. The character of Cohan's wife in the film was considered completely fictitious and unrelated to Mrs. Levey who was his first wife. There was, therefore, no true representation of the lady.

Use of a defamatory motion picture in a union organizing campaign was condemned in *DiGiorgio* v. *AFL*.[18] Here the film was found to falsely indicate conditions at the DiGiorgio Farm Corporation's 10,000 acre ranch in California. A jury held against the workers organization for $100,000 compensatory damages and $50,000 additional punitive loss. An Appellate Court upheld the verdict reducing, however, the compensatory damages from $100,000 to $10,000 while permitting the punitive award to stand. The limited and non-trade showings of the film, which was entitled *Poverty in the Valley of Plenty,* appeared to justify this reduction.

An effort of Albert DiSalvo to restrain Twentieth Century-Fox's version of Gerold Frank's *The Boston Strangler* on defamation and right of privacy grounds also failed. Mr. DiSalvo had signed an agreement waiving any claims in connection with the book, but claimed he was incompetent at the time of execution. The court differed and held him legally responsible for his acts. The court further pointed out that DiSalvo had actually received compensation under an agreement which bared his crime and that accordingly he was bound by it. In addition, it might be added that the incidents surrounding *The Boston Strangler* were clearly of broad public interest and short of wilful

---

[16] *Wheeler* v. *Dell Publishing Co.* 300 F.2d 372 (1962).

[17] *Levey* v. *Warner Bros. Pictures* 57 F. Supp. 40 (1944).

[18] *DiGiorgio* v. *AFL* 215 Cal. App. 2d 560 (1963).

falsehood no recovery on the part of this convicted murderer could be justified.

Our Changing Concepts

As in other areas, the law of defamation by performing arts is in flux. It is axiomatic to say today that we live "in a period of great change" and, while a cliché, the observation has validity. Defamation law is not immune to this change. What is and what is not defamatory clearly must change with the times. What is harmful to reputation today may be flattery tomorrow, and vice versa.

One need only look around to grasp the changing distinctions. Compare a charge of pro-German attitudes in 1914 or 1944 with an allegation of such sympathies today. Is adultery considered the same "crime" as it was in Grandma's day? What of homosexuality and lesbianism? Does reference to "marijuana user" have the same connotation in 1973 that it had but a few years ago? To ask these questions is only to indicate the constant variations of terminology that may apply in defamation. The law will and must change with the times.

The crucial point is that reputation must continue to be defended. It is still true, as Shakespeare wrote, "He who steals my purse steals trash," but he that filches from my good name leave me poor indeed. Unfortunately, a modern trend has set in which shows signs of undermining and destroying this long-established protection from defamatory assault.

The trend started with *Sullivan* v. *The New York Times* [19] which expounded the doctrine of freedom from liability except in the rarest of instances where a charge had been made against a public official. In this case, a pro-civil-rights advertisement in the *New York Times* on March 29, 1960 had made some erroneous charges against "Southern Violators" who were oppressing the black students in or about Montgomery, Alabama. The Commissioner of Public Affairs of Montgomery, unnamed in the ad and not identifiable by its terms, brought suit in libel and a local jury gave him an astounding $500,000 verdict against *The Times* and a group of Negro clergymen.

Instead of dismissing the case on any one of a number of simple grounds available, the U. S. Supreme Court reversed, establishing "The New York Times doctrine" that, short of intentional falsity or reckless

[19] *New York Times* v. *Sullivan* 376 U.S. 254 (1964).

disregard of truth or falsity, no public official can recover in libel as
to charges connected with the performance of his duties. This decision
granted a huge area of immunity in the law of defamation. It has since
been broadened and widened in its applicability.

In *Pauling* v. *National Review* [20] affirmed on appeal, the same
doctrine was applied, not to a public official but a professor who had
"thrust" himself into the public eye by his "peace" activities. So now
it is not only public officials but persons merely involved in public
issues who must accept defamation, except in the rarest of instances,
without the possibility of legal recovery. The charge against Pauling,
incidentally, was Communist sympathies—a charge long considered
libelous *per se*.

In *Rosenbloom* v. *Metromedia* [21] the same doctrine was applied
to a virtually unknown Philadelphia bookseller falsely accused on a
TV newscast of purveying obscene matter. Despite the erroneous
charge, Rosenbloom was found involved in a matter of legitimate
public interest and a verdict in his favor of $175,000 was reversed in
the U. S. Supreme Court.

The recent Goldwater decision is not contrary as it fits within the
exceptions stated in *The New York Times* doctrine. It is submitted that
this trend toward the destruction of the law of defamation, if continued, will have dire consequences. It is all well and good to talk of
free and robust discussion of public issues but it will be truly alarming
if this means that no man can venture into the political arena without
fear that his reputation will end in tatters, all without legal remedy.
I believe that cases such as *New York Times, Pauling, Walker* v. *The
Associated Press* [22] and *Rosenbloom* could all have been decided on
far narrower grounds, just as adversely to their plaintiffs, without
negating or diminishing the impact of the law of libel. Unfortunately
"hard cases make bad law" and these suits are no exception.

Another key issue is one of damages. *Corabi (Reis)* v. *Curtis
Publishing Company* [23] represents some kind of a record in strange
verdicts. A harsh piece in the late *Saturday Evening Post* had implications that "Tiger Lil" Reis was involved in hustling, murder, intimida-
tion of witnesses, burglary and assorted other offenses. At the end of

[20] *Pauling* v. *National Review* 269 N.Y.S. 2d 11 (1966).
[21] *Rosenbloom* v. *Metromedia* 403 U.S. 29 (1970).
[22] *Walker* v. *Associated Press* 18 L.ED 1094 (1967).
[23] *Corabi (Reis)* v. *Curtis Publishing Company* 273 ATL 2d 899 (1971); see
also 262 ATL 2d 665 (1970).

her case, the jury came in with an astounding verdict in libel for $250,000 compensatory and $500,000 punitive damages. They also granted her a judgment in unfair competition for $75,000 and for violation of her privacy $75,000 more. In addition, her two children, whose pictures were used in the exposé, were granted judgments for privacy violation for $300,000 and $600,000 respectively.

These fantastic awards did not stick on appeal. Initially the trial court insisted on reducing Lil's defamation claim to $100,000 compensatory and $200,000 punitive damages, and knocked out entirely her unfair competition verdict. Later the Appellate Court eliminated the children's verdicts entirely as well as Lil's award in privacy. The libel claim was sent back for a new trial.

Should the use of certain words or images permit the presumption by a court or jury of loss to the plaintiff? Or should the plaintiff be required to actually show his damages, like in practically every other sphere of law? On this issue authorities have suggested a reasonable compromise position, distinguishing between substantial and significant charges published in national media and insignificant unimportant allegations "published" to a handful of persons. When the charge is of the first character, a presumption of loss might be allowed. But when the allegation is of the second nature, there should be no damages granted, other than nominal, unless actual loss is shown. The best proof of loss remains in damages actually incurred, which can be shown specifically. Nonetheless, where the harm is potentially substantive, presumed damages should be available. Punitive damages should be assessed only in those limited instances where the most terrible allegations have been made as deliberate lies without the faintest justification. Apart from this, this type of assessment seems thoroughly unjustified.

The law of defamation must live. Protection of reputation must remain a crucial and important thing as long as human beings care about what other human beings think and say about them. The field of the performing arts, and film in particular, is growing and will be of increased importance in the future. As one medium of communication of defamatory matter it should be an area where reputation will be protected. It will be a very strange day, and indeed an unhappy one, if the arts—films, the press and all the other means of communication —will be entitled to destroy and undermine reputation without penalty or loss.

19

Film and Privacy

AT FIRST BLUSH the right of privacy seems quite alien in the area of film and the performing arts. In one sphere we are presumably talking of seclusion, or a right to be let alone, and in the other of public performances before general or limited audiences. Aren't the two areas entirely incompatible? While logic might so indicate, legal history differs. Both performers and presentations have played an active role in the development of the privacy right.

The right of privacy is a relatively new legal concept. Brandeis and Warren, in their classic 1890 article,[1] condemned the constant infringements of press and media on the solitude of the individual. They developed a limited concept of a personal right "to be let alone." Subject to the requirements of an interrelated society, certain aspects of life were to be legally held apart from public scrutiny. From their thesis there developed a common law and statutory privilege that is now recognized in all but a handful of American states. A person can sue for invasion of his right of privacy and secure damages or even enjoin the offense. The nature and extent of both the right and remedy, however, vary sharply from state to state.

Privacy must be distinguished from defamation. In privacy invasion the harm is to the personality and not to reputation. There is no

---

[1] "The Right to Privacy" 4 Harv.L.R. 193 (1890).

requirement of falsity in all cases, as appears to be the present, if not the past, rule in libel and slander. Nor need there necessarily be publication of the invading material. Defamation, in brief, holds a person open in his community to scorn, obloquy and contempt. Privacy invasion may injure his feelings and emotions but not necessarily his public stature. While the two offenses can be parallel and exist simultaneously, they remain clearly disparate.

A distinguished scholar [2] has characterized four aspects of the right of privacy, all dissimilar but with a common theme:

1. *The protection against intrusion on an individual's solitude.* Here the problem is with invasion of the purely personal realm. Questions arise involving such diverse applications as wire tapping and bugging, prohibition of contraceptive devices in the marital bedroom, abortion controls, data banks and compilations of personal information.

2. *The exploitation of the personality.* In this more traditional aspect we consider the misuse of a person's name, photograph or image for purposes of advertising or trade.

3. *False light in the public eye.* The concern here is with misrepresentation (but not defamation) of the individual or his point of view. The statement that one supports legislation when he does not, the unauthorized use of names on petitions, and the fictionalizing of biographical or other events involving living persons—all indicate the nature of the offense charged.

4. *The public disclosure of private facts.* This is the open resurrection of ancient, forgotten or justifiably concealed events for the benefit of public consumption with clear identification of the living parties involved. Here, too, there may be a privacy breach.

The categories are not all-inclusive and they do overlap. Nonetheless, they offer a broad spectrum of purported privacy protection against a large number of acts. How have they applied to film performers and performances?

Protection of an Individual's Solitude

Solitude protection is the newest category in definition but perhaps the most significant in general perspective. Its boundaries are far from enumerated for it involves a clash with certain public rights of broad and increasing significance, including the police power. One must speculate as to its impact in this precise selected area.

[2] Prosser: "Privacy" 48 Calif. Law Review 383 (1960).

The Blumenthal case [3] is indicative. A documentary motion picture was filmed on the streets of New York including shots of an old lady openly selling pretzels on a corner. The use of her image without permission was held a violation of her right of privacy. The case is dated (1932) and the decision questionable but it still stands as law in New York.

Its pattern has recently been followed in Massachusetts.[4] A distinguished documentary film—Fred Wiseman's *Titicut Follies,* was taken at the Bridgewater Mental Hospital. In revealing fashion the film probes life among the inmates of this institution. Wiseman had procured certain personal releases from patients and an oral consent, of a disputed nature, to film from state officers. Nonetheless, the Commonwealth brought suit as a "parent" to the inmates to enjoin public distribution of the film in the Bay State. Ignoring the modern doctrine, which calls for "free and robust" discussion of all public issues, the Supreme Court of the State upheld an injunction against public exhibition, on pure invasion of privacy grounds. Private distribution to doctors, sociologists and institutional personnel was permitted.

Although the film is frank and candid, and shocking in its nature (as are conditions in many mental institutions), the injunction appears unjustified. The hospital is a legitimate area of public concern and this fact should take priority over any alleged harm to privacy. The case, incidentally, is quite contrary to a holding on the same film in the Federal District Court in New York.[5] There, an injunction was denied against exhibition in view of the need for free and full dissemination of information as to such institutions. Just how much personal privacy is justified under these conditions remains in doubt.

An exception for newsworthy material was granted early in New York. Grace Humiston, female sleuth and attorney, objected to the use of her name and picture in the late Universal newsreel. The Court, however, found publication of her story involving a crime newsworthy and "not for purposes of trade." [6]

And the fact that a news item was created for the screen, in the form of a group of corpulent women exercising accompanied by caustic remarks, did not alter the rule. News is not confined to current

[3] *Blumenthal* v. *Picture Classics* 235 A.D. 570 (1932).

[4] *Commonwealth* v. *Wiseman* 249 N.E. 2d 610 (1969).

[5] *Cullen* v. *Grove Press* 276 F. Supp. 727 (1967).

[6] *Humiston* v. *Universal Mfg. Co.* 189 A.D. 467 (1919).

affairs but covers general matters of interest as well, including items of amusement, informational and educational.[7]

In the recent case of *Man* v. *Warner Brothers*[8] plaintiff had voluntarily performed on his flugelhorn at the festivities at Woodstock and sought to restrain showing of the distinguished Warner Brothers' documentary of the event. His picture was used without his consent. His claim, however, was denied and summary judgment granted to the defendant on the dual grounds that the nature of the affair was public and that he had volunteered his services as an entertainer.

Touching another aspect of the problem outside the film area, the recent Ralph Nader[9] decision by the New York Court of Appeals indicates that even a public act by an individual, such as withdrawing cash from a bank, may not be unduly "shadowed" or "watched" by private investigators. Such conduct runs the risk of a charge of invasion of privacy. It is not necessarily a defense that the party involved participates in public affairs. He may be performing what should be considered a purely private function even in public and, in that sense, is entitled to the same protection as someone less famous.

An interesting case in the parallel area of libel indicates still another side to this matter. In *Burton* v. *Crowell Collier*,[10] a magazine advertisement for Camel cigarettes ("get a lift with a Camel") featured a photograph of a steeplechaser holding a saddle in his hands. The lower edge of the saddle is approximately 12″ below his waistline and hanging from the saddle is a white girth strap. Unfortunately, an optical illusion was created that the strap was not attached to the saddle but to the steeplechaser's body at a most appropriate but surprising point. An "indecent exposure" was indicated. The rider brought suit for libel against the publisher and his complaint was upheld.

A similar potential would seem to exist for film, dramatic or televised performances. A normal or ordinary scene or photograph can create a thoroughly erroneous impression. If there be photographic libel by optical illusion the same may well apply to privacy.

Of course there is always the possibility in documentaries or live television of the camera invading precincts which are forbidden. One need only to think of the authorized invasion of homes and dining

[7] *Sweenek* v. *Pathe News* 16 F. Supp. 746 (1930).

[8] *Man* v. *Warner Bros.* 317 F. Supp. 50 (1970).

[9] *Nader* v. *General Motors* 25 N.Y.2d 560 (1970).

[10] *Burton* v. *Crowell Collier* 82 F.2d 154 (1936).

rooms in such shows as "Person to Person" to see the possibility for unauthorized invasion far beyond this area by peeping long-range cameras and recording devices. Private functions of public persons may be easily invaded.

Another aspect of solitude concerns bugging and wire-tapping. This is a wholesale abuse running far beyond the problem of film performances. In a recent New Hampshire case,[11] an inquisitive landlord placed a recording device in his tenant's bedroom. When assailed on privacy grounds, he stated that he hadn't committed any such offense because he hadn't published the information procured. The Supreme Court of New Hampshire disagreed and upheld freedom from such activity in the State. Private, if not public, wire-tapping is now officially banned under Federal Law. Need it be added in these days in particular, it still goes on.

Somewhat contrary in nature was a radio case where a commentator made use of the tapes of a private conversation with Charlie Chaplin.[12] Although the exchange was definitely not for broadcast purposes the court refused relief to the actor. The decision seems strange and unjustified. The media must be regarded as taking a substantial risk of privacy invasion as well as other offenses when they record, pick up and relay to the public purely private communications.

The use of real names of real people in the theatre could create future difficulties. This is a growing trend. The dramatic work, "In the Matter of J. Robert Oppenheimer," for example, named names, and while the public nature of those proceedings probably foreclosed legal action, other instances of less general interest could be envisaged. Similarly, in "MacBird," the highly unflattering portraits of Lyndon Baines Johnson and Robert Kennedy might have created both libel and privacy problems had the figures involved desired to litigate. Although being a public figure may oftimes be considered a waiver of the privacy right, this need not necessarily apply to the publication of personal and malicious matter in a less than public context.

A leading figure from a well-known libel case tried again in privacy when CBS offered a new version of Rasputin in the early 1960's. Felix Yousoupoff claimed that the story line used his personality without consent. His motion for summary judgment, or judg-

---

[11] *Hamburger* v. *Eastman* 206 ATL. 2d 239 (1965).
[12] *Chaplin* v. *NBC* 15 FRD 134 (1953).

ment without trial, was denied by a court concerned as to whether the Rasputin saga was "fictionalized" or used for "commercial purposes" under New York Privacy Law.[13]

It should be mentioned that purely incidental usage of a name is non-violative of the right of privacy. This means that every passing reference to a living person is not significant. Repeatedly the courts have held such limited usage immune. Examples in film include reference to "Shubert's Winter Garden" in *The Jolson Story*,[14] to "Little Wayne Damron's Saloon" in *Show Boat*,[15] and to picking up a "Punch Drunk Fighter Down at Stillman's Gym" in *The Country Girl*.[16]

Exploitation of the Personality

A second category of privacy invasion is more traditional in nature and has been the source of considerable litigation. That is the exploitation of the personality, generally for purposes of commerce and trade. This truly seems a misnomer for most performers as, ironically, the very thing they seek is publicity and promotion.

Illustrative is the famous Gautier case,[17] where a dog trainer performed his act between the halves of a football game in a huge stadium. Mr. Gautier's objections were not to the exploitation of his act, or its public viewing, but to the showing to additional thousands of his efforts over television without his authority or consent, or perhaps more significantly, without any additional remuneration to him. As the court put it, however, in fact "the last thing Gautier wanted was privacy." Suing under a privacy theory his cause of action was rejected.

Of course what Gautier truly sought was a "right of publicity" or the right, in his own way and for his own profit, to exploit his name and talents. He should justifiably have the legal means to prevent others from cashing in on these values. Such a theory has now been developed and is available in this type of case.

The new doctrine grew out of a controversy about baseball cards. Rival gum manufacturers utilized photographs of ball players in connection with the promotion of their products. One such producer had

[13] *Yousoupoff* v. *CBS* 41 Misc. 2d 42 (1963).
[14] *Shubert* v. *Columbia Pictures* 189 Misc. 734 (1947).
[15] *Damron* v. *Doubleday* 133 Misc. 202 (1928).
[16] *Stillman* v. *Paramount* 1 Misc. 2d 108 (1956).
[17] *Gautier* v. *Pro Football* 304 N.Y. 354 (1952) aff'g 278 A.D. 431 (1951).

an exclusive right to publish the likes of such diamond favorites as Yogi Berra, Monte Irvin and Gus Zernial. His competitors, however, published cards with the consent of these very same athletes. No one wanted to sue the players, who presumably had sold the same right twice, so one gum manufacturer sued the other. The controversy went to the Circuit Court of Appeals. The plaintiff saw his exclusive rights to the photographs infringed. The defendant felt that only the players could object to the use of their photographs as an invasion of their privacy and, as the players had not done so, the plaintiff had no legal complaint.

The late distinguished Judge Jerome Frank created a new right in these words:

> This right might be called "a right of publicity." For it is common knowledge that many prominent persons (especially actors and ball players) far from having their feelings bruised through public exposure of their likeness would feel sorely deprived if they no longer received money for authorized advertisements, popularizing their countenances, displayed in newspapers, magazines, busses, trains and subways. This right of publicity would usually yield them no money unless it could be made subject of an exclusive grant which bars any other advertiser from using their picture.

The gum manufacturer with exclusivity accordingly prevailed. A right of publicity was created, far more fitting to the case of performers in most instances, than any "right of privacy" for their protection against commercial exploitation.

Other situations pose different problems. In the Marion Kerby case, a film company sent out a flier to promote its motion picture, which read:

> Don't breathe it to a soul, but I am back in town and more curious than ever to see you. I promise you an evening you won't forget. Meet me at Warner's down town.

This missive was signed "Marion Kerby," who was a character in the film *Topper,* and mailed to 10,000 Los Angeles men.

Unknown to the producers, a real Marion Kerby also existed, an actress in Los Angeles. She objected to the use of her name. The

18 *Haelen Labs* v. *Topps Chewing Gum* 202 F.2d 866 (1593).

California court, applying the doctrine "it's not who you aim at, it's who you hit" held in her favor.[19] The reasoning should be questioned as the plaintiff was hardly identifiable, but the case still stands.

Identification is not always so simple. A Bronx street cleaner with a different name saw himself portrayed as Major Joppolo in John Hershey's play, "A Bell for Adano." He, like Hershey's hero, had served in Sicily as a civil affairs officer in the occupation, facing the problems of administration in a small Italian town. The court dismissed his claim for failure of identification but it should be kept in mind that in privacy there can still be a "portrait" despite dissimilar names, characters or other camouflage.[20]

One Joseph Anthony Maggio considered himself to be portrayed as Angelo Maggio in the James Jones novel *From Here To Eternity* filmed by Columbia Pictures.[21] The Court found no similarity, however, between the two Maggios other than their family names and their presence in the military service in Hawaii in 1941. A criminal remedy under New York Privacy Law was denied.

Rigid application of privacy rules are not infrequently a problem. A softcover book jacket of Eugene Vale's *Chaos Below Heaven* quoted a San Francisco newspaper critic, "Ayn Rand enjoys . . . the same kind of mystique analysis as Vale—their underlying drive is the same." Miss Rand took umbrage at the use of her name and sued for invasion of privacy. A literal-minded lower court, seeing the use of a name without consent, granted her judgment. The Appellate Court reversed on the grounds that the usage was appropriate and non-exploitive.[22]

In a fantastically absurd litigation, Notre Dame University, acting under a New York statute granting rights equivalent to privacy to certain non-profit organizations, succeeded temporarily in enjoining the release of Twentieth Century-Fox's filmed epic, *John Goldfarb Please Come Home*. In this situation a ridiculous football farce utilized the name and symbols of the South Bend institution. Justice Henry Clay Greenberg in Supreme Court, New York County, granted a remarkable injunction preventing a holiday play date for the film of December 17, 1964. The Appellate Division reversed, finding no commercial piracy and a free speech issue in the suppression of the film.[23] But the play date was long since gone.

[19] *Kerby* v. *Hal Roach* 127 Pac 2d 577 (1942).
[20] *Toscani* v. *Hersey* 271 A.D. 445 (1946).
[21] *People on Complaint of Maggio* v. *Scribner* 130 N.Y.S. 2d 514 (1954).
[22] *Rand* v. *Hearst Corp.* 298 N.Y.S. 405 (1969).
[23] *Univ. of Notre Dame* v. *20th Century-Fox* 22 A.D. 2d 452 (1962).

Another theatrical figure with a privacy problem was Shirley Booth. The noted actress, on vacation in the resort of Round Hill, Jamaica, consented to the limited use of her photograph in *Holiday* magazine. Following publication there, the monthly used the shot for an advertisement for itself in two other publications. Was Miss Booth's privacy invaded by the extended use? The court held no, considering the use merely incidental to a legitimate item published with consent.[24]

False Light in the Public Eye

Turning to the third area of protected privacy, the concept of false light in the public eye has posed serious problems for entertainers and entertainment. Here the issue is whether the matter published or disseminated falsifies the plaintiff's view or position. A trend has now set in against the recognition of this right except in the case of most extreme cases where there is the publication of willful falsehood or equivalent recklessness.

The key tests have been in the "fictionalizing" cases. In biographical matters, may film or other media fictionalize the characters, bringing them to life with non-factual or imaginary incidents or conversations? Or must the unauthorized biographer stick strictly to known facts and a narrative manner?

The decisions are conflicting. The trouble started early in the century with the classic New York case of *Binns* v. *The Vitagraph Company.*[25] In this situation a shipwreck at sea was reenacted for a filmed version. Archie Binns, the hero of the actual disaster, was portrayed without his consent in the performance of his heroic duties as wireless operator of the stricken vessel. Despite the flattering picture, his complaint for privacy invasion was upheld by the New York Appellate Court. Numerous cases thereafter accepted this line that fictionalizing the life of a living person without consent ran the risk of judicial condemnation.

The counter trend is exemplified by the *Compulsion* litigation.[26] In this novel, followed by a play and a film, the dramatic Loeb-Leopold story is retold. The plot was fictionalized, and while the characters were renamed, the work is clearly based on the famous Chicago case.

[24] *Booth* v. *Curtis Publ. Co.* 15 A.D. 2d 343 (1962).
[25] *Binns* v. *Vitagraph Co.* 210 N.Y. 51 (1913).
[26] *Leopold* v. *20th Century-Fox* et al 45 ILL 2d 434 (1970).

In his effort author Meyer Levin created two major imaginary incidents. In one instance Loeb and Leopold, seeing themselves as "supermen," exercised their right to choose who shall live and die by running down with their automobile an intoxicated vagrant on the street. In another, the character Leopold is indicated as participating in a sequence of attempted rape.

Nathan Leopold, rehabilitated and on parole, objected to these incidents as an invasion of his privacy and brought suit. Judge Brussel in Circuit Court, Cook County, Illinois, rejected his contention. He found Leopold a legitimate figure of public scrutiny and appraisal. More significantly, he saw a free speech issue in the defendant's right to publish and discuss matters of general concern. The court found no intentional or reckless falsity in Levin's version of the crime story. The Supreme Court of Illinois affirmed the verdict.

Contrary to Brussel's opinion, are the repeated holdings of the New York courts in the Warran Spahn litigation.[27] No motion picture was involved but the issues are similar. The eminent baseball pitcher objected to an unauthorized juvenile biography which fictionalized and embellished various aspects of his life. His charge was not defamation but invasion of privacy, and he was granted an injunction and damages against the publisher. The lower court, affirming on appeal, found that fictionalizing his life for publishing purposes took the work outside the scope of free speech immunity. In its view, there must either be consent to publication or pure factuality. After repeated appeals the Spahn case was reportedly settled on nominal terms. Nonetheless, the decisions on their face still grant a cause of action for "fictionalizing" the life of a living person in the Empire State.

The Supreme Court, however, has ruled to the contrary on the subject in a significant parallel litigation.[28] The factual base is interesting. To generate publicity for a theatrical opening, scenes from a play, "The Desperate Hours" were re-enacted for *Life* magazine in a home formerly occupied by the family of one James Hill. Years before, this very home in suburban Philadelphia had been the scene of an invasion by escaped convicts. The Hill family had been held hostage for 19 hours. Following the event, and abhoring the publicity, they had moved away. Now their story was publicly retold in *Life* by a

[27] *Spahn* v. *Julian Messner* 43 Misc. 2d 219 (1964); aff'd 23 A.D. 2d 216; aff'd 21 N.Y. 2d 124 c.f. 387 U.S. 239.
[28] *Time Inc.* v. *Hill* 385 U.S. 374 (1967).

dramatic re-enactment of Joseph Hayes' play based in part on their experience, but fictionalized and sharply altered. Of course no consent was involved.

Hill's suit went well all the way to the United States Supreme Court. Hill's lawyer, one Richard Nixon, alleged that the events depicted purported to represent his clients but in fact were false. To illustrate, the convicts in the *Life* story were portrayed as actively contemplating an assault on one Hill daughter. Mr. Hill is portrayed as having made a daring if unsuccessful effort to escape the criminals. Neither event actually occurred. Therefore, it was argued that privacy invasion had occurred by virtue of fictionalization.

Life pleaded that the matter involved was one of legitimate news interest and concern and had been published without malice or wrongful motivation. Accordingly, presentation should have been with constitutional immunity under the First Amendment. The Supreme Court agreed with this defense reasoning. Following the line of a famed libel decision,[29] the court held that in matters of general public interest (be they in the area of politics, amusement, enlightenment or stimulation) there can be no restraint under the Bill of Rights unless there is willful falsehood about an individual or equivalent recklessness in the presentation. It is emphasized that, for these purposes, there is no distinction between performing and entertaining or whether the material is for commercial, non-commercial or publicity purposes as here presented.

Under this rule it appears likely that the vast bulk of fictionalization cases will be immunized, and the performing arts and other media will be free to use live characters without legal responsibility unless they transgress the *caveats* stated above.

There are, of course, other aspects of "false light" that could involve film and performing artists. False impressions can be engendered in a number of different ways. In one case, the use of the photograph of a taxi driver in the *Saturday Evening Post,* in conjunction with a piece entitled, "Never Give a Passenger a Break" (dealing with the unsavory characteristics of Washington, D.C. hack drivers), was found objectionable.[30] The implication was clear that the driver was a part of the obnoxious trade. This case, however, seems closer to defamation than privacy invasion.

In another instance, Rabbi Julius Goldberg successfully objected

[29] *N. Y. Times* v. *Sullivan* 376 U.S. 254 (1964).
[30] *Peay* v. *Curtis Publ. Co.* 78 F. Supp. 305 (1948).

to a magazine piece indicating that he favored "a new era of sexual freedom" when, in fact, he favored nothing of the sort.[31]

Circulation of "Rogues Gallery" photographs of innocent persons has been the subject of privacy disputes.[32] It would seem that the performing arts may also run risks in connection with this type of activity. But the dangers have been sharply narrowed by the Supreme Court's ruling in the Hill case.

Public Disclosure of Private Facts

A similar rule should apply to our final category of privacy invasions involving the public disclosure of private facts. Once again, unless the material published is willfully false or recklessly prepared, it seems unlikely that such claims will be upheld in the future.

In this area, of course, generally the matters portrayed are truthful. Usually the issue arises by virtue of a resurrection of past sins and offenses long-since forgotten. The revelation of confidential, if truthful, data, however, occurring currently would seem to have an equal potential.

In the *Red Kimona* case,[33] which brought the privacy doctrine to California, Gabrielle Darley (*nee Melvin*) a former prostitute acquitted of murder, had abandoned her "life of shame." She married a gentleman of good manners and social standing (Melvin) and thereafter lived, according to the court, "an exemplary, virtuous, honorable and righteous life," vintage 1930.

Eight years after her indiscretions, the defendant, Dorothy Reid, produced the film entitled *The Red Kimona* based on Gabrielle's story and surprisingly using her maiden name. The film, of course, featured all the sex, shame, sin and slaughter of which Mrs. Melvin had been accused. The California court was chivalrous and upheld the suit of our redeemed lady. The release of the film was considered morally unjustified and presumably an invasion of her "rights," although not explicitly, referring to her privacy.

Similarly, in *Bernstein* v. *NBC*,[34] an ex-convict brought suit on revival of his long forgotten crime saga on NBC's "Big Story." His

---

[31] *Rabbi Julius Goldberg* v. *Ideal Publ. Co.* 210 NYS 2d 928 (1960).

[32] See *Itzkovitch* v. *Whitaker* 39 So. 499 (1905).

[33] *Melvin* v. *Reid* 297 Pac. 91 (1931).

[34] *Bernstein* v. *NBC* 129 F. Supp. 817 (1955).

case was dismissed, however, on grounds of a failure of identification as well as his status as a public figure.

The other side of the coin is the famous Sidis case.[35] A *New Yorker* magazine sketch entitled, "Where are They Now" with the sub-lead "April Fool," featured the exploits, 20 years after the fact, of a child prodigy who had astounded university professors at Harvard with his mathematical genius at age 8. What, the magazine asked, had happened to Robert Sidis?

In the years following his remarkable performance, Sidis had suffered a nervous reaction to his childhood fame. He sought to conceal his identity, found employment in a menial clerical position, and devoted his spare time to such activities as collecting street car tokens. Sidis' untidy room in a garret, his peculiar laugh and manner of speech, as well as his abiding interest in the lore of Okamakammaset Indians, were all portrayed. To justify the sub-title of the piece, a quote from Sidis was used, "but you know, I was born on April Fools Day."

Judge Clark of the Circuit Court of Appeals, found the article, "merciless in its dissection of intimate details of its subject's personal life. It is, in fact, a ruthless exposure of a once public character."

A split court refused to find the *New Yorker* guilty of privacy invasion. Balancing the equities, it considered:

> But despite eminent opinion to the contrary, we are not yet disposed to afford to all of the intimate details of private life an absolute immunity from the prying of the press. Everyone will agree that at some point the public interest in obtaining information becomes dominant over the individual's desire for privacy. Warren and Brandeis were willing to lift the veil somewhat in the case of public officers. We would go further . . . at least we would permit limited scrutiny of the "private" life of any person who has achieved or had thrust upon him the questionable and indefinable status of a "public figure."

The decision appears to predict that of the Supreme Court in the Hill case, although on somewhat different grounds. Immunity is granted where a once public figure is involved, if the report is reasonably true. In fact, under today's rule even truth is not required—only the absence of malicious falsehood.

This probably means that nearly all past events of any substantive interest can now be dredged up as a subject for motion picture or TV

---

[35] *Sidis* v. *F. R. Publ. Co.* 113 F2d 806 (1940).

presentation. The chances of privacy invasion have been reduced except in the extraordinary case to the near negligible.

As we have seen, the claim that privacy has been invaded is now subject to a multitude of defenses. We have already had reference to the basic constitutional doctrine that enforcement of the right in many instances conflicts with the guarantees of free speech. If a matter belongs in the forum of general public discussion, the fact that someone's name is used without authority in connection therewith no longer authorizes relief. And it matters not whether the motive of the publisher be commercial, informative or educational.

The concept of that which is legitimately public has also broadened. What was once deemed private and personal can now be seen to have public characteristics. Only a narrow area, generally criminal or sexual in context, could presently be considered private, and even this is a reducing territory.

In many cases "public figures" are denied a right of privacy, although they should have the commercial right to their publicity. Public figures are not merely those who seek the public eye but those as well who have the status "thrust" upon them by being involved in matters of general interest. A host of people are therefore public figures willy nilly, like it or not, with their privacy correspondingly reduced. Frequently the courts say such persons have "waived" their rights as having sought or received the very publicity they condemn.

The states differ among themselves, in any event, as to the degree of protection offered. Wisconsin and Nebraska, for example, afford no privacy protection at all by current judicial holdings.[36] New York, Virginia and Utah have statutes limiting protection under the concept to misuse for purposes of "advertising" or "trade." [37] These words have been interpreted with varying degrees of solicitude and the subject remains one of deep controversy.

Regardless of theory, truth has also become a significant defense. In the areas of false light and disclosure of private facts, it would seem there now must be extreme falsity if there is to be any liability. Mere publication of erroneous or distorted information is quite insufficient.

Waiver of privacy is, of course, a frequent defense. Where written and full consent has been given to the use of a name or picture, of course, no one should be heard to complain. But the waiver defense

---

[36] See Mayer: *Rights of Privacy*, Law-Arts Publishers 1972, Chapter 24.
[37] Supra: Footnote 36 to this Chapter; Chapter 23.

has not been limited to this. Courts, as we have seen, have implied waiver by virtue of public status. And even limited waivers for a particular use are utilized to justify uses far beyond their terms. Oral waiver is usually permitted as a plea only for the purpose of diminishing damages.

We have already discussed the defense of mere incidental use. Where a reference is brief and insignificant, of course, there should be no legal responsibility.

Ordinarily there is no right of privacy in a dead person. Neither his executor nor his heirs can claim a loss of this nature by virtue of the use of the decedent's likeness on film. In *Maritote* v. *Desilu Productions,*[38] Mrs. Alphonse Capone and her boy "Sunny" took offense at the TV production, "The Untouchables," which featured the infamous Al and his practices 12 years after his demise. Their claim was dismissed. The same result had previously followed in a legal attack on Allied Artists' memorable film *Al Capone* with Rod Steiger.[39] The screen portrait of the great composer, Robert Schumann, as suffering from mental disease was also held not to entitle his heirs to any recovery.[40]

The result might be otherwise in those states which specifically authorize by statute survival of the dead man's rights. But even under Utah's unusual statute authorizing suit by the dead for privacy invasion, Jack Donahue's heirs were denied recovery for his portrait in the biographical film *Look For The Silver Lining*. His "picture" was not considered use for commerce or trade.[41]

Assuming that the trend equating privacy invasion with defamation continues, the defenses now applied in that area will become even more significant. These include privilege (absolute and conditional), fair comment and an opportunity for retraction. The causes of action for privacy invasion are being limited while the defenses increase in scope.

In theory, three types of remedy exist for privacy invasion. In some states statutes exist asserting criminal responsibility for the act. These are most infrequently used and require no discussion. District

[38] *Maritote* v. *Desilu Productions* 230 F. Supp. 721, aff'd 345 F.2d 418 (1964).
[39] *Maritote* v. *Allied Artists Pict. Corp.,* unreported Illinois case (1962).
[40] *Schumann* v. *Loews Inc.* 102 N.Y.S. 2d 572 (1951).
[41] *Donahue* v. *Warner Bros.* 272 Pac 2d 117 (1954), see also *Donahue* v. *Warner Bros.* 194 F.2d 6 (1952).

attorneys have better things to do with their time than prosecute private controversies in this area.

Injunctions and restraining orders are more significant. In the fields of false light and public disclosure their doom, however, is clearly impending. Elsewhere, they remain useful. The *Titicut Follies,* as we have seen, has been unjustly enjoined in Massachusetts. A programmed CBS film, featuring the use of the name and figure of a former theatrical manager named Bullets Durgom, was restrained where consent was not granted to the portrayal.[42] When the right to use Mary Garden's name on a perfume product expired, the lady was able to enjoin continued use.[43]

But this remedy of restraint is so powerful and so destructive that it must be available in only the most unusual and clearcut cases. The normal remedy for privacy invasion is damages granted either by verdict or in settlement of a claim.

Verdicts have run the gamut from nominal, or one cent, to an original (reversed) jury verdict for the Hill family against *Life* for $175,000. It must be kept in mind that, as in defamation, once a privacy invasion is found, juries with reasonable discretion can determine damages without any showing of specific loss (proving specific loss would of course be helpful but it is not a prerequisite for judgment). This rule is quite understandable because the jury is measuring harm to a personality, which is hardly a tangible item. The jury can, in fact, even go beyond this determination of harm caused and in a flagrant case grant peremptory damages totally unrelated to loss in order to punish a wrongdoer.

Large damage grants in privacy cases are rare, and when they occur are likely to be reversed. An astounding verdict for a Missouri nurse allegedly portrayed in the film, *They Were Expendable* for $60,000 compensatory damages plus $225,000 punitive, was summarily reversed.[44] Similarly, a huge verdict based on a muck-raking *Saturday Evening Post* piece, "They Called Her Tiger Lil," about Lillian Reis (Corabi) was also sharply reduced on appeal. The trial jury in this combined libel-privacy claim had granted Miss Reis and her children a combined award of well over $1-million.[45]

[42] *Durgom* v. *CBS* 214 N.Y.S. 2d 752 (1961).

[43] *Garden* v. *Parfumerie Rigaud* 151 Misc. 692 (1933).

[44] *Walcher* v. *Loews Inc.* 129 F. Supp. 473 (1948).

[45] *Corabi* (*Reis*) v. *Curtis Publ. Co.* 273 ATL 2d 899 (1971); see also 262 ATL 2d 665 (1970).

More traditional are such verdicts as $3,000 (*Kelly* v. *Loews* for portrait in the film *They Were Expendable* previously discussed); use of a nude picture of a model in *U.S. Camera,* $1,500; [46] distortion of a prize winning essay, $2,250; [47] photograph of a professional dancer as an advertisement, $300; [48] an alleged endorsement of a photostat machine by a lawyer, $1,500; [49] and a story in *Time* magazine of an insatiable eater in a hospital, $1,500.[50] Substantial damages, while not impossible, are clearly hard to come by. Injunctions are even harder, and criminal proceedings most difficult of all. But the threat of such actions may, and frequently does, lead to compromise and cash.

Privacy invasion remains a vital matter in the performing arts, as elsewhere. One would hope that, with an added degree of clarification and sympathy from the courts, a better future might be substituted for its difficult and confusing past.

[46] *Myers* v. *U.S. Camera* 9 Misc. 2d 765.
[47] *Manger* v. *Kree* 233 F.2d 5 (1956).
[48] *Fisher* v. *Rosenberg* 175 Misc. 370 (1940).
[49] *Fairfield* v. *American Photocopy* 291 Pac 2d 194 (1955).
[50] *Barber* v. *Time Inc.* 159 S.W.2d 291 (1942).

20

Compensation for Ideas

THE IDEA PROBLEM ARISES out of the submittal or seizure of concepts for use in a motion picture (or other medium) and the legal problems thereby created. We are not talking here about federally copyrighted material or matters protected by patent law. Those problems are determined within the terms of their statutory provisions or practices. Raw ideas are quite another subject.

Assume a typical situation. A person has an idea for a film script. He communicates the concept to a studio executive with a vague allusion to possible compensation. No formal agreement as to use, however, is presented or reached. The idea, or something akin to it, is nonetheless utilized by the recipient. Is the studio indebted to the idea presenter or is the idea free and available for use? Similar problems are posed daily in the field of advertising slogans, titles for television programs, money-saving concepts to industries, and in a host of related areas.

The general and oft-repeated rule is that "mere" ideas are not protectable. The reasoning is that they are, and should be, as "free as air." How are old or new thoughts to be expressed and exchanged, and the broad knowledge of humanity as a whole increased, if each person is able to stamp a monopoly on these types of concepts. The answer seems apparent. It would stifle and hold back progress if any and all

169

thoughts and expressions were permitted to remain the property of any particular person.

Nonetheless, the rule has been subjected to numerous exceptions. Under certain circumstances, where it has seemed inequitable or improper to permit the use of an idea without compensation, the courts have granted a degree of protection. The determination of these extraordinary circumstances constitutes the idea problem.

The entire matter may, of course, be regulated or avoided by means of a written contract. As a rule, anyone is free to contract or traffic in ideas whether they be new, old, valuable or absurd. If he enters into a *bona fide* agreement to purchase or sell, under normal circumstances, the contract will control and the idea problem is at an end. There are even exceptions to this, however, as in some of the early cases the courts found that, where the idea was neither new nor valuable to the person to whom it was proffered, it was insufficient consideration on which to base a contract.

These cases, however, should not be regarded as currently binding and it is a fair conclusion that formal written acquisitions of concepts for consideration will be judicially respected. Law suits based on these contracts have been upheld.

Although they might prefer to avoid the problem by rejecting all unsolicited ideas, many users, such as advertisers and television networks in entertainment and elsewhere, feel that good public relations negates such an approach. They do not wish to offend their customers by telling them arbitrarily and in advance that they are not interested in the many suggestions, helpful or unhelpful, that are offered.

Accordingly, to avoid the idea problem these corporations frequently establish rules of procedure to control submissions. These are aimed at the avoidance of informal person-to-person approaches which have dangerous implications for users. Often approach through a recognized agent is required. Presentations are frequently channeled to screening personnel, usually non-creative in function, who make carefully phrased formal responses or send company forms to submitters to be executed before any material is inspected. The forms will feature such provisions as waivers of rights by the submittor, a general release to the prospective user or a broad provision leaving to the discretion of the company the compensation, if any, to be paid if the idea is used. An alternative approach is to place the company's discretion as to payment within certain limited financial areas ($250 to $1,000 if the idea is used and has not been previously presented).

Presumably, this is done so that no court can condemn the use of unbridled discretion in payment to the idea recipient which might void the entire form.

While the forms where executed have clearly limited the type and nature of claims filed, they are by no means a total solution. Where fair in principle, they have been upheld against eager submitters, but where considered unjust as granting too much power to the user, they have been set aside. While they do succeed in resolving some disputes, they are clearly no panacea for the problem.

Legal thickets and theories abound with reference to the disclosure and use of ideas not covered by express contracts or forms. As in other areas of the law, the particular individual situation involved is most likely to be the determining factor. Accordingly, it is necessary to glance at some of the cases.

Idea Protection in California

The center of idea litigation has been California and its courts have been unquestionably the most generous to idea submitters. We look, then, to the Golden State for so-called advanced thinking in this field.

A classic case of idea protection, although it might be regarded elsewhere as a dubious precedent, is *Desny* v. *Wilder*.[1] Here the defendant Wilder was a producer employed by Paramount Pictures in Hollywood. The plaintiff, seeking to contact Wilder with his story idea for a film, called his office but spoke only to his secretary. According to him, she demanded that he tell her his screenplay concept. The saga involved one Floyd Collins who, in real life, had had the unpleasant experience of being trapped in a Kentucky cave over a prolonged period of time. The secretary suggested that Desny send his script to Paramount Story Department but he followed a different procedure.

Two days later he called the secretary again. Now he told her he had prepared a three- or four-page outline of his story and at her instance he read it to her over the telephone. She took the story down in shorthand and informed Desny that she liked it and would discuss it with her boss, Wilder, and would let Desny know his reaction.

Desny claimed he made it clear to Wilder's secretary that the story could only be used if the company (Paramount) paid him its reason-

[1] *Desny* v. *Wilder* 46 Cal. 2d 715 (1956).

able value, and the secretary assured him that if Wilder made a film from it he would accordingly be paid. Desny never discussed the matter further with Wilder or any other person at Paramount except to complain, a year later, of lack of compensation when a movie was made that had relation to the outline he had suggested.

Paramount did indeed make a picture based on the Floyd Collins incident and Desny brought suit claiming the misappropriation of his idea. The lower court granted summary judgment to Paramount on the general grounds previously set forth that ideas are free for all to use and cannot be regarded as property unless expressed in copyrighted form. The Appellate Court reversed, however, holding that disclosure of the concept was consideration for a promise of compensation. Surprisingly, it found that Wilder's secretary had authority to negotiate a contract for Paramount for the purchase of this property and her statement that Desny would be compensated if the property was used was found, in theory at least, binding on the company. The granting of summary judgment for Paramount was rejected and a Pandora's Box in California opened for the idea submitter.

Similarly, in *Weitzenkorn*,[2] a concept for a new Tarzan film was presented to a producer featuring the jungle acrobat in "The Land of Eternal Youth." There was no formal understanding. This presentation, as well, was upheld as the prospective subject of an oral agreement to pay. It mattered not that there was no contract nor how slight or commonplace the idea might be.

In *Golding*,[3] an uncopyrighted play dealing with a demented ship captain was submitted to the RKO studios. Following production of a film based on this rather familiar theme, a complaint was upheld as cause for $25,000 damages despite the lack of any explicit agreement. This decision, too, is difficult to understand.

California courts also found a jury question in the issue of whether an audio production of "My Friend, Irma" was taken from a radio script of *My Sister, Eileen*. Despite a host of dissimilarities, the court refused to summarily dismiss a claim of idea seizure of the uncopyrighted property. More recently in California, the courts again found a jury question as to whether Ivan Tors Productions had contracted for, by using in their TV series, *Seahunt*, a submitter's raw concept for a number of underwater adventure stories for television.[4]

[2] *Weitzenkorn* v. *Lesser* 40 Cal. 2d 778 (1953).
[3] *Golding* v. *RKO Pictures* 35 Cal. 2d 690 (1950).
[4] *Minniear* v. *Tors* 72 Cal. Rptr 287 (1968).

The concept was uncopyrighted, unoriginal and not the subject of a written contract, but as it was presented to the user the court refused to dismiss the claim.

In *Fink* v. *Goodson Todman*,[5] the plaintiff submitted an uncopyrighted concept to defendant for a TV series featuring a cowhand and Indian fighter who had been court-martialed for cowardice in a prior battle with the redskins. The impact of his conduct carried over to affect his postwar activities. Defendant's TV series, entitled *The Coward*, similarly involved an act of cowardice which occurred in World War II. This failing of the hero also had impact on his postwar life as a policeman. Once again the court found sufficient basis for a claim of idea piracy on the theory of an implied contract and upheld the complaint.

Protection Elsewhere

Apart from California, it is only the rare case in which oral idea submissions are upheld. The surprising *Belt* litigation found "property" in a concept for a radio program featuring musically talented children.[6] The idea had been presented to a bank which thereafter sponsored a similar program over the air. As the court found the idea novel (!) and concrete as to form, it permitted protection as "property" despite the complete lack of any express contract or understanding. The case is, of course, dubious law and authority.

More traditional in impact is the decision in *Curtis* v. *Time, Inc.* which refused to protect an idea for a comic strip based on events in the lives of a series of Congressional Medal of Honor winners.[7] As the idea was neither novel nor concrete in form, it was in accordance with the general rule held insufficient to justify an implied contract.

In theory, implied as opposed to actual contracts can only be claimed where the idea meets a set of qualifications. It must be unusual or "novel" and definitive in form. It cannot be commonplace or a mere thought still in someone's mind in partial form. Ordinary and unspecified concepts are hardly things which reasonable men can be expected to pay for when they have entered no definitive agreement.

Once again, apart from California, custom in the trade has

[5] *Fink* v. *Goodson-Todman Ent.* 9 Cal. App. 3rd 996 (1970).
[6] *Belt* v. *Hamilton Bank* 108 F. Supp. 689 (1952).
[7] *Curtis* v. *Time Inc.* 147 F. Supp. 505 1957.

generally been found irrelevant to these disputes and idea submitters will not be protected merely because they allege it is ordinary practice to pay people who present them. It should, and usually does, require a degree of consent far more precise than this vague criterion.

The unjust enrichment theory (i.e. he became rich by using my property), as well, is easy to allege and hard to prove and should be judicially avoided. Nonetheless, courts which see conduct as inequitable and, searching for a handle on which to premise a plaintiff's verdict, may seize upon it as a technique to right an alleged wrong. Still another judicial theory used in some of these cases is to impose duties on a user as "fiduciary," such as a lawyer who allegedly steals his client's concept.

Many idea cases are actually claims of infringement of common law copyright. This is the legal theory of protection of unpublished, and uncopyrighted literary property which belongs in perpetuity to an author-owner. In such cases, no contract need be alleged if the material is used without license. If there is access to and actual copying of an unpublished writing, the plaintiff may assert a claim for infringement, but here his position far exceeds mere ownership and control of an idea. He has, in fact, created literary property which he owns.

In another chapter (Chapter 17) we deal with the protection of titles, which is still another aspect of this problem and which has been a fertile source of litigation. Titles are uncopyrightable but, nonetheless, are sometimes found protectable as a matter of unfair competition.

Recent cases have threatened the entire basis of idea recovery in the field of literary property. In an otherwise unrelated patent decision, the United States Supreme Court found that an unpatented lamp could not be protected against copying under the law of unfair competition. Without patenting, the proprietor was held to have no rights against even an exact replica sold by the defendant.[8] By *dicta* the court added that uncopyrighted material, as well, was subject to infringement without remedy. In brief, the finding is that federal patent and copyright legislation pre-empts the field, and that the states have no power to make that which is unprotected and properly available subject to remedy for use under other laws.

The full impact of this remarkable opinion is yet to be felt. Already it has been raised in idea cases with profound consequences. In the *DeCosta* litigation, a federal court, following this rationale,

_____

[8] *Sears, Roebuck* v. *Stiffel* (Supra).

reversed a $150,000 judgment for a show-business proprietor who for years had used the term "Palladin—Have Gun, Will Travel." [9] His claim against Columbia Broadcasting System for use of his uniform, as well as his uncopyrighted insignia in a TV show, was rejected as contrary to federal law. If he had no copyright, he had no protection. Elsewhere, the effects of this new doctrine are in dispute and yet to be finally determined.

There are, of course, other defenses to idea claims. The originality of the claimant is usually questioned on the grounds of "we thought of it first." The use is generally distinguished from the concept and therefore purportedly not a copy or invasion of it. A user may well have received the same idea from another public benefactor or one of its own employees. Then, of course, the form of the concept may be challenged as not "concrete." Finally, if the material is neither copyrighted nor copyrightable, the Supreme Court defense recited above may be asserted and, in any event, a user may always deny having access to the property or having copied it if he did have access.

One can see that idea litigation has been and remains a fertile source of controversy in the entertainment industries.

[9] *CBS* v. *De Costa* 377 F2d 315 (1967).

21

Characters and Sequels

AN AUTHOR OR a producer who has created an interesting or significant fictional character in his book or film today faces substantive if
not insurmountable difficulties in protecting this figure. This chapter
seeks to look at this vital problem and to offer some suggestions toward
a remedy. As the matter has been long and studiously considered by
others, no claims of originality or novelty are here presented.[1]

The problem frequently arises following publication of a novel or
the licensing for film production of a literary work involving a fictional
personality of a distinctive nature. The particular figure catches the
public's imagination. Such personalities are not hard to find. In the
detective area they range from Sherlock Holmes to Perry Mason. Elsewhere one thinks of Upton Sinclair's *Lanny Budd* or Herman Wouk's
Naval captain in his *The Winds of War*. Of course, there are many
others. One thinks of the possibilities in many members of the "Cor-
leone family" in *The Godfather*. In any event, the character develops
a value far beyond the work of fiction in which he has been involved.
The question arises what happens if, for example, a film producer or
any other person not directly authorized creates a new property utilizing the author's individual character? An agreement on sequel or

---

[1] See Roach: 2 Performing Arts Review 587 (1971); "Adams, Superman,
Mickey Mouse and Gerontology," 6 Journal of Bev. Hills Bar Ass'n. 6 (1972).

remake rights might or might not so authorize a producer, but what protection is there for the author or licensor against other parties?

The issue arose indirectly in the famous Sam Spade litigation.[2] Here Dashiell Hamett and his publisher had licensed Warner Bros. for all of $8,500 to make a motion picture of Hamett's novel *The Maltese Falcon.* This was the fantastic story of the wild search for a valuable bird figurine. The essential character in the drama is Sam Spade, private eye extraordinaire, played by the inimitable Humphrey Bogart. Spade's characterization proved a sensation on the screen and became of substantive value.

Warner Bros. had been granted the exclusive right to make motion picture, radio and televised versions of the work. The issue arose when Hamett continued to use Sam Spade in other novels and plays, and licensed the Columbia Broadcasting System and others to utilize him as a character on radio and in television. Did this impair Warner Bros.' exclusive rights to *The Maltese Falcon* "and/or its characters"? Warner Bros. saw copyright infringement and unfair competition in such presentations. The courts differed.

The judges found Warner's rights limited to the copyrighted literary property which it acquired but which did not include perpetual ownership of the character, Sam Spade. Unless unequivocally contracted, an author retains rights in his character and here the agreement was found ambiguous. Even more significant, however, is the ruling that characters are mere vehicles for a story told and that, even if Warner Bros. had acquired the entire copyright in *The Maltese Falcon,* it could not prevent the further use by the author of his characters in other stories. Sam Spade, in fact, was uncopyrightable.

This followed the reasoning of an earlier case involving a copyright dispute between two plays with similar themes—*Abie's Irish Rose* and *The Cohens and the Kellys.*"[3] In holding mere similarity of theme (i.e. Jewish-Catholic family rivalry upset by youthful inter-religious love) noninfringement of copyright, the court went further to deny any protection to the principal characters who it found incidentally to be insignificant and routine. As Judge Learned Hand put it so well:

> If *Twelfth Night* were copyrighted, it is quite possible that a second comer might so closely imitate Sir Toby Belch or Malvolio as to infringe, but it would not be enough that for one of

---

[2] *Warner Bros. Pictures* v. *CBS* 216 F2d 945 (1954).
[3] *Nichols* v. *Universal Pictures* 45 F2d 119 (1930).

his characters he cast a riotous knight who kept wassail to the discomfort of the household, or a vain and foppish steward who became amorous of his mistress. These would be no more than Shakespeare's "ideas" in the play, as little capable of monopoly as Einstein's Doctrine of Relativity, or Darwin's theory of the Origin of Species. It follows that the less developed the characters, the less they can be copyrighted; that is the penalty an author must bear for marking them too indistinctly.

It is doubtful, however, that no matter how well the characters are developed and particularized, they could be protected under current doctrines. The implied qualification that a well-developed character could be copyrighted has not been seriously followed in subsequent litigation.

Character infringement under copyright law, then, appears to present several problems. Firstly, as Judge Hand stated, the degree of singularity and importance of the character must be determined. Secondly, it must be shown that the specific character was precisely copied by the infringer. And, thirdly, more recent litigation would indicate that in any event the character is unprotectible.

Like most truisms, this is not universally so. Cartoon characters either on-screen or off may be sufficiently identifiable as to accomplish protection as opposed to those which are merely subject to verbal description. In an exceptional case,[1] the publishers of a cartoon character called "Wonderman," who appeared to encompass all the attributes of "Superman," were restrained from distributing books portraying the former in feats of strength or in similar costume to the giant do-gooder. Even here, however, the court did not go so far as to permit copyright of the mere character in and of himself. It thus appears that the courts are loath to grant such ultimate protection although the "unrestrained pilfering of characters" has been condemned.

A second technique of protection would be to regard significant fictional figures as "ideas" and attempt to protect their status under that legal umbrella (see Chapter 20 on Ideas). This was attempted in the DeCosta litigation.

Mr. DeCosta created a New England cowboy character of himself, and participated over the years in rodeos and other exhibitions. He used the name "Palladin" and handed out cards reading: "Have

[1] *Detective Comics* v. *Bruns Publications* 111 F2d 432 (1940).

gun, will travel, Cranston, Rhode Island." A similar use of a character with the identical name Palladin was developed by the Columbia Broadcasting System in a television series featuring Richard Boone (*Have Gun, Will Travel, San Francisco*). A lower court jury found the improper use by the Columbia Broadcasting System of Mr. DeCosta's idea to be of such significance as to entitle him to a $150,000 verdict. The judgment, however, was reversed in the Circuit Court on the essential grounds that unless copyrighted under Federal law, Palladin could not be protected.[5] This followed the language of the Sears, Roebuck [6] decision pre-empting the area of copyright law to the Federal domain in the case of published works. As DeCosta had clearly "published" by presenting his act nationally and handing out his card without copyright notice he had no claim to common law rights which exist only prior to publication. Once published, the court held, and not copyrighted under our system of law, the work is in the public domain and free for any or all to use.

There would also be other impediments to protecting characters as "ideas." Prior prerequisites in this field have included the requirements that the concepts be definite and concrete as well as original and novel. Serious doubts in these connections may be raised even if the devastating Sears, Roebuck doctrine were to be avoided. Unfortunately, the ancient rule of the *International News Service* case,[7] which prohibited direct copying even of uncopyrighted news reports, now appears to have been reversed if not by direct statement, by implication.

Common law copyright or state protection of unpublished material would hardly be applicable in most "character" disputes. In the instances where cited, the characters are generally parts of published or filmed works, and were subject to Federal copyright or have lost their status by virtue of publication without copyright notice.

In large parts of the world, authors are protected by the doctrine of *droit moral,* or certain rights running far beyond ordinary copyright protection. These would include the right to be known as the author of their own creations, to prevent others from being so named, and to prevent "deforming changes" of their creative works. The doctrine is aimed at respect for the creator of literary and artistic works and insists that a work not be mangled or mutilated by others. Under such

[5] *CBS* v. *DeCosta* 377 F.2d 315 (1967).

[6] *Sears, Roebuck* v. *Stiffel Co.* (Supra).

[7] *International News Service* v. *Assoc. Press* 248 U.S. 215 (1918).

a doctrine it would seem possible that rights of characterization, such as discussed here, might prove protectible. While at the present time *droit moral* is not recognized in American law, except occasionally by indirection and as such could provide little protection, the genius of the law has been to develop reasonable and responsible remedies to serious offenses. It would seem quite conceivable that fair-minded American legislatures and judiciaries might some day find that it is the inherent right of an author to own and control his characters as created by him. Pending that day, however, it would be an optimistic assertion to claim character protection pursuant to this concept.

In the area of unfair competition, it has always been considered improper for one author to seize the well-designated character of another for his own competitive use. This would, in effect, involve the cardinal sin of "palming off" or presenting one's product as that of another. Under such circumstances, it seems that the courts might find grounds regardless of copyright to see that the original owner of rights is protected. But palming off is difficult to identify and there can be no certainty of protection even in this area for identifiable characters.

A reasonable solution presented by some authors would be to modify present rules by statute or administrative fiat to specifically permit the copyright of specific fictional characters. If proper standards could be established and this could be done, authors and businessmen would know where they stand when transactions are accomplished, and litigation might be avoided.

Not all characters, of course, could conceivably be covered by copyright. Those of nominal or mere background importance (stock characters) certainly would be omitted from any fair interpretation. It would be only the truly delineated character whose full representation, including physical appearance, weight, height, facial expression, name, as well as conduct patterns and miscellaneous idiosyncrasies, who might specifically be subjected to copyright as an author's "writings."

Such characters are clearly sufficiently "tangible" and are the product of intellectual labor. Essential novelty has never been required under U. S. Copyright Law. They are visually perceptible. The requirements for "character registration" could be set up by a progressive Copyright Office.

By such a decisive technique major individuals from important works could be protected, and the entire matter simplified and taken out of the argumentative stage. Transfers of sequel rights would have to include the specific characters or they would remain with the copyright owner. Rights in them not transferred would remain with prior authors or owners. A profound step toward the protection of creative rights could be accomplished. As such protection is deserved by the artistic creator, action should be taken to make it a reality.

22

Copyright and Film

THE COPYRIGHT SYSTEM SEEKS to protect the rights of proprietors and creators of artistic works. Under the 1909 Federal statute, following publication, two 28-year terms of exclusivity are assured the qualifying claimant provided only that he meets the statutory formalities.

Under a parallel and somewhat contradictory system common law copyrights are preserved, where there is no publication, in perpetuity, for the authors and creators of literary and other material. This power exists under state law.

While the dual system has not worked without difficulty under modern technological conditions, it has succeeded in protecting to a great degree a large number of authors and film-makers. Revision of the law to strengthen and encourage the rights of artistic creators remains a "must" for the national legislature, albeit a long delayed phenomenon.

In view of the two copyright system (i.e. statutory and common law) the fact of "publication" becomes a critical point of distinction. For if there is publication, all common law protection is eliminated and one must rely entirely upon the statute. If, on the other hand, there is no "publication," common law protection continues in perpetuity and no one can ever copy the protected material.

The word "publication" sounds simple, but in fact it is a complex concept in this area of the law. There is, of course, publication within the traditional concept when a book is physically published and sent out to retailers for marketing. That is the common idea of publication. But is it publication when a play is produced on the New York stage? The answer is that it is not. Nor is it necessarily publication when a television script is shown over the air on hundreds of outlets or on a more modest basis, or when an outline is merely forwarded by agents for submittals to interested persons. Nor has the distribution of sheet music to interested publishers traditionally been considered publication.

Dispute exists over whether the distribution of a film (as opposed to the sale of a print) is, in fact, a publication. The modern trend is to so consider it. Accordingly films distributed by licensing have been regarded as "published." They should be copyrighted.

To emphasize the importance of all this, if a book is published in the United States without proper copyright notice, it is in the public domain and free for anyone to copy, use or otherwise deal in to his heart's content and without liability. That is one reason why the courts are frequently restrictive in their interpretation of the word "publication." Very few judges are anxious to see the hard-working creator sacrifice all of his rights by virtue of some inadvertent act which might be construed as publication without notice of copyright. Therefore, for the purpose of divestiture of statutory copyright, the court rules are rigid and generally seek to prevent that unfortunate event.

On the other hand, where there has been a clear infringement by a third person and the plaintiff seeks remedies under the copyright law, the tendency is to say that yes, indeed, there was a prior publication and the plaintiff's work should be protected—this is true, even where the situation might otherwise be considered somewhat less than a full and complete publication.

It might be added that were the proposed amended Federal copyright law to pass, a good many of these distinctions would be unnecessary. The new statute would abolish the common law copyright and set a flat term of copyright protection starting, in most instances, from the date of creation. The proposed general rule is a term of the owner's lifetime plus 50 years, which follows the European pattern. Were this rule in effect now there would no longer be perpetual ownership of unpublished material but only ownership for the period of life plus the term of 50 years. The effort to construe various releases of material as something less than publication, in order to retain perpetual rights, would then become pointless.

But even under the proposed copyright law, in the case of

anonymous works, pseudonymous works and works for hire the rule would still be 75 years' protection after publication, with a 100-year maximum—so the publication problem would not be entirely obviated.

Under the present copyright law, a 28-year term of protection is granted to published (and certain unpublished works) with a 28-year renewal term if refiled during the last year of the original term.[1] Pending the copyright reform bill there have been repeated legislative extensions of time to prevent copyrights from falling into the public domain, so that the renewal period is presently exceeding 28 years for a good many works. But this must be considered a temporary rather than a permanent condition. The extensions, sooner or later, will stop, whatever eventually happens to the copyright reform movement.

Copyrightable and Non-Copyrightable Items

Copyrightable items under the 1909 law include books, periodicals, lectures, dramatic compositions, musical compositions, maps, works of art, reproductions, technical drawings, photographs, prints and motion picture-photoplays as well as other types of motion pictures. Recordings are a new addition. Each of these categories may therefore be subject to copyright protection. Forms for filing are available at the Copyright Office (Library of Congress, Washington, D.C.).

Certain types of material, however, are outside the scope of the law and are in the public domain no matter whether copyright is claimed or not. Such items would include the following:

1. Materials published without copyright notice.

2. Publications where the copyright is not renewed, after the initial 28-year term.

3. Works of foreign authors (and those of U. S. citizenship, in certain cases not qualifying under the statute or the Universal Copyright Convention or treaty.

4. Works of total unoriginality (this phrase is so difficult of definition that its inclusion in this list is questionable, but it could pose problems on occasion and therefore should be mentioned).

5. Nominal works, including such things as titles (see our chapter on this subject), standard information as to wages, etc.

6. Raw ideas as opposed to specific descriptions of ideas (see chapter on ideas).

[1] 17 U.S. Code Annotated Sect. 903 et seq. (Section 24 of Copyright Act).

7. Blank forms.

8. Recordings and performances; while music is protected by copyright, recordings have not been until a recent amendment of the law permitted copyright protection, in some instances, to prevent record piracy.

9. Government publications (again the distinction between governmental and private publications is frequently difficult to make).

10. Obscene and seditious material (this also poses serious problems of definition which seem to be ignored by the Copyright Office).

11. Material in which copyright has expired.

Copyright secures a large bundle of rights in any particular property which include publishing, adapting, performing and recording. In this respect, it should be noted that "publishing" involves printing, reprinting, copying and vending—and not the mere technical act of publication itself. Similarly, adapting would include translating, dramatizing, converting into another form such as a drama and arranging a musical work. Performing also involves public performances (as defined by the courts) of dramas, and performances for profit of non-dramatic and musical compositions.

Motion Pictures and Musical Compositions

With specific reference to motion picture photoplays, these have been held to be dramas which are protectible against duplicating public performances. Serious problems have arisen, however, as to what constitutes a public performance. In an early case, an unauthorized performance of a motion picture at a private yacht club in Maryland where only members were present was held not to be a public performance, and the use of an admittedly infringing print was thereby immunized.[2] The case appears illogical and unfair to film distributors, and its importance as a precedent is now dubious. Public performance should merely require unauthorized projection on a screen of a copy of a copyrighted work where the public is present. The revised copyright law, if passed, would broaden this definition and cure the problem.

Other difficulties have arisen as to the class of nondramatic or documentary motion pictures. Some early cases found these types of films uncopyrightable under any specific provision of the law. An

[2] *MGM* v. *Wyatt* 21. Copyright Office Bulletin 203 (1923).

inventive bit of judicial construction, however, managed to squeeze them into its terms and the presentation of an unauthorized copy may now be regarded as infringement.[3]

Accordingly, then, motion pictures are an appropriate category for copyright registration. Under the law it is not mandatory although it may be wise to file copies with the Copyright Office in order to secure this protection. Publication with copyright notice is the act that creates a legal right. However, prior to suing on a copyright, it is essential that the published material be filed and a certificate acquired. In other words, filing is a precondition of suit but not a precondition to acquiring a valid copyright. Agreements with the registrar to file prints are often utilized.

In another significant area, the widespread use of musical compositions originally in bars and nightclubs, and thereafter on radio and television, caused the necessity for the creation of performing rights societies to license musical compositions. Obviously, the authors of these compositions could not keep track of all individual performances of music for profit and it was necessary that they act collectively to do so. Following widespread abuses under the antitrust laws by these societies (ASCAP, in particular) various judicial decrees have been established regulating their conduct in licensing compositions. Nonetheless, they continue as effective protectors of the rights of publishers and authors of musical compositions in connection with their performance particularly in the broadcasting medium.

Other problems arising within the context of the performing societies include, of course, the division of revenues between members. These are now generally based on a use formula, i.e. the composition that is most played would be credited with the most revenue. Prior systems whereby successful composers achieved a large priority by virtue of their standing over young new authors have been minimized. Publishers and authors generally share in such rights on a 50-50 basis.

There is an interesting feature of the copyright law involving recording rights. The present rule is that, once a recording of a musical composition has been published by a copyright owner or his licensee, any person may then record and publish his version of the same composition if he notifies the copyright owner of his intention to use the same and pays him a royalty of 2 cents on each record. Of course, many copyright owners deal directly with such users at vary-

[3] *Patterson v. Century Productions* 93 F.2d 489 (1937).

ing rates apart from the law, but the statutory protection does exist. It prevents any monopoly in song recordings. It does not apply to movie sound tracks.

An anomaly of the copyright law is the absurd jukebox exemption, which allows the ubiquitous machines to play any number of songs any number of times without compensation to the publisher or author. All the jukebox owner must do is buy the record. In other words, there is no recognized performing right in the use of music on jukeboxes. The reasons for this perversion of justice are shrouded in the absurdities of history, but apparently relate to a potential monopoly in the field back at the time when the copyright law was originally passed. Since that date, the jukebox business has grown to mammoth proportions and fortunes have been made without any regard to the rights of authors and publishers. The vested interests in jukebox ownership and licensing, of course, would like things to stay as they are, but even they cannot justify this *reductio ad absurdum* and a compromise provision has been worked out for a new copyright law in this connection. If passed, the bill will grant a modest participation to authors and publishers in the use of their music in jukeboxes.

Copyright is, of course, limited by the doctrine of fair use. No complete monopoly is granted. Unauthorized users are permitted to utilize portions of copyrighted materials for valid reasons. Critics, teachers and others are permitted advantage of these provisions and should not be considered infringers of copyright merely by virtue of their limited takings. Meaningful or substantial use, however, which inhibits the revenue as well as the reputation of the copyright owner during the copyright term is not exempted by this provision.

Copyright Technicalities—Infringement

As a technical matter the copyright laws have sometimes required strict observation. This is particularly true in the area of copyright notice. While the notice is simple, it must be accurate and properly placed. On a book, for example, the copyright notice, or preferably the letter "C" in a circle, accompanied by the name of the copyright proprietor and the year of publication should be on the title page or immediately succeeding page. Failure to include the notice at the proper place may throw the work into public domain, and allow any person to copy it for any purpose with full legal immunity.

Other illustrations of technical defects would include postdating the copyright—i.e. setting a copyright date subsequent to actual publication, such as 1974 for a 1973 book. If one does this he has, in effect, extended the copyright term by an additional year. The courts have held this conduct improper and have, in fact, negated the entire copyright where the owner has sought thereby to extend his protection. As antedating the notice with a prior date causes no such harm, and in fact reduces the copyright term, it has not been held equally illegal There have been many problems as to copyright notices on toys and labels not properly affixed to the work and, in the particular area of fabric designs, this has proved a singular and difficult problem.

Another substantial difficulty under copyright law has been the "manufacturing clause" which, although modified, still requires in general that books in the English language be printed in the United States. While this is subject to some exceptions, it remains as an absurd carry-over to protect American manufacturers and users against foreign competition, and should have no real status in a new law.

Copyrights, of course, may be transferred, bequeathed or assigned and endorsements of transfer may be recorded in the Copyright Office. The duration of the first term is 28 years from publication or, in the case of an unpublished work, from registration. The renewal term is an additional 28 years. There have been problems with copyright renewals when the author is dead and rights have been previously transferred, as the statute sets forth priorities in the persons who may file for renewal (widows and children, executors, next-of-kin) regardless of prior licensing. A licensee may be inside looking out at refiling time if he lacks the requisite approvals.

Infringement is the act of using the copyrighted work without authority. This includes purloining certain parts of the protected matter for a new version, as well as the creation of identical copies. Mere superficial changes in names and characters will not avoid judicial condemnation. There have been several classic copyright cases in film and elsewhere where, despite minor differences in story outline and changed names of individuals, copyright was nonetheless found infringed and substantive damages granted. Even parody has been found, in some instances (i.e. the famous *Gaslight* case), to violate the rule and subjects the offender to penalties.[1]

Copyright, of course, protects methods of expression rather than ideas or concepts. Many people can use the same ideas provided that

[1] *Benny* v. *Loews Inc.* 239 F.2d 532 (1956), aff'd 356 U.S. 43 (1958).

they do not express them in precisely the same way. The subject of idea protection is dealt with elsewhere in this volume.

The illegal use of a motion picture print has always been found to be a copyright infringement.[5] Even a technical hold-over of a picture beyond the agreed time of its engagement, or an unapproved "move-over" to another theatre, would be a copyright violation. The constant trade in "hot" or illegal prints opens the door to numerous infringement actions. The present development of brand-new media for making cheap copies, such as videotape recorders, emphasizes this difficult and growing problem.

Copyright liability is broad and applies, in theory at least, to all parties participating in the infringement. This would include, in the case of film, the distributor, the exhibitor and even the projectionist of the infringing picture. Innocence of intent is not a bona fide defense, although it might certainly affect the nature of any damages granted.

Ordinarily the plaintiff in copyright infringement must prove access to his material. There is a possible exception to this in that access may be assumed where the works are so identical that the copying of the plaintiff's work is apparent. In the usual case, however, it is up to plaintiff to show that defendant saw or had the opportunity to see his work before preparing his own. The validity of copyright is ordinarily assumed *prima facie* by the presentation of a certificate from the Copyright Office.

While the damage provisions of the Copyright Law are confusing and difficult of interpretation, they are nonetheless potent. Although infrequently utilized there are, in fact, criminal penalties for infringement. Under some circumstances, infringing works can be seized and impounded by judicial authority while the case pends, and destroyed if the finding is in favor of the plaintiff. Injunctions are available against the use of infringing material, and both damages and any profits that a defendant may accrue by virtue of plaintiff's work may also be granted to the victim. In the famous Lettie Lynton case on which M-G-M's *Dishonored Lady* was based, a vast award in the form of defendant's profits from the motion picture was granted by a righteous court.[6] Other examples of large copyright-infringement verdicts are available.[7]

[5] See *MGM* v. *Bijou* 59 F.2d 70 (1932). Cases cited in *Nimmer on Copyright,* Matthew Bender 1971 (Section 109.4 et seq.).

[6] *Sheldon* v. *MGM* 106 F.2d 45 (1939), aff'd 309 U.S. 390 (1940).

[7] See cases cited in *Nimmer on Copyright* (Supra) Section 150 et al.

If proof of damages or profits is unavailing, the plaintiff is still not without remedy. The law specifically grants certain statutory damages which may be awarded where it is recognized that neither actual damages nor profits may be sufficiently provable. Large judgments founded on these statutory provisions are not uncommon, although the law is far from specific and requires rewriting. In addition, unlike most other areas of American law, the plaintiff is entitled to a counsel fee in the court's discretion when he proves his case, and this can be a substantial added cost to the infringing defendant. In fairness, the law also allows a successful defendant to secure a counsel fee from an unjustified plaintiff if the cause of action lacked merit.

The United States is a signatory to the Universal Copyright Convention (UCC), which means that works originally properly protected in their own country of origin are protected under our law here. Securing U. S. copyright, therefore, protects a motion picture or other work throughout the world in the member countries comprising a large number of important nations under their own rules. There are still, however, territories in which such copyright is not recognized—The USSR joined the UCC only in mid-1973. Many of the new national states have been pressing for a change in the rules which would allow them the broad use of copyrighted material with but limited compensation to the owner.

Copyright reform is long overdue, and a constant subject of Congressional attention, if not action. A revised statute would abrogate the old common law protection and federalize all copyright. The term of protection would be specified as from creation, and the issue of "publication" diminished if not destroyed. Modern means of communication would be permitted copyright, including sound recordings pantomimic and choreographic works. Authors' rights would be embellished with new provisions permitting termination of grants after a period of years. The rights granted by copyright would be clearly defined and so would the privilege of fair use. The remedy provisions, which today appear close to inexplicable, would be restated and clarified. Technical rules that have harmed authors and copyright holders would be abolished or modified. The jukebox exemption would end.

Significant issues, such as CATV transmission, photocopying computer input and output, and educational exemptions, have to date held up this happy event but it is difficult to believe that, even in this balky and unwieldy democracy, the pressures for progressive change will not eventually prevail.

23

Music and Film

THE ESSENTIAL NATURE of music as an element in motion pictures is, of course, self evident. In the "musical" film it is, moreover, the key element of vital consequences. But even in the dramatic or comedy type endeavor music is increasingly important in setting pace, increasing tensions or creating romantic atmosphere. In the era since sound there is little or no escape from this magic component. Even pre-sound pictures, in fact, were frequently accompanied by a noisy piano.

The powerful position of publishing affiliates of the major production companies is some evidence of the importance with which producers view this condition. Practically without exception every important film company owns or has controlled a major publishing house to market its music. The power of these companies, long dominated the American Society of Authors, Composers and Publisher (ASCAP) and their affiliates are also members of rival performing rights societies including Broadcast Music, Inc. (BMI). Through such mechanisms major production companies frequently control, to a substantial extent, the exploitation of their music originally created for film.

Composers share interest in film music with producers in view of the vast potential for popularity created by the film medium in their work. A film can "make" a song, thereby opening the door for large sheet music sales, performance royalties and mechanical earnings.

Prestige can be created practically over night for a minor piece or insignificant writer. There are other benefits as well for composers at the long end of the movie rainbow.

To utilize music in his film the producer must acquire two vital rights from the musical creator. While theoretically one might think that the right to synchronize with the film implies the right to perform the music, for practical reasons this is not the case. Film synchronization is a separate and distinct right. It authorizes recording in timed relation to film. In addition to this, however, there must be granted a right to publicly perform the music so recorded in the motion picture. Unless one wishes to create a film with music for his own personal use and not for public exhibition, the performing right is essential.

The significance of the performing right is emphasized in many countries by the power of performing rights societies, such as ASCAP and BMI. In Europe, theatres pay to such local organizations royalties for the use of music before their audiences. Large sums are involved which are shared by authors and publishers within the societies. In France, for example, payments are made to the French Society (SACEM) based on the gross of the motion picture at the box office. While payments by theatres in the United States have been eliminated by an unfortunate antitrust decision against ASCAP, the domestic television industry still pays vast royalties to the American performing rights societies for the use of their members' music.

It should be pointed out in connection with foreign-made films— particularly from France, Italy and England—that the local performing rights societies abroad hold musical performing rights by assignment of their members, and quite properly claim that they alone are entitled to license this use in the United States. A distributor should, although some do not, acquire a license from these organizations before distributing any such film in the United States.

Producers seeking music for their films frequently cause its creation by hiring composers for the specific task. Here their music does not previously exist and is expressly written for the film. Under present constructions of law the producer, as employer, has been held entitled to copyright such music in his own name and acquire all rights in it including, of course, synchronization and publicaton. In effect, the producer is the author and by his creation he has earned the status of copyright proprietorship. This, however, has become a disputed item under pressure of the Composers and Lyricists Guild which has entered into contracts with producers. Under these terms, important rights are reserved to composers and writers of film music.

In 1972, in an out-of-court settlement of a pending litigation, the Columbia Broadcasting System (CBS) announced that it will re-negotiate its exclusive rights in music and lyrics composed and written for the network's television shows and motion pictures. This followed a lawsuit against both broadcasters and motion pictures charging anti-trust violations and restraint of trade in the standard terms allegedly acquired of composers and lyricists when they deal with motion picture companies as "employees for hire." The suit, then, challenges the very privileges we have set forth above on antitrust grounds, and the agreement by CBS to permit the composers to retain all the rights in their music except those essential to producing for television or for films is a break in the existing practice. It is too soon to say whether other producing entities will also surrender the other rights granted to them in motion picture music and confine themselves to the essential rights necessary to production and use. It seems likely, in any event, that the rights granted will hereafter be sharply limited.

Another interesting, if theoretical point, arises in connection with the use of motion picture "sound-track" music. Under the copyright law there is a compulsory license provision whereby music, once recorded, may be utilized under the statute by any third party, subject to the payment of minimum royalties to the owner and other statutory requirements. The question arises whether another publisher may similarly utilize his own arrangement of the music on a sound track of a film on simple payment of the 2¢ royalty per use. There appear to be no square rulings on the subject although the courts and authorities have implied conflicting conclusions as to the point. If, as seems reasonable, the music track is recorded as but a part of the integrated total film, the compulsory license provision should not apply as the music is hardly separable from the totality which is clearly entitled to exclusivity under copyright law. To date we have had no instances of any effort to so utilize sound-track music under the minimum royalty provision established for recordings, and industry practice is to the contrary.

Rather than hire composers and lyric writers, a producer may seek existing music to synchronize and perform with his film. If the music or its arrangement is in the public domain, being either uncopyrighted or copyright having expired, he is free to acquire it and use it without payment to the composer. Such music is frequently easily available through sound libraries and other trade facilities. Of course, this assumes that the music has been "published." Unpublished work, musical and otherwise, as defined in copyright law retains its common law copyright indefinitely. Use of music protected either by copyright or common law copyright (unpublished) must be cleared with the appropriate owner. Violation of this essential principle is not only morally reprehensible but a substantial risk to the film-maker. It is to be noted with chagrin that a handful of independent low-budget producers are simply seizing existing copyrighted music for backgrounds and otherwise with callous disregard for composers' rights. They will richly deserve the fate that will be theirs when the law eventually catches up with them.

A producer's dealing with the owners of musical copyright is quite distinguishable from his creation of rights as an "owner for hire." He must acquire, for a consideration, the synchronization and performing rights previously discussed. The other rights under copyright are subject to negotiation but will generally remain in the hands of the copyright owner—in the usual case, this will be the publisher. The license to a producer will set forth the composition, the right to record it on a particular film or films, the type of use and number of uses involved, and the territory covered as well as the price. The license will also grant a non-exclusive right to perform the music as recorded in the film in the territories and will be subject to any obligation to any performing rights society to collect license fees from television or theatres or otherwise. In the United States, as indicated, synchronization and performing rights are licensed together. The grant will frequently be expressly subject to a reservation of all other musical rights to the copyright proprietor. Accordingly, unless otherwise agreed, these valuable privileges will continue as the province of the publisher or composer.

In connection with the grant of musical licenses, many publishers utilize the services of The Harry Fox Agency of New York as agent for their properties. This office specializes in this field and is able generally to quote prices and other terms on behalf of its clients. Accordingly, many such mechanical licenses are secured in this manner. Some publishers, however, license music for film on their own behalf and must be dealt with directly. The ownership of music rights can and should, in any event, be checked with attorneys specializing in copyright search who are well known and active in this area. The risks of dealing with a former owner or non-owner are substantitive and definitely to be avoided.

The price for a license will relate to many factors including the nature of the use of the music. For example, a vocal use is more important than an instrumental background use and the license price will reflect the difference. Similarly, an important piece may draw one price while an unknown effort draws quite another.

An important element of revenue may well be long-play sound-track recordings. They not only popularize their film sources but, in some instances, outgross any sales revenues of the movie from which they derive. The film company's publishing affiliates, accordingly, make every effort to retain these monies and limit the participations of composers and conductors. Generally, they have proved successful in this purpose. Occasionally, however, an independent publisher will own all rights in a composer's work and will insist on sound-track rights for the publication and use of his music. This may also occur with independent or international film productions where there is no producer-affiliated music publisher involved, and the sound-track rights may be up for grabs. In connection with domestic sound-track recordings, regard must also be had for the re-use rights of the musicians' union which wants a separate payment for published recordings over and above the amount paid for the original sound-track recording. Although only one recording may actually be made, the producers and the publishing companies sometimes are charged twice for the act.

To summarize, in the vital matter of music rights it is essential for a producer to secure synchronization and performing rights for the music involved. If he can acquire other rights as well, he is far ahead in the game. Acquisition may be in the form of a creation of music through a contract for hire (subject to union requirements and existing litigation), by use of uncopyrighted or public domain music, or by direct license from the copyright proprietor or his agent. There must be clearly drafted contracts setting forth the rights acquired. The use of skilled attorneys in the music field is highly recommended.

Part Four

CONCLUSION AND NOTES

24

Charting a Future

DISASTER HAS ALWAYS been close at hand for the theatrical feature. The coming of sound created chaos in the film industry and fears were expressed of an early doom. The rise of the record industry with its threat to keep people at home by their victrolas also clouded the movie scene. Then came the television revolution with its ferocious negative impact on the total average audience. Since that time, the coupling of declining markets on the down-side and lopsided budgets for production on the up-side created another crisis in the late 1960's.

Can we foresee a future for feature films in theatres? What will be the impact of the new media—bigger and better television; wall screens; hotel closed-circuit; community antenna television; cassettes; and other forms of pay television?

The Debit Side

Looking at the debit side of the ledger, initially a number of negative factors emerge that becloud the future. The first such item must, of course, be the vastly increased selectivity of audiences. It is cliché to point out that huge numbers of people simply will no longer pay money at the box office just to see "a movie." It is only a particular movie they wish to see. Parenthetically, it might be added that ticket prices appear to be only a minor factor in combating selectivity.

If the theatre has *The Godfather* or *Last Tango in Paris,* audiences will apparently pay an increased tariff to see that which they wish to see. If, however, the attraction is of little interest, price reduction is no panacea—the idea of a $1.00 price for all features at all times seems to have come and gone without significant result.

The problem of selectivity is emphasized by shocking grosses in the domestic market in recent years. Whether the figures are precisely accurate is not crucial—it is their sweep and trend that is alarming.

A survey took ten films for several six-month periods and compared their relative box office take with total gross for all films distributed in the period. For the first half of 1970, the figures indicated that these top ten features were responsible for *over 31%* of the total gross business done. In the first half of 1971, with a different list of winners, a nearly identical situation existed. (Ten features garnered 31% of the market.) In 1972, the proportion of gross rose to 48% for the top 25 films. Nearly half of an industry's domestic theatrical take was estimated to come from merely 25 features! With hundreds of films in release sharing the balance it seems an understatement to call this business a giant "crapshoot." [1]

The alarming factor is not that grosses are down—in fact 1972 was ahead of 1970—but if the business is not to become a large-scale copy of the legitimate stage, where there is boom or bust and little or nothing in between, it is difficult to foresee a viable future unless there are other substantial markets for motion pictures. Either a producer-distributor has a major hit or he is, in effect, out of business.

Coupled with this fantastic selectivity is the near impossibility of prediction of success. A major film is generally planned and prepared at least two years in advance of release. What could be popular at the moment of selection may prove anathema 24 months later. We have already discussed the elements of popularity and indicated their ephemeral nature. The copying of past successful formulas, the acquisition of top literary properties, the attempt to ride current fads and trends, the vast expenditures of huge budgets for production and advertising—none has indicated any reasonable, much less sure-fire path to success. High selectivity is bad enough for business as a whole, but joined to near total unpredictability it comes close to becoming disastrous.

The theatrical market is also adversely affected by the large

[1] See *Variety* magazine 5/9/73.

demand for films and other entertainment on "free" television. Major films are playing on the TV medium sometimes well within two years of general theatrical release. People cannot be two places at the same time and if they are home watching *Patton, Love Story* or *Thunderball,* they cannot be paying patrons in a theatre. Huge packages of theatrical films and features made for television have been and are being licensed to television, and they must continue to hurt theatrical business and hurt it badly.

While no comfort to most exhibitors, the redeeming aspect of all this is the vast revenues going to producers and distributors. Television revenues, paradoxically, have kept them alive while their theatrical customers suffer. There is no convincing evidence that television viewing creates a substantial theatrical audience for film. The converse seems more likely.

Antitrust restrictions still remaining in effect (see Chapter 13) generally prevent broad theatre ownership or control by distributors as well as the booking of films in blocks. While far from fatal in themselves these, too, are limiting factors in developing markets in difficult conditions. Reasonable exemptions in this area under governmental sponsorship could be of modest help in surmounting the crisis and are to be encouraged.

Major problems also remain in the continuing high costs of distribution and the relative shares of revenue received from theatrical sources. Although the major distributors have quite properly embarked on a significant cost reduction program in the past several years to eliminate many exchanges and unnecessary procedures, the distribution of a film still remains a disproportionately high-cost item. The so-called ratio of distributors' gross to profitability continues near an average 2.6—meaning that, for a hypothetical film, the distributor must take in revenues 2.6 times the production cost before there can be a "profit" on the production. This has been reduced under some of the new formulas, such as "First Artists" but it is still a huge burden for a producer to carry. In distribution charges, in prints, in advertising and in a multitude of other expenditures, obviously large sums are needed, but must the ratio remain so high before a producer can share in profits? (He may, of course, share in gross under the so-called "gross deal" previously discussed.)

There is a profit built into the distribution fee, as well there may be, in view of the numerous pictures on which distributors suffer losses. The question persists, however, whether the costs of distribution must remain so large as to nearly prohibit profits on the vast bulk of films not overwhelmingly popular in the mass markets.

Akin to the problem of distributors' costs is that of his revenues. We have already pointed out the re-negotiability of the financial terms of exhibition contracts which constantly dilute the distributors' share. Only a handful of "firm" commitments and non-negotiable, competitively-bid playdates avoid this drain. In addition, it must in candor be added that there are exhibitors, and not just a mere handful, who withhold monies due distributors for long periods of time, improperly report grosses, or take advantage of other available gimmicks and devices to reduce distributors' share of revenues. There should be no room in this industry, particularly at this difficult time, for these practices—whether they be clearly illegal or merely immoral.

Whether "pornography," as so frequently alleged, has actually decreased theatrical business is a doubtful point. While it may have discouraged some family trade at some theatres, it has obviously paid off handsomely for others. In this area, as elsewhere, selectivity is ever present. Some sex-accented films will fare well—others will not. The rating system, or some variation, will certainly remain to warn parents or easily offended adults of film content. A new series of court decisions seems sure to limit "hard core" obscenity in any event as we have indicated. There are many difficulties in the film business but increased candor and sexuality do not seem the root of the problem.

The decline of the American city has also taken its toll in the theatre business. Supermarkets and bowling alleys have replaced older houses in urban areas. The fear of street violence, mugging and purse-snatching keeps thousands in their homes who might be out downtown enjoying a show. Perhaps the new suburban theatres take up some of this slack but certainly a huge audience is lost when "center city" decays.

Paradoxically, 1972 saw a rise in downtown business in New York and other cities. A primarily black audience came out in strength to view a host of racially oriented films patterned on the success of *Sweet Sweetbacks* and *Shaft*. This phenomenon seems more in the nature of a "flash in the pan," however, than a permanent development and it can be safely assumed that downtown will continue to decline unless a host of expensive alleviative measures are taken under both public and private auspices. Theatre groups should be in the forefront of the movement to cure this disastrous condition.

Completing the difficult picture for theatres, if not for distributors, would be the unpredictable impact of the new technology. If the home will have large-scale wall screens for color television or Community Antenna Television (CATV), pay TV or cassettes, will masses of people still attend theatres? Will a multiplicity of fare on numerous cables hold the audience home? If, as indicated, hotel viewing of films for a fee is proving popular, how far can this extend and with what impact? Where else can the new media extend to limit theatrical patronage? While far from predictable, the future is clearly hazardous.

The Credit Side

What are the pluses or affirmative factors toward the continuance of a viable theatrical film industry? Turning our first negative point on its head, it should immediately be stated that, for the film that really succeeds, there appears to be no limit to gross on the up-side. The hit picture has an unprecedented market. This is reflected in figures showing a growth in total box office take, even after adjustment for price rises, in the period 1970-1972. The audience is clearly there. If enough such popular films can be created, despite the previously stated difficulties, a successful future is obviously quite within reach. How to provide these films is the unanswered question.

It cannot be overstressed that people like the medium of film. Millions see and enjoy it in theatres, on television and in the non-theatrical markets. Its remarkable ability to hold, transport, amuse, move and delight an audience is evident. Producers and distributors and exhibitors have a product that clearly appeals to people. Translating that general popularity into box office returns is the key to the problem.

Another positive factor for the theatre business is the age-old desire of people to "go out" and be sociable. While this sentiment may have declined, its existence should still guarantee at least a significant audience for theatres and other "outside-the-home" amusements. Similarly, a reduction of working hours and a shortened work week should add up to an increase in leisure time that could be spent by millions more at the cinema—if they are not captured by competing attractions such as night sports, ice shows and other amusements.

The foreign market has long cushioned the shock of difficult domestic conditions for film revenues. Recent estimates are that in excess of 55% of distributor returns come from abroad. The indefinite continuation of this condition, however, remains a question. It is subject to some of the same difficulties which we have already discussed as applicable to the domestic market. Without this vast source of revenue the attrition in distribution might well have proved far greater in recent years. Foreign distribution, however, must still be considered a major positive factor helping the industry's posture.

Attendance may also be helped by the improvements in the new theatres (primarily at shopping centers). Compared to the aging downtown and neighborhood monstrosities, these houses contain major pluses in their comfort, ease and availability. Projection has been improved and the screens are wide and attractive. Complexes or theatre clusters also are convenient and economical, and give the patron a healthy choice of fare. That the public likes these houses is evident from the vast building boom in theatre construction despite all the problems we have related. Drive-ins have slipped in importance and now appear to emphasize the sex-horror trade. They still retain a modest appeal. A new breed of downtown and neighborhood theatres can, however, prove a stimulation to business despite the fact that the picture remains the major attraction. People do like comfort and convenience with their entertainment and, of course, they are clearly entitled to it. Furthermore, by time-honored tradition if not logic, the candy concession belongs to the exhibitor or his licensee and can provide a vast increase in his total take.

On the positive side, as well, are the indications that producers and distributors have shown in recent years of an ability to limit their risks by reducing fantastic budgets and operational costs. Major films, despite rising prices, are being produced far below budgets of but a few years back. Few are the features in today's market budgeted over $4- to $5-million. The $2-million production budget maximums are now a rule rather than an exception. Going, if not entirely gone, are the wild expenditures for epics such as *Cleopatra, Catch 22* and *Tora, Tora, Tora,* all in the eight-figure bracket. As previously indicated distribution costs, as well, have been cut by the reduction of exchanges and unnecessary manpower abroad. While the costs may nonetheless remain too high, the industry has shown an admirable ability and willingness to stand up to this aspect of the problem.

This struggle has been aided by the rise of the powerful conglomerates as a factor in the trade. No longer is a Paramount or United Artists, for example, dependent on its films alone. The assets of Gulf & Western or Trans-America stand back of the company's efforts. While the unproven charge is made that these entities interfere with production with their alleged computerized methods of doing business, the bulk of evidence would seem to indicate that they stand as powerful bulwarks against the frightful losses that can occur in one unpredictable film division. They also can assure financing for important properties that might not otherwise be produced.

The glamour appeal of film as an industry to certain individuals and groups should not be underestimated. New sources of financing have arisen from diverse organizations, all of which know the risks inherent in this trade. Nonetheless they invest and take their chances. Something is compelling them towards film. Could it be that the desire to be involved in this exciting trade, or to have fun with the starlets, or some wild type of gambler's instinct has achieved priority? Obviously there is an intangible here that cannot be easily explained.

Film as an industry will go forward and will prosper. The huge television, non-theatrical and foreign markets will assure production's future if nothing else does. New technology will make film or tape readily available to a vast consuming public that likes and wants the medium. And the public will pay for what it wants. Producers and those who distribute their film, in whatever manner, are here to stay.

The theatrical side, however, remains a question. My own conviction is that despite all the stated difficulties there is a future indeed. The struggle may be difficult. This may become a far more specialized and limited business with each theatre catering to a particular audience. Its practitioners must sharpen their tools of exploitation, publicity and showmanship. The operator can no longer be a mere janitor or permanent beach dweller in Florida but must work diligently to find his market—be it family, action, revival or exploitation film in nature. There may well be fewer theatres. The "downtown" (and uptown) problems of crime and decay must ultimately be met. They threaten not only "downtown" but our entire society in a thousand ways more important than film. Exhibitors must be leaders in solving these problems.

Showmen have been overcoming crisis since the day the first one-reeler was displayed on Forty-Second Street. One should not lightly assume that those who survived the panic of sound, the revolution in antitrust and the disaster of free competition on television will not continue to prominently and profitably exhibit motion pictures in the decades ahead.

Index

206

Bizarre film, popularity of, 37
"Blind buying," 99, 102
Block booking, 98-99, 101
Blow Up, 65
Blumenthal v. *Picture Classics,* 154 and *n.*
BMI (Broadcast Music, Inc.), 191, 192
Bob & Carol & Ted & Alice, 37
Bogart, Humphrey, 177
Bond films, 11, 27, 34, 36, 39
Bonnie & Clyde, 37
Boone, Richard, 179
Booth, Shirley, 160
Boston Strangler, The, 148
Brando, Marlon, 34, 40
Breathless, 77
Bridge on the River Kwai, 11, 40
British Commonwealth, 27
Broadcast Music, Inc. (BMI), 191, 192
Brown, Grace, 145
Brown, Helen Gurley, 136
Brown v. *Paramount Publix,* 145 and *n.*
Burton, Richard, 40
Burton v. *Crowell Collier,* 155 and *n.*
Butch Cassidy and the Sundance Kid, 32, 34, 38

California, 134, 135; idea protection in, 171-73
"Campiness" in film, 37
Canada, 44, 45, 48, 66
Candide, 77
Cantinflas comedies, 59
Capone, Alphonse, 146, 147, 166
Cardozo, Benjamin, quoted, 142
Carnal Knowledge, 40, 129
Cassettes, 73, 80, 86-87, 105, 201
Catch-22, 40, 202
Catholic Legion of Decency, 119, 131
CATV (community antenna television), 59, 73, 80, 83-85, 89, 90, 105, 190, 201
CBS (Columbia Broadcasting System), 156, 175, 177, 179, 193
Censorship: newspaper, 114; prior-restraint, 119, 124-26; self-, 118; U.S. Customs, 126

Censorship in Denmark, 129
Chaos Below Heaven (Vale), 159
Chaplin, Charlie, 120, 156
Chaplin, Geraldine, 33
Characters, fictional, infringement of, 176-81
Children of Paradise, 77
Christie, Julie, 33
Churches, films shown in, 73
Cinema International Corp., 68
Claire's Knee, 64
Classification statutes, for control of film content, 119
Clearance, as trade practice, 101, 102
Cleopatra, 202
Clockwork Orange, A, 36, 40, 123
Clubs, films shown in, 73, 74, 75
"Cohens and the Kellys, The" (play), 177
Colleges, films shown in, 73, 75
Collins, Floyd, 171, 172
Columbia Pictures Corp., 68, 99, 113, 159
Comedie Française, 59, 77
Comedy, as film's popularity factor, 37
Commission, Presidential, on control of film content, 120, 128
Community antenna television, *see* CATV
Compco Co. v. *Day-Brite Lighting, Inc.,* 90*n.,* 137 and *n.,* 138
Composers and Lyricists Guild, 193
Compulsion, 160
Computerization, and conglomerate-dominated films, 108
Concert for Bangladesh, The, 36
Concession income, exhibitor's rights to, 55
Conformist, The, 64
Conglomerates: 106-10; attracted to film industry, 107-08; concern about impact of, 108-09; positive effects of, 109-10
Connery, Sean, 11, 34, 39
Consent decrees, and anti-trust laws, 101-04
Cooperative advertising, 115
Copyright, 90, 93, 94, 95-96, 132, 137, 179, 180, 182-90; common-law, 182; and film, 182-90